Praise for *Off the Edge*

"A deep dive into the world of Flat Earth conspiracy theorists . . . that brilliantly reveals how people fall into illogical beliefs, reject reason, destroy relationships, and connect with a broad range of conspiracy theories in the social media age. Beautiful, probing, and often empathetic . . . An insightful, human look at what fuels conspiracy theories." —Jennifer Golbeck, *Science*

"Fascinating . . . I learned a lot about why people believe what they believe." —Brian Stelter, author of *Hoax* and former host of CNN's *Reliable Sources*

"Kelly Weill is one of the best observers of the fringes of modern American life, making her the perfect chronicler of the Flat Earth movement. Her deep reporting and gift for storytelling make *Off the Edge* a gripping read—but what sets Weill apart is her ability to cover her subjects with great empathy, all without losing sight of the enormous damage and personal consequences of their actions. If you want to understand how the fringe has become our new normal, you should read this book." —Charlie Warzel, co-author of *Out of Office*

"Even-handed . . . Perfectly encapsulates disturbing implications of conspiracy theorists and their beliefs." —*Minneapolis Star Tribune*

"In lively prose, Weill untangles the most complicated webs, revealing the real people who believe the unbelievable." —*Booklist*

"An inquisitive, empathetic, deeply reported, and disturbingly funny tour through the farthest reaches of the most-fringe-possible conspiracy community. While Weill's subjects frequently risk falling off the edge of their own self-created map of the known universe, she follows them deftly to the brink, showing what their delusional explorations can teach us about belief, community, and the long history of pseudoscience around (sorry!) the world." —Anna Merlan, author of *Republic of Lies*

"Thorough, sensitive . . . Weill's historical excursions into Flat Earth reinforce a desperately needed correction within the recent public conversation about conspiracy theories."
—Trevor Quirk, *Guernica*

"Extraordinary."
—*BookPage*

"Provocative . . . A timely and disturbing study of flawed, dangerous thinking."
—*Kirkus Reviews*

"Insightful and surprisingly empathetic . . . An illuminating take on a much-scrutinized subject."
—*Publishers Weekly*

"Weill's elegant writing, informed by both historical research and deep-delving reporting, offers a complex and vivid portrait of a conspiracy community that serves as a metonym for this moment—when so many of us are in dispute about the very nature of reality. An essential and enjoyable read."
—Talia Lavin, author of *Culture Warlords*

"Entertaining and informative . . . An invaluable and deeply human look at a movement which, while divorced from reality in many ways, inhabits the same (spherical) space as the rest of us."
—*The Skeptic*

"An illuminating study that locates the common human psychological impulses behind conspiracy culture."
—*Library Journal*

"In this delightful deep dive into Flat Earth culture past and present, taking in YouTube recommendation algorithms, amateur rocketry, and a rat's nest of conspiracy theories, Kelly Weill explains why, after several millennia of set-backs, the idea that the Earth is flat is burgeoning once again."
—Michael Strevens, author of *The Knowledge Machine*

"Alert, informed, and up to date, *Off the Edge* is aptly describable as on the ball."
—*Skeptical Inquirer*

OFF THE EDGE

OFF THE EDGE

Flat Earthers,
Conspiracy Culture,
and Why People Will
Believe Anything

KELLY WEILL

ALGONQUIN BOOKS OF CHAPEL HILL 2023

Published by
ALGONQUIN BOOKS OF CHAPEL HILL
Post Office Box 2225
Chapel Hill, North Carolina 27515-2225

an imprint of WORKMAN PUBLISHING CO., INC., a subsidiary of
HACHETTE BOOK GROUP, INC.
1290 Avenue of the Americas
New York, New York 10104

Library of Congress Cataloging-in-Publication Data

Names: Weill, Kelly, [date]– author.
Title: Off the edge : flat Earthers, conspiracy culture, and why people will
    believe anything / Kelly Weill.
Description: First edition. | Chapel Hill, North Carolina : Algonquin Books
    of Chapel Hill, [2022] | Includes bibliographical references.
Summary: "A history of the Flat Earth movement and a look at the recent boom
    in conspiratorial thinking in America"— Provided by publisher.
Identifiers: LCCN 2021035867 | ISBN 9781643750682 (hardcover) |
    ISBN 9781643752198 (ebook)
Subjects: LCSH: Conspiracy theories—United States. | Earth (Planet)—Figure. |
    Earth (Planet)—Philosophy.
Classification: LCC HV6275 .W45 2022 | DDC 001.9/8—dc23
LC record available at https://lccn.loc.gov/2021035867

ISBN 978-1-64375-337-9 (PB)

10 9 8 7 6 5 4 3 2 1
First Paperback Edition

To J. and C., who were with me the whole way.

CONTENTS

PROLOGUE

THE SUMMER BEFORE he fell from the sky, Mike Hughes was experimenting with amateur jet propulsion. It was going badly.

"Problem again today," he texted me in August 2019.

"With the rocket, or weather?" I asked.

"Rocket."

This was his second failure in two days, and I'd lost count of the times he'd run into trouble with wind or parachutes or spare rocket parts he'd purchased off Craigslist for $325. Most people would have given up years earlier, maybe taken up a less lethal hobby. I certainly thought he'd quit.

"He's gotta know, right?" I remember asking my husband. I was standing in our kitchen, texting Hughes with one hand and brandishing a spatula with the other, making an omelet while trying to talk Hughes out of launching himself into low orbit. "Deep down, he's gotta know Earth is round. That's why he keeps having these 'rocket failures.' Earth is round, and he doesn't want to prove it."

I liked Mike. He was an offbeat guy, but a good one. We'd met the previous year at a conference for people who believe the earth is flat. I was there as a journalist for the *Daily Beast*, the news website where I reported on extremist movements and conspiracy theories. He was there to drum up support for a self-manned rocket launch into the upper atmosphere, during which he would decide the planet's shape for himself. He and I sat around talking trash and the particulars of rocket science. Throughout the next year, he'd send me updates: pictures of rocket designs, gossip from the conspiracy scene, and invitations to more conspiracy conventions. This wasn't a guy with a death wish. This was a man who'd lived six bombastic decades and had no intention of stopping. So when he texted me about a summer's worth of rocket troubles, I thought it was his good sense finally rebelling against a bad idea. After all, who *truly* thought Earth was flat?

But "Mad Mike" Hughes was a believer—in thrifted rocket parts, in back-of-the-envelope flight calculus, in himself, and most famously, in Flat Earth.

Flat Earth theory, the idea for which Hughes was willing to shoot himself into the stratosphere, represents a profound misunderstanding of the world. But the theory and those who believe it are also misunderstood, by the world at large. I've spent years hobnobbing with Flat Earthers at conferences across the United States and interviewing them on the weekends, becoming the friend of some and the enemy of others. Some have called me for legal advice, and others have labeled me a saboteur out to sink the movement. Ally or archnemesis of Flat Earthers, I've spent enough time among them to sympathize with them on one key grievance: nearly every common assumption about Flat Earth is wrong. Maybe you learned as a kid that people expected Christopher Columbus to sail off the edge of a flat planet. Or maybe you've seen people refer to Flat Earth an example of a backwards-thinking ideology held in Europe's Middle Ages. The truth is that, by at least the fifth century BCE, Greek astronomers and mathematicians had already determined that the earth was round and had popularized the formulas that proved their calculations. By Columbus's day, the globe model had been the default for centuries. (In fact, we can credit the Columbus Flat Earth myth to "Rip Van Winkle" author Washington Irving, who seems to have more or less invented it in his heavily embellished Columbus biography in the 1820s.) Flat Earth theory is a new idea, one that emerged in a utopian commune in England decades after

Irving's account of Columbus. It simmered in hard-core religious communities in the United States in the early 1900s, found a home with moon-landing skeptics in the back half of the twentieth century, and skyrocketed to popularity in the late 2010s, the same time Mike Hughes was teaching himself rocket science.

Hughes was a walking reminder of the other mistake people make about the movement: that Flat Earthers are wackos, denizens of society's fringes. But Flat Earthers exist among us—often so inconspicuously that you'd never notice unless you asked. Some are parents, some are self-taught aerospace engineers, and some are professional athletes. Some are clever, some are kind, some are neither, and at least two have released bad rap songs that praise both Flat Earth and Adolf Hitler. On the whole, however, Flat Earthers comprise a spectrum of people who are seldom much different, or any dumber, than the rest of us.

Their theory typically claims Earth is as flat as a Frisbee, surrounded by ice at its perimeter, and maybe enclosed by a great, impenetrable dome. The details vary from believer to believer. Most Flat Earthers (but not all) do not believe in outer space. Though many are dismissive of gravity as a concept, some claim that the planet is constantly accelerating upward, while others disagree and claim that the only reason we don't drift off the ground like escaped party balloons is because humans are heavier than air. But unless you find yourself in an argument over the theory's nuances at a Flat Earth conference, they are of secondary importance. Flat Earth is best understood not as a viable science with meaningful specifics but as the ultimate incarnation of conspiratorial thinking. Members of the movement believe governments and scientists are actively peddling a "globe lie" in order to control the world by tarnishing religious teachings or by making people feel insignificant next to the great expanse of outer space. For the past 150-odd years, this bizarre theory has grown by borrowing age-old mistrusts and exploiting new forms of communication, from newspapers to radio to—eventually, explosively—the internet.

Today's world looks different than it did when I began work on this book, and not just because I've spent that time among people who believe the earth is flat. Widespread civil unrest, a contentious presidential election, and the outbreak of a catastrophic pandemic have seeded the United States with so much suspicion that I need to clarify, up front, how I use the term "conspiracy theory." Jan-Willem van Prooijen, a psychologist specializing in conspiracy theories, lays out five criteria that qualify a belief as a conspiracy theory: the theory must explain correlations between events and actors; the perpetrators must have acted deliberately; multiple people must have been involved in the plot; the plot must be ominous in its deception (and not a benevolent cover-up, like concealing a surprise birthday party); and the cover-up must be ongoing. "Conspiracy theory," for the purposes of this book, refers to an unproven allegation of a secret, deliberate, and malevolent plot, like a scheme to conceal the true shape of the world. Conspiracies theories are ways to construct order and meaning in times of uncertainty. They let us shape our fears into something we understand.

Belief in conspiracy theories is highly common. Study after study, across multiple continents, has found that more than half of respondents support some conspiracy theory or another. Some of those theories turn out to be true. The United States has been involved in damning and demonstrably true plots on its own soil (like the FBI's plot to discredit Martin Luther King Jr.) and abroad (like the Reagan administration's plot to illegally sell weapons to Iran in order to support counterrevolutionaries in Nicaragua). In light of these revelations, suspicion might seem justifiable, even reasonable, to many Americans. I'm no exception here. For instance, I am militant in my unproven belief that Oklahoma City bomber Timothy McVeigh was aided by sympathetic, uncharged members of the white power movement. Given an hour and a strong drink, I will talk your ear off about this, possibly while drawing maps and diagrams on the nearest surface. My belief probably means I can be classified as a conspiracy theorist.

But conspiratorial belief is not without consequence. Flat Earth can result in devastating effects to its followers, people driven by religious conviction or distrust of authorities or belief in faulty science. A pastor lost his job after he went to a Flat Earth conference. A female Flat Earth internet personality fell in love with a male Flat Earth internet personality but became the subject of new conspiracy theories when she claimed—and he denied—that he was sexually brutal with her. An aspiring Flat Earth community leader was arrested for trying to distribute Flat Earth leaflets at an elementary school. A pop star's ex-husband became curious about Flat Earth and other conspiracy theories, tipping him into a rabbit hole that led to his participation in a conspiracy-fueled rally in Washington, DC, that ended with other participants invading the US Capitol building. When I first met Mike Hughes in 2018, he showed me a model of a "rockoon," a rocket/balloon that he intended to fly to the atmosphere's upper reaches in order to take a picture that would prove the planet's flatness. A year and a half later, he was killed in a rocket launch, likely the result of the secondhand parachutes that had given him so much trouble the previous year.

When Hughes died in February 2020, I realized that even after years immersed in Flat Earth theory, I was still incorrect about it. I'd assumed that, on some subconscious level, Hughes didn't really believe Earth was flat; that his rockets would always conveniently fail the morning before he had to shoot himself into space to prove the theory, or that his flights would always stay low enough to avoid danger and the sight of a curved horizon.

I was wrong. Flat Earthers are as serious as your life.

1 | In the Beginning

THEY WERE BEGGARS and scholars and out-of-work lace makers, dreamers and drunkards, decent farmers and hopelessly bad ones. They were bricklayers, some honest and some exploiting an obscure loophole in brickmaking law to commit tax fraud. They were at odds with the local press, accused of sex scandals, and eternally feuding among themselves. And from 1838 to 1841, they were all stuck there together in the worst little utopia in all of Cambridgeshire, England.

"They paid much more attention to the beer shops and the company of the lowest prostitutes" than to their work, one griped about his neighbors.

"To make a successful Community all parties must be economical and industrious, and must not, like Mr. Kirk, frequently get up *after* breakfast," others complained of a comrade in an anonymous collective letter to the commune newspaper.

This was Manea Fen, a short-lived socialist commune scooped out of the wetlands. Staffed by soft-handed idealists rebelling against England's Industrial Revolution and local laborers seeking more than starvation wages, Manea Fen was a beacon for people chasing a new world. They found it, though not in a way they could have imagined. By its second year, the whole project would become an embarrassing flop that would send its founder into debt and most of its members slinking back into polite society. But as the weeds reclaimed Manea Fen's homesteads, the commune's real export would blossom across the country. Up from Manea Fen's marshy plains rose modern Flat Earth theory, a conspiracy theory so audacious it could eclipse a planet. It was entirely one man's fault.

Samuel Birley Rowbotham was twenty-two, radical, and according to a socialist newspaper's account, occasionally high off his mind on laughing gas when he began imagining a new world in 1838. That year, he was one of the first to answer a local farmer's call to build the planned utopian society of Manea Fen. Rowbotham and the farmer comrade, William Hodson, were followers of Robert Owen, a utopian socialist who envisioned grand, sweeping paradises made up of cooperative worker communes. (Working before socialist heavy hitters like Karl Marx, Owen argued not for society-wide class struggle and revolution, but for model communes that would show the world how to live peacefully.) The year 1838 was a boom time for English utopians. Workers, dirt-poor and fed up near the end of the First Industrial Revolution, banded together in experimental live-work settlements where they hoped they could break the accelerating wheels of capitalism.

Few photographs exist of Rowbotham. If you ask around at a modern Flat Earth conference, someone might be able to sell you an old pamphlet with a picture of him as a stern, round-faced man of middle age. I like to imagine him in his early years, however, not as an aging man from an old book, but as a young idealist who would have gotten by just fine in the twenty-first century. The young Rowbotham liked to get high and litigate obscure political arguments with other socialists in their niche newspapers. Substitute those newspapers for social media, and he'd be indistinguishable from dozens of people I know in modern life. Rowbotham had one more commonality with contemporary Twitter users: he lived in a moment ripe for conspiracy theories.

Conspiratorial thinking is not a weird pathology, experienced by some and absent in others. It's part of a mental process hardwired into all of us, from Rowbotham's era and beforehand and afterward. The same powers of abstraction that make humans good at detecting patterns (like anticipating storms when dark clouds gather) can make us imagine patterns where they don't exist, especially when we're feeling stressed or powerless. Rather than languish in the unknown, we tell ourselves stories about the secret causes of our troubles. All of us do this. For instance, after failing my driver's test three times, an explanation emerged in the back of my mind: maybe the Department of Motor Vehicles secretly had to flunk a certain quota of student drivers. The stress of the situation (being demonstrably bad at driving), coupled with a misunderstood pattern (the apparent impossibility of passing a road test) and a comforting explanation (*I* wasn't a traffic hazard; *I* was being oppressed by the iron boot of the state) turned my botched parallel parking into a conspiracy theory. I passed on round four.

In short, conspiracy theories help us feel safe by providing an explanation for things that feel incomprehensible and beyond our control. This dynamic can influence us in measurably silly ways. Dutch psychologists, for example, found that if students were asked to describe a situation that made them feel powerless, they were more likely to subsequently believe conspiracy theories about a controversial train line near campus.

Moments of rapid industrialization and income inequality—like Rowbotham's and arguably our own—are prime sources of precarity and uncertainty. In the United States during the Second Industrial Revolution in the late 1800s, for example, newspapers logged a spike in conspiracy-minded letters to the editor, which contemporary researchers attribute to laborers' worries that new technologies would cast them into unemployment. Though newspapers were not yet in widespread circulation during Rowbotham's youth, the First Industrial Revolution produced many of the same anxieties as the Second, including those that inspired Owen to build worker-friendly communities.

Seeking to build an anticapitalist utopia in rapidly industrializing England, Rowbotham and Hodson took a tour of existing Owenite communes in an attempt to drum up support for their own efforts in Manea Fen. But while Hodson, a devout socialist who would eventually bankrupt himself for the cause, was focused on earning membership and finding financial backing, Rowbotham might have been hatching a secret plot. It was one, he would later write, that he had fomented since childhood.

Since he was a boy, Rowbotham would later claim, he had always believed he lived on a flat planet. Even in the early 1800s, this was supposedly enough to get the young Rowbotham into trouble at school. Though twenty-first-century Americans love to portray Brits from past centuries as Flat Earthers (for instance, a 2020 Super Bowl commercial depicted English peasants talking about Flat Earth), people have known the planet was round for thousands of years. By Rowbotham's time, schools had long been teaching a fairly modern model of the solar system.

Rowbotham claimed he never took to his school's teachings, and that he tried sneaking out of a school astronomy lesson, which he believed was bogus. Those doubts compounded when he searched the Bible for confirmation of his beliefs. He concluded that if Sir Isaac Newton's model of the solar system—round planets orbiting a round sun—was true, then God was dead. "Again and again, the feeling came over me that as the Newtonian system appeared so plausible and so grand in its extent and comprehensiveness, it might after all be correct," Rowbotham later wrote of his path to Flat Earth, "and, if so, there could be no heaven for man's future enjoyment; no higher existence than on this earth; no spiritual and immortal creatures, and therefore no God or Creator."

Was Rowbotham really a childhood Flat Earther? We only have his perhaps unreliable word for it. But even before Manea Fen broke ground, Rowbotham had begun shaping it in a way that would doom the commune and put Flat Earth theory on the map.

His early membership in Manea Fen gave the young Rowbotham considerable power over the collective. Hodson named him secretary of the group, and Rowbotham went to work looking for a suitable location for the project. He found it on the shores of Cambridge's Old Bedford Canal. Rowbotham was adamant about starting the commune on the canal banks. They "would form a beautiful promenade in the summer evening," Rowbotham told his comrades. When other Owenites panned his choice (not enough winding river bends and birdsong for a paradise), Rowbotham doubled down, his conviction becoming tinged with fanaticism; he had to have his commune there.

Why not, in the spirit of revolutionary harmony, just move Manea Fen to one of swampy Cambridgeshire's many natural waterways? Rowbotham's fixation on the Bedford Canal might have been more than socialist devotion. He may have been guided by ulterior motives. Pin-straight and pancake-flat to the untrained eye, the Bedford Canal, nick-named the Bedford Level, looked rather like a flat line stretching across the visible length of a flat planet. It was a gift to anyone who hoped to argue that Earth is not a globe. Early in his work to build the Manea Fen colony, Rowbotham began making repeat trips to the canal to conduct experiments.

Earth curves at approximately eight inches per mile squared. (Real mathematicians use more precise formulas, but for very short experiments like Rowbotham's, approximations are fine.) If you lie on your stomach and gaze at the horizon from one mile away, a barely perceptible eight inches of Earth will be hidden behind the planet's curve. If you can see two miles away, thirty-two inches of Earth will have curved out of view. Six miles away, the ground will have dropped twenty-four feet below your line of sight. This has been more or less the established model of the planet since Pythagoras proposed a spherical Earth, around 500 BCE.

Rowbotham, however, saw the world differently. When wading neck-deep in the canal with a telescope, he could see the full height of boats sailing at the far end, he claimed. When the canal froze in winter, his telescope could spot ice-skaters six miles away. Those damp sojourns would go on to haunt the future. One hundred eighty years after Rowbotham's experiments on the canal, I've met dozens of Flat Earthers who have cited the nineteenth-century experiments in their own writings or, despite their internet connections, traveled to the canal themselves to re-create the "Bedford Level test." These modern Flat Earthers may as well have been citing a fantasy novel. Rowbotham was incorrect (archaeologists who studied Manea Fen are doubtful he even had an adequate telescope) or outright lying (those same archaeologists tried replicating his experiment and found it to show a round earth). For years, he wouldn't even discuss his findings with the masses, and none of his commune peers appear to have adopted his burgeoning theory.

At the time, however, Rowbotham had other problems on his plate. Manea Fen was, functionally, a mess, and people blamed him. When the colony opened on the canal banks around Christmas 1838, Rowbotham recruited a sordid crew, many of them more interested in drinking than working. Visiting socialists were appalled and accused him of gathering the laziest leftists he could find. (The accusations were a little unfair. The laziest man on the commune was probably not a Rowbotham recruit, but a man named Kirk, who moved in of his own accord and immediately demanded the right to build a cave and live in it as a hermit. And even the commune's most ambitious workers were likely cutting corners: archaeologists who studied the commune suspect the Owenites routinely dodged their taxes by selling bricks mislabeled as "drainage" materials, in what looked pretty clearly like a scheme to cash in on a tax loophole for toilet products.)

Regardless of fault in recruitment strategy, the utopia had other issues. Despite the commune's socialist mission, some early workers claimed they received no pay for their labor. "I am without home and without bread," one man complained when he abandoned the commune after three unpaid months. As for Manea Fen's intellectual aims, its early occupants spent their time "finding fault with one another and with everything about them," engaging in "useless discussions," and micromanaging their comrades, member E. Wastney later wrote. Other

Owenite communes and newspapers, already suspicious of Rowbotham's project, latched on to these stories.

The sex scandal made matters worse. Hodson, Manea Fen's official founder, believed in equality for women. Like so many male feminists of his moment and the future, however, his ideological commitment wavered in practice, and Manea Fen never had any significant female leadership. For some time during Rowbotham's tenure, though, commune leadership condemned the institution of marriage as oppressive to women, and encouraged more independent sexual relationships. At this, all the leading Owenite newspapers pounced. The commune, already unpopular, was now practicing free love and polygamy, they alleged. The scandal spread. Owenite committees across the country held inquiries. Hodson's and Rowbotham's names began to float to the top of these investigations, and disillusioned Manea Fen members began quitting the commune en masse. Hodson was ultimately able to shake free of the allegations. But Rowbotham, who had made a name for himself by picking an undesirable plot of land by the canal and staffing it with hard-drinking layabouts, was not so fortunate. In a desperate plea to keep his spot in the commune, he wrote an April 1839 letter to Owen, asking the socialist leader to help resolve "a little confusion in our Society" with regard to whether or not marriage was bad. He did not receive a response.

By summer, the Manea Fen commune had cast him out. Rowbotham "is neither secretary to, nor a member of this society," a curt article in the commune's newspaper announced. The whole utopia was bankrupt and abandoned less than two years later.

So there Rowbotham was, drifting around the wetlands with little to his name besides a handful of counterscientific beliefs. For a short time, he tried his hand at social missionary work, but complaints against the argumentative young man piled up. He dropped out in a matter of months, abandoning his efforts and denouncing Owenism. Further fringes were already calling him. Casting off the name that had become associated with a socialist sex scandal, Rowbotham rebranded as "Dr. Birley." His lack of any doctoral degree was irrelevant. Rowbotham was about to plunge into a career that, to this day, rubs shoulders with the Flat Earth movement and other conspiracy scenes. He was about to become a huckster of miracle cures.

Medical hoaxes prey on many of the same thought processes as conspiracy theories. Faced with frightening diagnoses or unaffordable treatments, we go looking for the One Weird Trick that will put us back in control of our health. It's easier than accepting the harsh reality that a cure might not be within our reach.

Sometimes bogus medicine is actually an extension of conspiracy theory. The anti-vaccination movement that gained popularity in the late 1990s falsely claims that vaccines cause autism and can lead to a host of illnesses, and that governments and medical authorities are covering it up, for nefarious reasons ranging from pharmaceutical profits to population control. Never mind that research has repeatedly discredited these claims; the anti-vaccine movement continues to this day. Theories like these help people grapple with feelings of powerlessness by positioning other human beings, with agendas and motivations, as responsible for medical conditions. In doing so, believers can avoid the uncomfortable truth: that life and death can lie with something like a virus, which cannot be voted out of office or sued for medical malpractice.

Miracle cures, meanwhile, treat the other side of conspiratorial health beliefs, falsely claiming to be the *real* solution to an ailment—the one that governments or pharmaceutical companies allegedly try to hide. One modern conspiracy kingpin, for example, sells a book claiming you can beat diabetes with a secret cure that doctors hide because "drug companies would much prefer to keep you dependent on insulin and diabetes drugs. The moment you beat this disease, they lose a customer." While killing time at a Flat Earth conference in 2019, I wound up talking to a woman who was convinced that natural foods could eradicate several serious medical conditions. When the COVID-19 pandemic hit the

United States in 2020, justifiably frightened people suggested combating the mysterious virus with useless treatments like turmeric powder or, in the case of one of my acquaintances, "essential oils" that she was conveniently selling via a pyramid scheme on Facebook. Likewise, in Rowbotham's moment of industrial upheaval, as new factories belched soot into the skylines and people crowded into dirty cities, an emerging industry of quack doctors stepped up to sell hope and snake oil.

Rowbotham offered nothing less than immortality. Aging was actually the result of the body solidifying, he claimed in his 1845 work *Biology: An Inquiry into the Cause of Natural Death, Showing It Not to Arise from Old Age, but from a Gradual Process of Consolidation* . . . To effectively live forever, all one needed to do was follow his special diet of phosphoric acid and lime. He said medical experts secretly agreed that phosphates were a miracle cure, though they never prescribed them because they were too fussy to work with. But Rowbotham said he had a unique way of diluting the chemical in water, making it easy to drink. "It is, to all intents and purposes, a true and literal 'life water,' surpassing, beyond all comparisons, the so-called *Aqua vitae* of the alchemists," he wrote in another publication, claiming his creation boosted brain power. "It may truly be called an *aqua sancta*—a new and chemically generated 'holy water.'"

In actuality, all he'd invented (not even invented—similar products were already on the market!) was soda. Still, he threw himself into the sale of carbonated drinks, billing them as the cure for everything from asthma to old age. If followed to the letter, Rowbotham's miracle diet would probably have caused bone loss and mineral depletion. Indeed, in one tragic case in 1844, Rowbotham prescribed his miracle cure to a ten-year-old boy suffering from the aftereffects of a stroke. The boy later died, and his parents accused Rowbotham in court of having effectively poisoned their child. A jury cleared Rowbotham after he successfully argued that the parents couldn't prove that his phosphorus played any role in their son's death. Future medical research did not vindicate

Rowbotham. Modern medicine finds that today's consumers likely ingest too much phosphoric acid, often from soft drinks; if Rowbotham's miracle cure worked, much of the United States would be experiencing pleasant indestructibility. Unfortunately, you can't Mountain Dew yourself to eternal life—you can only increase your soda-based risk of osteoporosis, like many modern consumers. Today, a group called the Flat Earth Society sidesteps these medical facts in its literature on Rowbotham by referencing only outdated nineteenth-century texts that suggest that phosphoric acid is actually good.

Rowbotham made steady money as a phosphorus grifter before returning to his more ambitious conspiratorial project: Flat Earth. In 1849, a decade after his first experiments on the Bedford Canal, he published his supposed findings in a pamphlet titled *Zetetic Astronomy: Earth Not a Globe*. The sincerity of this Flat Earth founder's belief is up for debate. Rowbotham's theory was steeped in extreme biblical literalism, which historian Christine Garwood describes as unusual for someone who once mingled with Britain's socialist upstarts, and as a Flat Earth preacher, Rowbotham tried to hide his legal name. Instead, he wrote under the pen name Parallax, which refers to a phenomenon of shifting perspectives, especially when measuring the position of stars. As for "zetetic," the Greek word refers to a pursuit led by skeptical inquiry. When Rowbotham took up the term, it was already associated with a radical British atheist crew: the exact sort of people who would want nothing to do with Rowbotham. Under their definition, "zetetic" suggested a brand of nothing-is-sacred skepticism, calling into question every revered figure from the Queen to Christ. Rowbotham borrowed the definition but inverted the intentions, using the term to promote biblical literalism in the form of Flat Earth. "Zetetic," by his philosophy, meant trusting only what one can personally observe with one's own senses. "To proceed only by inquiry," he wrote in an 1881 version of *Zetetic Astronomy*, "to take nothing for granted, but to trace phenomena to their immediate and demonstrable causes." He described the term as the opposite of "theoretic," "the meaning of which," he wrote, "is, specu-lative—imaginary—not tangible,—scheming, but not proving."

This mode of reasoning, with its accusatory labeling of theory as "scheming," has obvious shortcomings when it comes to scientific inquiry. For example, I have never personally visited New Mexico. Under Rowbotham's model of zeteticism, I should regard New Mexico, as a concept, with deep suspicion. After all, my belief in New Mexico is based entirely on accounts from other people. Who's to say New Mexico isn't a large-scale hoax, perpetrated on me for rea-sons unknown? Of course, I could construct a theory of New Mexico, researching it from afar. I could interview friends who were born there, send inquiries to New Mexico politicians, and consult sworn testimo-nies from New Mexico court cases that imply the state's legal existence. While this time-consuming project might move New Mexico closer to accepted reality under Rowbotham's model, it would always leave room for doubt, unless I booked a flight to Albuquerque to confirm New Mexico's reality with my own eyes.

I've been on the receiving end of this mode of inquiry in conver-sations with my Flat Earth acquaintances. "If I asked you how fast the earth is going around the sun on the globe you believe in, what would you say?" one asked me on a phone call one summer afternoon. I hap-pened to be in Midtown Manhattan, looking up at skyscrapers that I trusted not to plummet down on me, despite my limited knowledge of construction codes.

"No idea," I replied.

"You have no idea. You have no freaking clue what you believe in," he shot back. I wanted to ask him whether he knew his exact GPS coordi-nates, and whether his not knowing them meant that he wasn't actually standing anywhere, but I remembered that GPS—Global Positioning System—was no good in his model of the universe.

Anyway, it was a rhetorical argument. Knowledge does not work this way. For the sake of sanity and advancing beyond a toddler's grasp of object permanence, we are constantly evaluating information out of our limited fields of view. When a friend relates a funny story, we likely trust that it happened even if we weren't there to witness it, just as we don't go around grabbing power lines to ascertain whether they are still delivering electricity. Healthy skepticism allows for doubt without making doubt one's default position.

In practice, not even Rowbotham's zetetic model lived up to its ideals. From his earliest pamphlets, he relied on cherry-picking passages from the Bible and applying a literal reading so that they appeared to reference a flat planet. The opposite of skeptical inquiry, this practice demanded that readers discard everything they believed in and put their blind trust in Rowbotham's limited interpretation of one faith's much-debated holy text.

Rowbotham would need all the blind faith he could get. His *Zetetic Astronomy*, which he constantly revised over the course of his life, expanding it from sixteen pages to hundreds, proposed a wildly inaccurate version of the world. On the basis of his experiments in the Bedford Canal, he claimed that the earth was completely flat, and located at the center of a small, dark universe. His map of the planet looked as though he'd sliced through a globe's southern tip with a saw and tried to flatten it on a table. The North Pole lay at the center of the pancake Earth, he said. All other land masses radiated outward from the pole, like jagged spokes on a wheel. Antarctica, the greatest casualty of his rearranged map, spanned the outer rim of the world like a great ice ring containing the world's oceans. The whole planet floated on the waters of some bigger, darker ocean: the "great deep," as he termed it.

As for the sun, stars, and moon, all were minor lights in the near sky, within four thousand miles of the ground. These low pinpricks of light traced circles above the disc Earth, bringing daylight when the sun passed over a continent and nighttime when the moon and stars passed above. (The moon emitted its own light, Rowbotham said, contrary to accepted science, which tells us that moonlight is just a reflection of the sun's glow.) Many of these claims were, of course, grounded in questionable readings of the Bible. "The sun, moon, and stars, are described as lights only to give light upon the earth," he wrote in *Zetetic Astronomy*, pointing to his own arguable reading of Genesis 1:16–17.

Though future Flat Earthers would tinker with his model, proposing that Earth is encased by a dome or nixing his theory about the "great deep," Rowbotham's general map of the world has endured within the movement. (I've met a Flat Earth artisan who sells vast rotating Flat Earth sculptures based on Rowbotham's map. One of those sculptures— three feet across with a maple frame and an LED panel—is listed online as having sold for $3,900.)

Rowbotham's theory also had a strong strain of apocalypticism. He asserted in *Zetetic Astronomy* that the earth was "approaching destruction by fire." For once, the biblical literalist wasn't talking about hell's flames. He claimed that Earth was made up of combustible chemicals and that natural occurrences like volcanoes suggested that a burning underbelly of the flat planet was clawing its way to the surface, where it would imminently ignite. He warned of future "mental and moral confusion, followed by decomposition and chemical and electric action, sufficient to ignite a great portion of the earth, and to reduce it to a molten, incandescent state." (Born well before contemporary science warned of human-produced climate change, Rowbotham had no way of knowing that he was at least a little correct about the planet's fiery future.)

Rowbotham might have taken inspiration from texts besides the Bible. Although he would introduce the flat model to the world at large, an anonymous author had self-published a short booklet called the *Anti-Newtonian* in 1819, which proposed a near-identical map. That anonymous author wrote that he "condemned the Newtonian System of the universe as being the father of all philosophical errors and evils that have already befallen mankind." The *Anti-Newtonian* never hit wide circulation, and Rowbotham never cited it in his work, but its specific arguments are so similar to Rowbotham's that he really appears to have taken large parts of it for his own purposes.

Plagiarized or not, Rowbotham's theory was as observably wrong in 1849 as it was in 1819 and as it is today. Even without pictures of the round Earth from outer space, Rowbotham's nineteenth-century readers could debunk Flat Earth with their own eyes. You can, too. Go to the beach and watch for boats near the horizon. As they sail away, you'll see them disappear hull-first behind the curve of the earth. Approaching ships will appear sail-first as they emerge around the curve. Differences between the night skies in the Northern and Southern Hemispheres also prove the globe. Stargazers in the United States or in Rowbotham's Great Britain can watch the stars appear to orbit a "northern celestial pole" over the course of a night. Observers in the Southern Hemisphere watch a different set of stars orbit a "southern celestial pole." All of this makes perfect sense on a globe and no sense on a flat model like Rowbotham's, where the sky is enclosed by a dome or "firmament." In that dome model, stars in the Southern Hemisphere would not slowly orbit a celestial pole but would zoom through the sky at meteor speeds like the outer rim of a record whizzing around to keep pace with its slower-moving center. Modern-day debunkers can also prove the globe by affixing a camera to a weather balloon, which can fly high enough to capture Earth's curve. But perhaps the easiest way to debunk Flat Earth is just to watch a sunrise or sunset. If you have a clear view of the horizon, you can watch the sun move above or below the curve, degree by degree as the day breaks or the night begins. If Flat Earth were just about the shape of the planet, we could bury this theory using its own zetetic model over the course of an evening.

But conspiracy theories—sources of meaning making and blame casting—are about more than whatever they claim on their faces. Rowbotham introduced the theory precisely when some of his countrymen were looking to discredit the emerging world. Early evolutionary biology was beginning to challenge old orthodoxies about creation, calling into question the literal truth of the Bible. Emerging theories of evolution were beginning to pave the way for thinkers like Charles Darwin, who would release his revolutionary work *On the Origin of Species* ten years after Rowbotham first began preaching Flat Earth. For some, this march of new theories looked like an assault on Christianity's privileged place in the world, led by a godless scientific elite. Even if Rowbotham, the former commune rabble-rouser, didn't believe wholeheartedly in his Flat Earth theory, its biblical literalism made it easy to sell to the religiously anxious.

"Because the Newtonian theory is held to be true they are led to reject the Scriptures altogether, to ignore the worship, and doubt and deny the existence of a Creator and Supreme Ruler of the world," he wrote in *Zetetic Astronomy*. He seeded his conspiratorial writings with a strong note of anti-elitism, firing missives at scientific types who "may see nothing higher, more noble, more intelligent, or beautiful than himself . . . Such atheism exists to an alarming extent among the philosophers and deep thinkers of Europe and America; and it has been mainly created and fostered by the astronomical and geological theories of the day."

Rowbotham's writing proposed the existence of a broad—literally worldwide—pattern of immorality and delusion among intellectuals and academics. It was among an emerging wave of conspiracy theories that made such far-flung claims. Many theories of previous centuries were narrower in scope, but grew in scale with an increasingly interconnected planet. The French Revolution in 1789 awakened the world to the potential for society-shaking upheaval, and gave rise to tales of more abstract plots of evil and intrigue. The new set included conspiracy theories about the Illuminati, a Bavarian secret society of little importance that nevertheless became a conspiratorial buzzword in Rowbotham's youth. At the end of the eighteenth century (at which point the Illuminati had already ceased to exit), a pair of popular conspiracy books accused the group of being a powerful occult movement responsible for the

French Revolution. One such book even reached the hands of George Washington, who wrote in a letter that he believed the Illuminati's doctrines had spread to the United States. These post-revolution theories focused less on specific individuals and increasingly on shadowy societies whose aims and operations were unknown. Conspiracy theorists of the time claimed that rather than seek immediate goals like political office, the alleged plotters were trying to enact vague and often worldwide evils, via enormous networks of fellow schemers.

Rowbotham's nebulous theory fit the emerging model of a plot implicating unnamed actors in unspecified evils. And it was audacious enough to draw a crowd when Rowbotham started a Flat Earth lecture circuit, especially because he targeted working-class audiences who had reason to be suspicious of the elite institutions that Rowbotham accused of deception. He delivered his first Flat Earth lecture at a mechanics' institute, a technical education hub for workers. Rowbotham might have been talking nonsense, but he could talk it well. "On Monday and Tuesday evenings last two lectures were delivered by a gentleman adopting the name of 'Parallax,'" read the *Wilts Independent* newspaper after Rowbotham's first lecture, according to a flattering set of press clippings Rowbotham included in his own book, "to prove modern astronomy unreasonable and contradictory: that the earth is a plane or disc and not a globe, the sun, moon, and stars, self-luminous . . . The lectures were well attended, and were delivered with great skill, the lecturer proving himself thoroughly acquainted with the subject in all its bearings."

Rowbotham's days of social ministry, followed by a decade of smooth-talking medical quackery, had made him a gifted speaker and debater. Maddeningly calm, he could appear to puncture arguments by Globe Earthers who showed up at his lectures to heckle him. If Earth is spinning hundreds of meters per second, he'd challenge his challengers, why does the ground feel so steady? (He'd later try to prove his point by firing a gun directly into the air and watching the projectile fall nearby, not hundreds of meters away.) He dismissed centuries of global circumnavigation with a wave of his hand. Sure, explorer Ferdinand Magellan had sailed in a large circle, he'd tell questioners. Anyone can sail in a flat circle. It doesn't mean they've circled a globe.

When indignant globe fans challenged Rowbotham to prove his theories with a lighthouse on a long stretch of beach, he used an obscure quirk of light refraction to claim that the lighthouse lantern shone out farther than a curved Earth would allow. (Actually, the trick of the light made the lighthouse *less* visible, but Rowbotham used the anomaly to cast doubt on math and claim victory.) From the beginning of his days as Parallax, Rowbotham also boasted of having had his papers read before the Royal Astronomical Society. The claim gave him an air of legitimacy, like a contemporary scholar publishing their work in an academic journal. He probably wasn't lying, but the likely truth would have been mortifying to most self-respecting scientists. Early after publication, a copy of *Zetetic Astronomy* found its way to mathematician Augustus De Morgan, secretary of the Astronomical Society, who read excerpts of the Flat Earth manifesto during a Society meeting as a joke.

Rowbotham didn't always win his debates. During his first round of lectures, he promised a two-night extravaganza in a town called Burnley. His theories were still young at the time, and he wasn't prepared to account for all the holes in his Flat Earth ideas. When someone pushed him too hard on why the hulls of ships disappear over the horizon before the sails, Rowbotham bailed on his own lecture. He did not show up for the second night. His would-be audience passed the time by telling each other that Rowbotham had slipped off the planet's icy edge.

If a credentialed scientist had had their work disproven during a conference and vanished ahead of their second speech, they could have likely kissed their career and credibility goodbye. But Rowbotham was a showman at heart, not a scientist, and he courted controversy for the paying crowds it could draw to his lectures. In this, the press was often his biggest ally. Flat Earth boomed when newspapers did. This is likely no coincidence. Heavily taxed and confined to small presses, newspapers had largely been the territory of rich men at the beginning of the century. But after cuts to stamp taxes, newspapers began flourishing in the 1840s, bringing a culture of voracious readership to the masses for whom the printed word had once been a luxury.

As would happen with subsequent dam bursts in communications, like the emergence of the internet and social media more than 150 years later, sensational nonsense like conspiracy theories floated to the top. In this time of booming readership, Rowbotham received free advertisement on the regular; even the skeptical papers covered his lectures as a source of amusement, a big multiday in-joke that would inevitably turn out crowds. Rather than lean away from the papers' colorful descriptions, Rowbotham welcomed arguments. Posters for his upcoming speeches invited "philosophers and Scientific men" to attend, alongside people of all faiths. On at least one occasion, he tried goading a prominent astronomer into attending a lecture by falsely claiming that *another* revered astronomer had already converted to belief in Flat Earth.

He didn't need any of these people to agree with him; all he needed was the spectacle. And while some newspapers treated him like a joke, other newspapers were openly flattering, at least according to quotes Rowbotham included in reprints of his own work: "The lecturer is not a theorist, and the matter is sufficiently important to claim the attention of the scientific world," a Liverpool paper fawned in 1850. The *Athlone Sentinel* in 1851 poured out its praise, likening Rowbotham to Hamlet. Listeners might have shown up to mock Rowbotham and his ideas, but their intentions didn't matter. By the end of the night, they'd all paid six pennies for the lecture (and possibly an additional three shillings for a copy of *Zetetic Astronomy*), and some of them had converted to Flat Earthism. Whether Rowbotham believed his theory had become irrelevant. His converts believed, and they were willing to pay good money for his sermons.

Not everyone was amused. Some early interventionists saw Flat Earth as a dangerous ideology. One of them, a vicar from York called

Rev. M. R. Bresher, disbelieved Rowbotham's theories on theological grounds. Bresher understood the biblical verses Rowbotham cited in Flat Earth sermons, and he was also a respected member of his local philosophical society who dabbled in astronomy. When Rowbotham came preaching in his town, Bresher was rattled by how many locals accepted the Flat Earth arguments immediately. "Many of those who listened to the Lecturer's fervid denunciations of the newtonian system as utterly absurd in itself, and subversive of all belief in the inspiration of the Bible, seem to have been carried away by his declamation, and to have become converts to his system," he noted.

Bresher was so alarmed that he churned out a 173-page rebuttal to Rowbotham's main claims. In addition to using a highly selective reading of the Bible, Bresher argued, Rowbotham also took liberties with a reference book about lighthouses, using it to claim that lighthouse beacons were visible beyond the point at which the earth's curve should have obscured them. Bresher noted that contrary to zetetic science, Rowbotham had not personally observed those lighthouses. If Rowbotham had investigated or consulted scientists, he might have learned that the book was inaccurate, that his calculations were wrong, or that he had not considered how atmospheric refraction would warp the light. But, Bresher continued, Rowbotham was more concerned with sowing doubt in scientific models than he was with proving his own theory. "I have carefully looked over the book alluded to, and find that out of above 2000 cases, the few selected by 'Parallax' are nearly the whole that do not verify the truth of the doctrine in question," Bresher wrote after cross-referencing Rowbotham's lighthouses with the more than two thousand listed in the book *Lighthouses of the World*. "And what do these few, about thirty out of upwards of 2000, prove?"

In other words, approximately 1.5 percent of lighthouses in *Lighthouses of the World* seemed to support Rowbotham's theory, and Rowbotham cited all of them—not a very zetetic thing to do. Bresher hoped his rebuttal would free believers from the grip of Flat Earth fanaticism. He was wrong, and modern Flat Earthers still make fun of him on conspiracy forums 150 years later, an unfortunate legacy for the well-meaning vicar. "This is supposed to be meaningful?" one Flat Earther complained of Bresher's math on a forum in 2019.

While the preacher stumbled, Rowbotham was building his empire. He incorporated multiple zetetic societies, including a branch in New York in 1873. The officers of this American chapter almost certainly signed up as a prank. Many were respected lawyers. One, G. H. Colton Salter, was a US consul to China. Another member, Hans Powell, was a famous doctor who had recently served as the surgeon general of the Grand Army of the Republic. Rev. John Nelson McJilton was the superintendent of Baltimore's public schools, and Lemuel Crane was the president of a literary society. The men may have been mocking Rowbotham, but he got the last laugh when he printed their names and titles in an official-looking announcement of the Zetetic Society's New York chapter in his newspaper the *Zetetic*.

He also gained earnest apostles in the United Kingdom. One invaluable follower was William Carpenter, a Greenwich printing press owner who attended one of Rowbotham's lectures as a joke and emerged a Flat Earth diehard. Mimicking Rowbotham's Parallax pen name, Carpenter started publishing his own Flat Earth works under the name Common Sense. He dedicated his first major work, *Theoretical Astronomy Examined and Exposed*, to Parallax.

"Time was, they said the Earth was *flat*; but now they say it's *round!*" begins an introductory poem. "But strange enough, though true, it is, no *PROOF* has yet been found." Carpenter took up Rowbotham's biblical arguments and found new places to poke at established science. Legendary astronomers Nicholas Copernicus, Johannes Kepler, and Isaac Newton had all estimated different distances between Earth and sun. Carpenter claimed the discrepancy should call the entire field of modern astronomy into question. (Copernicus, Kepler, and Newton never had the chance to compare notes because none of them lived at the same time, and all were using inexact estimation methods.) Where Rowbotham styled himself after conventional scientists with sober prose, Carpenter went after his opponents with a verbal hammer and all the derision of a modern-day internet troll. "*Fiddle-de-dee!*" he wrote of a scientist who praised science's ability to measure distances with relative accuracy. "We are to be *thankful* that there are men who can *calculate* and *correct* certain 'quantities:' but what have they done, by their own showing, but *mis-calculate*, and 'correct' their *mis-calculations?*"

Critics were quick to praise his work for its entertainment value, if not its ideas. "'Common Sense' argues his position in a very able manner: the highest authorities are quoted, and, to our minds, demolished like a pack of cards," read an 1864 review printed in the front of Carpenter's book. Another wrote that "he ridicules modern astronomy, and caustically comments on the unreliable character of the views its professors advance for our guidance."

For all his devotion, Carpenter wouldn't even be the most aggressive Flat Earther of Rowbotham's era. That title fell to John Hampden, one of the first people whose lives would be ruined over Flat Earth theory.

Hampden had one of the easiest incomes in Britain. The oldest son in a wealthy family, he was set to inherit a significant fortune. All he had to do was not land himself in a catastrophically expensive and embarrassing legal drama. On this count, he would eventually fail in spectacular fashion, landing himself in prison and going bankrupt—all in Flat Earth's name. A divinity school dropout cushioned by his privileged circumstances, Hampden spent his much of unemployed adulthood writing militant pamphlets on the need for a stricter Church of England. *Zetetic Astronomy*, which he first read in 1869, opened new possibilities in biblical literalism. Hampden began snapping up Flat Earth literature and started a correspondence with Carpenter. For his first year of Flat Earth belief, Hampden churned out pamphlets, their texts half borrowed from Rowbotham's and Carpenter's works. But by the following year, he had hatched a more attention-grabbing scheme.

In a January 12, 1870, edition of *Scientific Opinion*, Hampden placed a bet in an advertisement offering £500 (approximately £60,000 or $82,000, present-day) for proof that the earth was round. For Globe Earthers, the wager seemed like free money. Three days later, Hampden had a challenger in the form of the revered scientist Alfred Russel Wallace. An esteemed naturalist and evolutionary biologist, Wallace had the famously bad luck of proposing the theory of natural selection around the same time as Charles Darwin. Wallace was also openly skeptical of religious zealotry and was an ideal foil for Flat Earthers looking to discredit scientific elites.

Wallace suggested several locations for a test that would prove Earth's rotundity. But over a series of letters, Hampden refused them all, demanding instead to host the tests at the Bedford Canal, the mecca of England's Flat Earth scene. They agreed to meet in March 1870, each bringing their own "neutral" referee to validate the experiment's results. Wallace brought another respected naturalist. Hampden brought Carpenter. The conflict of interest was even greater than it seemed on its face. After Carpenter's Flat Earth book sold poorly, Hampden bought up the copyright and all the remaining stock, placing Carpenter in his debt, figuratively speaking. Neither man informed Wallace of Carpenter's Flat Earth sympathies, nor of the copyright connection. Wallace agreed to the terms of the experiment with no idea what he was wading into. Naively, he believed that "a practical demonstration would be more convincing than the ridicule with which such views are usually met," he later wrote.

Wallace brought with him a £500 check, surveyors' tools, a telescope, and a series of flags and markers, which he set up at strategic distances along the canal. The morning after his arrival, he prepared to view the flags through his telescope and demonstrate once and for all that the distant markers were obscured by the earth's curve.

The plan started falling apart as soon as he met with Carpenter, the supposedly impartial referee. Carpenter promptly set about wreaking childlike havoc on the experiment. When entrusted with holding a tripod leg, he kept dropping it at critical moments. When Wallace's team got fed up and relieved Carpenter of his setup duties, he repeatedly bumped into a telescope, forcing the Globe Earth crew to start the surveying process anew. When Wallace's telescope inevitably showed that the distant flags were hidden behind the earth's curve, Hampden's team made an irrelevant observation about the telescope's crosshairs and claimed it invalidated Wallace's measurements. Hampden proceeded to declare victory for Flat Earth. Carpenter and the other referee "gave diametrically opposite decisions on the same facts," an exasperated Wallace later recounted.

After a tortured process of finding new referees, Wallace was finally awarded the full £500 prize, much to Hampden's fury. The Flat Earther embarked on a feud against Wallace, sending letters full of appallingly violent abuse to him and many of his friends, claiming to have won the wager and charging Wallace with fraud and conspiracy.

One of the worst letters was addressed to Wallace's wife. "If your infernal thief of a husband is brought home some day on a hurdle, with every bone in his head smashed to pulp, you will know the reason," Hampden wrote in the letter. "Do tell him from me he is a lying infernal thief, and as sure as his name is Wallace he never dies in his bed. You must be a miserable wretch to be obliged to live with a convicted felon. Do not think or let him think I have done with him."

Wallace pressed libel charges and won several judgments against Hampden, who was repeatedly jailed and released, each time reemerging to send Wallace new letters with supervillain-like zeal. "I make no secret of having written thousands of letters declaring your conduct to be that of a cheat and a swindler," he wrote in one. "No lawyer or Law Court in England shall prevent my doing so. . . . I only wonder your wife and family are not ashamed to live with you. How much longer is this to last? Do not dream of my getting tired."

Hampden declared bankruptcy as the result of the many court proceedings. Even Wallace, who had hoped to make a quick £500 from the bet, ended up hundreds of pounds in the hole. And although Hampden's fellow Flat Earthers supported him as if he were a martyr for the cause, Wallace's peers came to regard the whole incident with disgust, accusing the scientist of taking advantage of an idiot.

The bet and its ensuing legal battles "cost me fifteen years of continued worry, litigation, and persecution," Wallace later wrote. "And it was all brought upon me by my own . . . ignorance of the fact so well shown by the late Professor de Morgan—that 'paradoxers,' as he termed them, can never be convinced."

Even Rowbotham had become roped into the dispute. Shortly after the contentious bet on the Bedford Canal, Hampden financed a trip for Rowbotham to visit the canal and make his measurements again. Rowbotham, by this point, appears to have been phoning it in; instead of wading out onto the canal as he did as a young man, the now-aging Flat Earther made his measurements from a bridge on another part of the waterway and declared that, yes, it was all still as level as it had been when he was a young Owenite imagining a utopia along those same banks. He jotted off a new pamphlet, *Experimental Proofs (with Illustrative Engravings) That the Surface of Standing Water Is Not Convex but Horizontal*, about his supposed findings. Rowbotham opened the text, however, with a lengthy scold against Hampden, whose increasing appearances in newspaper headlines had begun to eat into Rowbotham's fame. He wrote that he had been "startled" to learn via newspaper of Hampden's wager with Wallace, and that he had written Hampden "enquiring as to the nature of the experiments to be made and the place and time and persons concerned in the matter: but could get no information. I was kept in entire ignorance of the whole affair until it was over."

Rowbotham was either conducting damage control for the failed experiment or else earnestly offended to see his work take on a life of its own outside his control. "Were they not bound in honor, as gentlemen, . . . to have informed me of their intentions and to have invited me to take part in their proceedings? Their not having done so was to myself individually a needless insult," Rowbotham wrote. "There never was an instance where in deed and in truth it could have been more justly said 'save me from my friends.'"

Whatever his intentions when he first publicized Flat Earth theory—earnest belief or the potential for quick cash—Rowbotham had created a movement larger than himself. With zetetic societies (even joking ones) on either side of the Atlantic, a crowd of devotees publishing their own Flat Earth works, and a growing public awareness for his theory fed by tabloids' love for Hampden and Wallace's wager, Flat Earth was now self-sustaining. As disciples like Carpenter and Hampden took on the Flat Earth movement's battles, Rowbotham moved back into the medical fraud field, selling his phosphorus drinks to the desperate. His miracle cures brought him money but not the near immortality he promised his patients. In 1884, he slipped while getting out of a carriage. Once the leader of a movement that could shake the earth to its foundation, Rowbotham was incapacitated by the fall. His health suffered beyond what his glorified soda water could repair, and he died two days before Christmas, at age sixty-eight.

But the theory he had brought into being as a young man on the marshes was about to go global.

2 | The Tyrant

SAMUEL ROWBOTHAM HAD been despised at Manea Fen, the commune where he'd first dreamed up Flat Earth theory. But if he'd survived just a few more decades, he would have lived to see his vindication in another, even more borderline-cultic community, which went absolutely fanatical for his idea.

Much like Manea Fen, the little town of Zion, Illinois, was a would-be utopia. A planned community on the shore of Lake Michigan, Zion was established with lofty ideals of moral righteousness and self-sufficiency. Unlike Manea Fen's short-lived commune of marriage-scorning, laughing-gas-huffing British socialists, however, Zion operated with ruthless puritanical efficiency. And rather than implode after a few short years, Zion operated for decades under a genuine Flat Earth dictatorship.

In the beginning, Zion's central fiction wasn't Flat Earth. It was faith healing, a practice championed by the town's founder, John Dowie. Born to a Scottish preacher in 1847, Dowie was a noted religious wacko from his teens onward, when his family moved to Australia. At twenty years old, the young man began preaching for new Christian revivalist movements, and rather than try to ingratiate himself with local worshippers, he instead made himself a local joke for fighting with his congregants and giving dramatic, shouting sermons. After being kicked out of multiple ministries, he tried establishing his own church, but quickly landed in an all-out war over its ownership, during which his rivals locked themselves inside the building while his supporters waited in siege outside. The feud eventually landed Dowie, by then in his thirties, in jail for a month. By the late 1880s, he was deep in debt and embroiled in another church ownership dispute. Conveniently, the church in question burned to the ground, and Dowie, a militant anti-alcohol crusader, claimed "liquor interests" had started the blaze. Others accused Dowie of arson, and he left Australia for the United States before investigators could take a close look at the incident.

Despite the arson allegations against him, Dowie began to attract a band of American followers, as well as followers at offshoots of his church in Australia and South Africa. Many were likely drawn to his boasts of mystical healing abilities. In this, he was like Samuel Rowbotham, who advertised his glorified soda drinks as a miracle cure. But instead of singing the praises of a proto-Pepsi, Dowie credited the divine, claiming to work miracles via his unique friendship with Jesus. He might have been an eccentric, but belief in faith healing and quack cures was, and is, far from unusual. Around the time Dowie was building his empire, the *New York Times* ran multiple stories on faith healing all across the country, reported with varying degrees of skepticism. (In one Brooklyn case, in 1885, the paper noted that a woman claimed prayer had cured her of a tumor, while her doctors told the paper she never had a tumor in the first place, just a local infection.)

More than one hundred years later, belief in faith healing and alternative medicine persists at unusually high rates among Flat Earthers, so much so that a Vanderbilt University researcher in 2018 used Flat Earth forums for a study on anti-doctor sentiment. In my own years traversing the conspiracy scene, Flat Earthers must have pitched me on half a dozen cure-all diets, from raw foods to veganism. (Myself a vegan for years, I agreed to pay a Flat Earther twenty dollars for a PDF of his vegan health food cookbook. The product he texted me was eleven pages long and contained recipes like one for eating a package of store-bought vegan chili. "Just heat up, and enjoy with some toasted bread," the recipe's single step instructed. "Super easy.") A spectrum of extra-medical beliefs are also common outside the Flat Earth community. In a 2007 Pew poll, 36 percent of Americans who believed in a god said they'd personally witnessed "a divine healing of an illness or injury." In a 2010 Baylor University survey, nearly 80 percent of respondents said they'd prayed for their own health at some point. We may live in an era of unprecedented scientific discovery, but this counterscientific habit is as enmeshed in American culture as our tendency toward religion and our instinct toward hope.

Many of Dowie's fans followed him because he promised to cure them. Across several decades and two leaders of Dowie's movement, these followers' lightly superstitious belief in faith healing would be twisted into devout Flat Earthism.

If Dowie ever considered Flat Earth theory, he made no note of it. The Flat Earth movement floundered after Rowbotham's death in 1884, with no clear heir to Parallax's throne. William Carpenter moved to the United States in 1880, settling his family in Baltimore, where he became a local oddity and gave classes in shorthand writing, earning him the nickname "the Professor." He continued publishing Flat Earth writings in great volumes and was notorious for hanging around university campuses, trying to sell his books and encouraging people to take them for free if they refused to buy. "One of his characteristics was to try and draw into argument on the question some of the leaders of religion and science, and when they refused to debate with him Professor Carpenter would generally write an open letter roundly denouncing them," a *Baltimore Sun* obituary recalled after his death in 1896. John Hampden, haggard from decades of legal feuds, died in 1891.

The year after Hampden's death, some minor-league Rowbotham followers launched the Universal Zetetic Society, which came to be led by Lady Elizabeth Anne Mould Blount. Born to a land surveyor in 1850, Blount was an unusual candidate for Flat Earth militancy, but she became one of the movement's pioneering female voices. She obtained her ladyship through a marriage to an older nobleman, Sir Walter de Sodington Blount, a baronet and a staunch Roman Catholic. Lady Blount, meanwhile, was a Protestant, a biblical literalist, and by 1892, when she wrote a pamphlet equating globe belief with heresy, a Flat Earther. Some (or all) of the couple's religious beliefs appear to have come between them, with Sir Walter's family cutting him off for marrying outside his faith. The couple moved into separate houses in 1901, three years after Lady Blount published *Adrian Galilio; or, A Song Writer's Story*, a Flat Earth novel infused with sheet music. The book remains probably the most creative text ever to emerge from the Flat Earth movement. While not strictly autobiographical, the book likely made for some uncomfortable Blount family dinners, if the couple even discussed it at all. *Adrian Galilio* is about a beautiful Protestant Flat Earth lady unhappy in her marriage to a mean, older Roman Catholic nobleman, who hates her for being Protestant. The protagonist, Lady Alma, finds true love and acceptance while having an affair with a handsome priest who praises her theories.

I adore this bizarre little book. Every few pages, someone will break out in song, for which the sheet music is helpfully provided. Hoping to hear the cadence of Lady Blount's thoughts, I conscripted a friend to record a version of a song. She sent back a chaotic, rollicking soprano show tune with lyrics railing against godless "globites." (As it happened, we were not the only twenty-first-century readers trying to raise Blount from history. I later discovered that the Flat Earth Society had uploaded, and subsequently deleted, a recording of its own piano-and-violin version of a Blount song. And a large Flat Earth YouTube channel has also brought back Lady Blount, enlisting a British woman to read passages of her writing, pausing occasionally to make jabs at Flat Earth theory's modern-day critics.)

The novel's plot is just as unusual as its musical interludes. In one representative passage, Lady Alma name-drops Parallax during a rendezvous with the priest and bursts into a song she wrote about Flat

Earth. Her lover responds that she is very pretty and talented, and that if she believes in Flat Earth, there must be some truth to the theory. Just then, a previously unintroduced character shoots both of them in a jealous rage, and Lady Alma goes on to become a famous and respected Flat Earth lecturer.

In real life, Lady Blount did indeed become a Flat Earth lecturer, but to less success. Although she was, unsurprisingly, known to intersperse her speeches with song, she lacked the sheer bombasity of Rowbotham or the headline-grabbing legal delusions of Hampden. When she announced in 1909 that she had invented a "flying machine" modeled after a bird, "studded with valves, which open when the machine is going up and close when it is coming down," the *Washington Post* afforded her a three-sentence article. (No one appears to have built a test model of the machine, which is fortunate, because it almost certainly would not work.) Under Blount's leadership, the Universal Zetetic Society launched a publication, the *Earth Not a Globe Review*, which was polite and professional-looking, and never obtained any serious readership. The UZS fizzled out in the early twentieth century, and even Blount appears to have ended her Flat Earth evangelizing long before her 1935 death.

While the UZS was fading, however, Dowie was unintentionally planting the seeds for the most hardline Flat Earth group ever to exist. In the United States, Dowie embraced the absurd, dressing in ornate robes like a priest from some long-forgotten sect and calling himself Elijah the Restorer. As with Rowbotham, the press ridiculed him (*Harper's Weekly* in particular referred to him as "a weird little fat man" pushing a "curious jumble of religion and get-rich-quick activities"), but the bad press gave him more notoriety. As in Australia, legal troubles followed him. Two of his "patients" sued him when his miracle cures turned out to be bogus, and he was repeatedly arrested, including once during a sermon, for practicing medicine without a license. Critics accused him of literally stealing money from sickly patients' pockets while laying hands on them in prayer. None of that slowed him. He launched a newsletter called *Leaves of Healing*, became a multimillionaire, and amassed so many followers in his Christian Catholic Apostolic Church that in 1900 he announced designs for the city of Zion, an obsessively planned religious community about fifty miles north of Chicago. Most of his ten-thousand-or-so-member Chicago congregation followed him to Zion. There, he carried out a massive property scam, forcing new Zionites to sign overpriced eleven-hundred-year leases, which contained strict rules (no alcohol, no pork, no doctors). Rule breakers could be evicted without compensation, and followers had to deposit their savings into Dowie's unincorporated bank, which he personally controlled. The cult-like con laid the groundwork for the inescapable push of Flat Earth doctrine that was yet to come.

Still, Zion was not so unique at the outset. Dowie's movement emerged near the end of the Second Great Awakening, a nationwide revival of evangelicalism that led to a host of sects and settlements. Another Chicago-area group preceded Zion in building a cultlike atmosphere based on an alternative model of the earth. Members of this group, the Koreshan Unity movement, believed they lived inside a hollow Earth. To Koreshans, the skies were the inner walls of a vast sphere, and the sun was an electric light near the top of this great ceiling. (Blount's *Adrian Galilio* also references Koresh. "There are those who believe that the earth is a hollow globe, and that we inhabit its inner portion," the fictional Lady Alma tells the audience at a lecture. "These last are the 'Koreshanites' of America.")

Though Zion was not founded as a Flat Earth society, the man who would convert the city to the theory was at Dowie's side even before Zion's blueprints were revealed. Wilbur Glenn Voliva was suffering a crisis of faith when he found Dowie's teachings. Born in Indiana in 1870, he turned to preaching in his teen years. Like Dowie, he came into conflict with his congregants, whom he believed too shallow for his vision of fundamentalist Christianity. He was considering quitting ministry to become a lawyer when he first read an issue of *Leaves of Healing* in 1899. The alleged miracles Dowie described were enough to renew Voliva's faith, and he joined Dowie's movement. He rose quickly in Dowie's estimation, and in 1901 was dispatched to Australia to deal with a mutiny among Dowie's followers there.

It's not clear when, or how, Voliva became a Flat Earther. He made no mention of the theory before his trip to Australia. If he believed in the theory at the time of his trip, he would have believed himself sailing toward the outer circumference of a flat disc. He wouldn't have been the only Flat Earther in the Southern Hemisphere. Paul Kruger, the controversial president of the short-lived South African Republic (also known as the Transvaal) from 1883 to 1900, was a staunch Flat Earther, for reasons of biblical literalism, and was known to berate people who described sailing "*round* the world."

Flat Earther at the time of his Australia trip or not, Voliva built a small empire of new Dowie devouts, who sent thousands of dollars back to Zion. The city needed every penny. Voliva was in Australia for four years, and Dowie spent all of them in Zion on a shopping spree. He built himself an elaborate mansion in the center of town, spending $90,000 (the equivalent of almost $3 million dollars, adjusted for inflation) on the twenty-five-room home, which he stuffed with $50,000 of luxury furniture and $40,000 in books. He hosted a miserable touring circuit, including a failed New York City event that cost the church $300,000. The city had its own industries—a lace factory and a factory that made off-brand Fig Newtons—but they couldn't keep up with Dowie's expensive habits. Desperate for funds, the faith healer repeatedly ordered followers to mortgage everything they owned and place the proceeds in the city bank, where he could access them. Though Zionites bore the city's heavy financial demands in its early years, many grew disillusioned as their wealth melted away, while their leader lived in a lavish home.

Dowie's claims to faith healing were the next to fail him. In 1902, his daughter Esther suffered third-degree burns while using an alcohol-burning hair-curling device at the University of Chicago. Dowie rushed to her bedside, but in keeping with his movement's disdain of doctors, they refused professional medical assistance. Esther died within the day.

Then Dowie's own health failed. During a 1905 sermon, he had a stroke in full view of his followers, leaving him partially paralyzed. He left the city for an expensive recovery-slash-vacation, first in Mexico (where he dabbled in plans for a new religious settlement), then in Jamaica. Sick and alone abroad, he realized he was in danger of losing Zion, the very heart of his empire (which spanned four continents, with branches in Australia, South Africa, and Switzerland). He needed someone capable and trustworthy to act in his stead. He wrote to Voliva in Australia, instructing him to return.

But Dowie misjudged Voliva's loyalty. During Dowie's spending spree, some of his followers had, disgusted, returned home to Australia, where they tattled to Voliva about the goings-on in Zion. As soon as Voliva stepped foot in Zion in February 1906, he began a coup against its founder, with support from fed-up Christian Catholic Apostolic Church elders. Finding Zion effectively bankrupt, with up to $3.4 million in city funds unaccounted for, Voliva purged Dowie from the church. ("Quietly retire. Further interference will precipitate complete exposure, rebellion, legal proceedings," Voliva warned him in a letter.) Voliva's first sermon in the city strongly implied that Dowie was under Satan's grasp. Voliva also accused Dowie of being a shameless polygamist, who was trying to create a harem of wives. Even Dowie's wife signed on to the allegation, producing love letters her husband had supposedly penned to his would-be partners, although she later recanted and came to her husband's side. *Leaves of Healing*, now under Voliva's control, published out-of-context quotes from Dowie's old sermons, which had been unfairly doctored to look like he was advocating polygamy.

In a bid to reclaim his crown, Dowie returned to Zion with plans for a great sermon, only for Voliva to counterprogram him with a larger sermon at the same time nearby. Meanwhile, a group of apparent Voliva supporters rushed Dowie's stage, injuring Dowie's son. During Dowie's final months, church elders in Zion scrubbed his name and picture from city buildings. Little did they know that the city's true tyrant was just taking his throne.

A funny thing sometimes happens with cultic religious groups in disarray. Rather than dissolve when a spiritual leader disappoints them or a promised paradise turns to hell, many groups double down on their beliefs. In the early 1840s, for instance, an apocalyptic Christian sect called the Millerite movement warned of the imminent apocalypse. When the prophesied Judgment Day came and passed without incident, many members only became more fervent in their belief, proclaiming that the real end was still coming soon. While waiting for a rescheduled doomsday, believers let their crops rot and their friendships fail, in the belief that none of those earthly ties would matter soon. These groups often find trivial factors to blame for their disappointments, like a preacher for misinterpreting a prophecy, or themselves for possessing insufficient piety. They seldom find fault with their underlying belief system, proclaiming that something else, not the prophecy, has failed.

Fanatical political movements, I suspect, can function much in the same way. In November 2020, then president Donald Trump lost reelection but claimed, via an increasingly ludicrous series of conspiracy theories, that he was the rightful winner and that his opponent had cheated. As Trump's election loss became evident to everyone outside his thrall, I spent my day job as a journalist interviewing Trump supporters who believed him. They were more devoted to him than ever before, buying his false claims that Democrats had registered fake voters, and that the companies that manufactured voting machines were distorting the count on behalf of the left. One Trump supporter, a Republican state senator from Virginia, told me she was certain that Democrats had stolen the election, and that Trump should declare martial law in order to restore his presidency. (After I wrote an article dismissing her

statements as lunacy, she posted my cell phone number on her government Facebook page.) Another Trump believer, a gambler who bets on
political outcomes, told me she put money on Trump's victory even after
most news outlets had declared him the loser. Several months later, I
spoke to a Trump-loving Arkansas cop who, by her own admission, had
trespassed on the grounds of the nation's Capitol during the January
2021 pro-Trump riot. Despite having marched into the area alongside
some of the rioters who would later breach the Capitol building itself,
she expressed her (incorrect) conviction that the riot was a conspiracy
between police and anti-Trump militants, or "antifa."

Speaking all day to the hard-core believers of a doomed political
sect, I began to understand how Zionites entered mostly willingly into
an alternate reality, divorced from the world outside their city limits.

When Dowie turned out to be an obvious fraud who left congregants penniless, many Zion dwellers did not abandon the city. Instead,
they threw themselves completely into Voliva's new leadership and,
soon, his Flat Earth philosophy. With city coffers empty, many worshippers worked without pay in the belief that Voliva would deliver
them from bankruptcy. During sermons, churchgoers were encouraged to dump their worldly possessions on a pair of tables. One service
saw the tables piled with jewelry, coupon books, a violin, and checks
for up to $3,500. As their possessions dwindled, so did their rights.
Although he never held any elected title like mayor, Voliva assumed
control of the Theocratic Party, Dowie's old political gang. By way of
this puppet government, helmed by a loyal mayor, Voliva began to
enforce Zion's morality rules—no drinking, dancing, or doctors—with
a fervor unseen under Dowie's reign. In a last gasp of resistance against
what some started to realize was a burgeoning dictatorship, a group
of anti-Voliva political candidates ran for office in April 1909 and beat
Voliva's stooges in city hall by a narrow margin. But in a Trumpian
turn, Voliva and his preferred candidates simply refused to accept the
results of the election.

"It means war," Voliva thundered in a speech that could have been uttered by the forty-fifth president of the United States, accusing his opponents (without merit) of sneaking fake voters into the city. "We are fighting for the right and for religion, and we do not intend that these men shall gain control of the city through illegal voting. The old city officials were reelected and must be given the offices. I've hired two big attorneys to prosecute those who perpetrated these election frauds. I mean business."

For several tense weeks, Zion was in the grips of civil war with two competing mayors, each of whom announced their own police chiefs. Captain A. K. Walker, the illegitimate pro-Voliva police chief, set up camp in the city's main jail "with doors and windows barricaded and a large store of food and water to withstand a long siege," the Chicago *Inter Ocean* reported. The city's real police chief, the newly appointed Captain John Jaap, rallied two hundred of his own supporters to drive Walker and his forces from the jail, a standoff that led to the two men shouting at each other from opposite sides of the barricade.

"Don't come a step nearer or I'll shoot," Walker bellowed from an upstairs jail window.

"I'm the regularly appointed chief of police," Jaap yelled back.

"You are not!"

"I demand that you give up the city jail!"

"You'll never get this jail," Walker countered. "I'm here to stay for two more years!"

Both men threatened to release any prisoner the other police chief arrested, and the city remained in limbo until June, when a court ruling forced Voliva's side to admit defeat.

In a final push for power, Voliva supporters tried swearing in defeated pro-Voliva officials in a barricaded city hall room on the grounds that, because they didn't know where the ballots were, none of the ballots counted and, therefore, they could decide the election as they pleased. Instead, hundreds of anti-Voliva activists rushed city hall, physically forcing Voliva's faction to hand over power in a riot that left hundreds wounded. BARE FISTS FROM EARLY EVENING UNTIL AFTER MIDNIGHT, one headline from a Chicago newspaper read.

Ultimately, the effort to unseat Voliva did no good. Though independents did briefly manage to hold power in Zion after the election, their reign of sanity was short-lived. The following year, in 1910, Voliva resumed control when he bought back the city's property from the state receivership that was holding it during bankruptcy procedures. (So no one forgot their financial savior, Voliva attached his name to deeds on all the newly repurchased city property, and raked in the profits from Zion's various industries.)

This new takeover also placed him at the head of Zion's educational system, a fact that would prove fateful by 1914, when his Flat Earth philosophy started leaking into his leadership. Voliva launched verbal crusades against astronomers in his sermons, attacking the idea that the sun was a distant star. By 1915, he was preaching a Rowbotham-like model of the world, based on selective scripture readings.

"I get my astronomy from the Bible," he ranted in a sermon the day after Christmas that year. "I believe this earth is a stationary plane; that it rests upon water; and that there is no such thing as the earth moving, no such thing as the earth's axis or the earth's orbit. It is a lot of silly rot, born in the egotistical brains of infidels. Neither do I believe there is any such thing as the law of gravitation: I believe that that is a lot of rot, too. There is no such thing!"

Around the time of Voliva's first Flat Earth sermons, he ordered the closure of the city's high school, and in 1916 launched an alternative: the Zion Educational Institutions, which would be completely under his control. A church elder wrote the schools' Flat Earth curriculum, which required teachers to instruct students in this alternative model of the world. References to conventional geography were prohibited. Voliva also banned other scientific areas of study on the grounds of his biblical literalism. "Teach a child he is kin to the ameba [*sic*] and he will take on the characteristics of the ameba. Anyway, such teaching is a flat contradiction to the plain word of God. The Bible doesn't even mention ameba," he wrote. (Of all Zion's bizarre institutions, its schools would trigger the greatest alarm from Illinois officials. In 1919, state investigators were startled to learn of the Flat Earth curriculum in Zion schools, but they did not intervene at the time.)

Voliva's militancy about childhood Flat Earth education remains more or less consistent in modern Flat Earth circles. I am an obsessive lurker in Flat Earth Facebook groups, where I've witnessed multiple parents complain that their children's Flat Earth maps received failing marks in school. Some allow their children to attend public school anyway: "She goes to school with 12 other children (All within 2 grades of eachother) [sic] who are taught Flat Earth at home," one commenter on a Flat Earth forum wrote of her daughter. A parent in a Facebook group I monitor told the group, "I was thinking about sending my kids to school with a letter to say that I do not want my children participating in any lessons to do with the solar system! Would this be wise?" Other Flat Earthers simply leave public education in disgust, opting to homeschool their children outside the sinister influence of the globe. In the check-in line for a Flat Earth conference in Dallas, I stood next to a group of women gathered over a toddler in a stroller. "*You* won't be fooled," they cooed to the child.

Classes in Zion were permitted to use two maps: a speculative map of the world imagined by a Flat Earther in 1890 and an obscure nautical chart that showed the world from a top-down perspective, with the North Pole at its center. (The latter map was technically correct, but essentially useless to everyone besides Arctic explorers and Flat Earthers who wanted to imagine how the planet would look as a flat disc with the South Pole as an ice ring at the perimeter.) Issues of Dowie's old newsletter, *Leaves of Healing*, which went to Christian Catholic Apostolic Church members worldwide, included pleas for donations to the schools, alongside clip-out contribution forms that were personally addressed to Voliva. The same church elder Voliva had placed in charge of the schools was also tasked with flattening the city's religious hymns. A familiar Zionite song that went "Let every kindred, every tribe, / On this terrestrial ball, / To him all majesty ascribe, / And crown Him Lord of All" was rewritten as "Let every kindred, every tribe, / On this terrestrial *plane*, / To Him all majesty ascribe, / And *praise His Holy Name*." Modern astronomy was among the disciplines Voliva labeled the "Devil's Triplets," an unholy trinity that also included the study of evolution and literary study of the Bible.

The Christian Catholic Apostolic Church devoted an entire special edition of *Leaves of Healing* to Flat Earth in 1930. Topped with a picture of Voliva in a scholarly pose, pointing to a Flat Earth map, the newsletter described Flat Earth belief as a matter of salvation or hellfire. WHICH WILL YOU ACCEPT? a headline read. THE BIBLE, THE INSPIRED WORD OF GOD OR THE INFIDEL THEORIES OF MODERN ASTRONOMY?

Voliva riffed on previous Flat Earthers' fears that modern science would come to replace Christianity, particularly focusing on emerging fields like the study of evolution. "While it is true that Evolution has slain its thousands, it is equally true that Modern Astronomy has slain its tens of thousands!" Voliva wrote in the newsletter's introduction, referring to Christians who had apparently lost their faith after learning about outer space. "Multitudes of hitherto professing Christians, unable to reconcile the theories of Modern Astronomy with the plain declarations of the Bible, have accepted these theories and rejected the Bible, so that it can be truthfully said that the faith of millions in God, in Jesus Christ, and in the Bible as the Inspired Word of God, has been uprooted and completely destroyed."

The newsletter also turned to the old tactic of cherry-picking Bible quotes that appeared to support a Flat Earth. Many of these quotes were just references to circles. "It is He that sitteth upon the circle of the earth, and the inhabitants thereof are as grasshoppers," reads Isaiah 40:22. It's a poetic turn of phrase, but probably not one to be taken literally, since it likens people to insects.

Voliva's Flat Earth manifesto recycled a significant number of talking points from Rowbotham and his crowd. The Christian Catholic Apostolic Church had reprinted William Carpenter's *One Hundred Proofs That the Earth Is Not a Globe* just one year earlier, and the special edition of *Leaves of Healing* borrowed his old arguments about mathematicians who differed in their estimations about the distance to the sun. Because these mathematicians, who never communicated with each other, offered different guesses about the distance between the sun and the earth, none of them could be trusted, the Flat Earthers argued.

The newsletter also updated Rowbotham's zeteticism for the modern world. In Rowbotham's day, air travel was limited to hot-air balloons and blimps, none of which were much good for long-haul flights. But between the time of Zion's founding and the publication of *Leaves of Healing*'s special Flat Earth edition, manned airplanes had been invented, popularized, and flown internationally. These new revelations forced Voliva to "debunk" even more Globe Earth material, including the fact that explorer Richard Byrd had flown over the South Pole in Antarctica the previous year, with a crew member filming the expedition. One headline argued BYRD'S FLIGHT NO PROOF, the article accusing Byrd of conspiring to conceal the planet's true shape: "Commander Byrd must know that the sea is a vast outstretched plane, ill fitted to become any part of a globular surface." (In a boon to Flat Earthers since, Byrd's claim of flying over the *North* Pole in 1926 has come under dispute, with his own diary suggesting that the expedition secretly ended in failure.)

Cameras had also become commonplace and affordable since Rowbotham's lifetime, and Voliva worked the new technology to his advantage. *Leaves of Healing* included a huge photograph of Wisconsin's Lake Winnebago, spread across a two-page centerfold. The picture showed a long expanse of water, then a blurry shoreline emerging from the lake's opposite edge in the distance. "This photograph proves that no curvature exists on the surface of Lake Winnebago, Wisconsin, and that the surface of the standing water is level—horizontal," the caption read. "The lake is twelve miles across at this point. The necessary curvature for this distance on a globular earth is ninety-six feet. No curvature is shown in this picture as reference to objects on the shoreline easily proves. The lens of the camera was three feet above the water."

I'm no zetetic. I've never been to Lake Winnebago, and I have never replicated the experiment for myself. But thirty minutes in a library with a topographic map of the area left me unimpressed with *Leaves of Healing*'s claims. For one, the newsletter's math was wrong: by placing the camera three feet above water, only sixty-five feet (not ninety-six) would be obscured from view. Not that those specifics matter much. Superseding all my math is the fact that Lake Winnebago has steep shorelines, rising more than three hundred feet over their first mile in some places. Almost all of that shoreline would have been visible to a camera on the opposite shore.

Like Rowbotham, who exercised the new powers of the mass-produced newspaper, Voliva also spread the Flat Earth gospel by becoming a media pioneer. In 1923, he launched WCBD, one of the country's earliest radio stations. Armed with a powerful $50,000 broadcasting center (about $750,000 today), the station could reach listeners across the United States, in Central America, and even reportedly on ships on the ocean as they chugged along relying on Globe Earth measurements to navigate. Still a young technology, radio had a following of dedicated hobbyists, whose attention Voliva courted. WCBD passed out collectors' stamps as well as radio directories, and Voliva's control of Zion city finances meant he could regularly update the station's systems to give it one of the clearest sounds on the air. WCBD passed out flyers advertising that it had "achieved a reputation for perfect modulation, and excellent enunciation."

When Voliva first applied to register WCBD, he described it as a religious station, and he upheld some of that promise with broadcasts of sermons and Sunday school lessons. But from its first moments on the airwaves, the supposed religious programming was dense with Voliva's anti-globe views. As the radio scene rapidly grew, WCBD gave Voliva—and by extension, Flat Earth—a wide audience. And when broadcasting authorities temporarily made WCBD share the same channel as a big new Chicago station in 1924, the Zion station was able to piggyback its way to even more ears.

In 1927, Voliva set out on the first of two world tours, which he described as Flat Earth fact-finding missions. The trip received some media attention, mostly mocking: "If Voliva finds the earth is flat, as he contends, his discovery may solve the mystery of lost golf balls," the Moline, Illinois, *Dispatch* quipped. When his ship landed in New York after his second voyage in 1931, he was even firmer in his beliefs (he'd determined somehow that Antarctica was like a "rim of mashed potato" around a plate) and spoiling for a fight. He tried picking one with the world's best theoretical physicist. "Learning that Prof. Albert Einstein, a rival savant who goes in for curves, was in town, Mr. Voliva at once dispatched Carl L. Huth, his secretary, in search of the German scientist with a challenge to debate," the *Chicago Tribune* reported. "Unfortunately Prof. Einstein was preparing to sail." In Einstein's absence, Voliva attempted to save face by announcing that he'd studied Einstein's theory of relativity and that "it is pure bunk. Just stuff on paper. The man has no proof."

Through radio and world tours, Voliva hoped to spread his gospel across a flat planet. Those international ambitions were especially successful in South Africa, where Flat Earther Paul Kruger had previously held power. In this, Dowie was an unwitting Flat Earth accomplice from beyond the grave. By the time he founded Zion, Dowie had a sizable audience in South Africa. That audience grew even after his death, due in part to John G. Lake, a former Zion dweller, who'd been involved with Dowie's church before pivoting to a different local religious sect under the leadership of another self-proclaimed prophet. This group, the Parhamites, had even greater troubles than the Zionites. After their leader, Charles Parham, was accused in 1907 of "unnatural offenses" (the

legal term then used when charging someone with engaging in homo-
sexual acts, which was considered to be a crime), the group (many of
them former Dowie followers) began experiencing something like a collective psychosis, performing brutal exorcisms that led to three deaths.
One exorcism victim was literally torn limb to limb by her children and
three others.

Voliva blamed Lake for the deaths, and although he was never
charged in the slaying, Lake wisely decided to leave the hemisphere in
1908 and become a minister in South Africa, where some fifty thousand
Dowieites still remained faithful to the movement's founder. Though
Lake was not a Flat Earther, he reinvigorated the country's Dowie fans,
and Voliva exploited the steady South African base from abroad. *Leaves
of Healing*, which became a Flat Earth publication under Voliva's guidance, saw a sustained readership in South Africa.

But as Voliva's movement was expanding abroad, it was also falling
apart at home. After the 1909 election failed to permanently oust Voliva,
the Flat Earther grew even more militant about his religious rule over
Zion. Even the name of his newspaper advertised his aggressive stance:
in addition to taking over Dowie's *Leaves of Healing*, whose title suggested a certain gentleness and generosity, Voliva founded a new paper,
called the *Battle Axe*. By 1914, he had abandoned all pretense and added
an additional paper, published under the title the *Theocrat*.

While Dowie had been a deeply flawed eccentric, he was still a char-
ismatic speaker, capable of faking miracles and enchanting crowds until
his downfall. Voliva, by contrast, was a total buzzkill. Grim and venge-
ful, he soon gave the city an ominous reputation. "There has been slowly
growing a belief that Voliva lacks an important ingredient essential to
his position," the *Chicago Tribune* had reported while Voliva was ousting
Dowie in 1906: "A check upon bitterness, a saving element of mercy and
kindness."

A reporter from *Collier's* magazine sent to cover Zion's Flat Earth
mania in 1927 described the community like something out of the early

pages of a horror novel. "I had slogged no more than a quarter of that dismal mile eastward [into Zion] before the heavy Puritanism of the place fell upon me. I passed houses, but saw no human being except a small boy who followed me," *Collier's* reporter Walter Davenport wrote of his descent into the city. "Within three minutes the boy had been joined by three others who seemed to have sprung hip-booted out of the ground. The unpaved streets, instep-deep with bluish mud, were punctuated frequently with water holes. The only human beings in sight were the boys behind me. Another minute and I looked back again. Instead of four boys there were eight. Obviously something was wrong and, just as obviously, it was wrong with me." Shortly thereafter, he was confronted by a local woman, who threatened to call the police on him for smoking.

Davenport was lucky to stub out his cigarette before the cops came. Flat Earth and anti-smoking were two of Voliva's greatest crusades, and he enforced both with a borderline-fascistic fervor. Voliva preached that smokers would suffer in a specialized hell, locked in great tubs of tobacco juice. When trains stopped in Zion, the city's police would search them for smokers, who were subject to arrest. Voliva also had a secret police force at his disposal. The eight-hundred-strong Zion Guard, whose members carried Bibles in their pistol holsters, patrolled the streets in search of anyone having a conspicuously good time. Chewing gum and whistling on Sundays were prohibited, as were standing outside in groups of more than two, watching unapproved films (although Voliva made this easy by banning movie theaters), driving faster than five miles per hour, joining a union or secret society, eating oysters, wearing tan shoes, and bathing within fifty feet of a person of the opposite sex (including one's own spouse). Women lived under a strict dress code, which banned makeup and short hair, and required them to keep their arms, necklines, and full legs covered at all times.

Some of Voliva's rules for himself were even stricter. In the belief that it would sustain him to the age of 120, Voliva claimed to eat nothing besides Brazil nuts and buttermilk. He let loose on his sixty-fifth birthday when, the *Chicago Tribune* reported, he ate two poached eggs "and on the insistence of his grandchildren nibbled a small piece of birthday cake—the first cake he had eaten in several years."

"I never felt better in my life," Voliva told the *Tribune* at the birthday party. "If you don't believe the world is flat, just try a diet of buttermilk and Brazil nuts."

The organs of power Dowie had abused became even more corrupt under Voliva. Because he'd repurchased the city under his own name, typically public institutions like parks were his private property. He couldn't completely expel the city's "independents" (nonmembers of the Christian Catholic Apostolic Church), but he could do everything in his power to make them miserable. His tactics included harassing independents and their children, who used his privately owned parks, and building dramatic billboards in areas where independents congregated: THIS CITY FOR ZION PEOPLE AND FOR ZION PEOPLE ONLY!!! one billboard read. THE ZION FLAG FLOATING OVER EVERY BUILDING—OVER EVERY FOOT, INCH AND PINCH OF THE ORIGINAL CITY SITE. TRAITORS, THIEVES AND THUGS WILL FIND THIS CITY HOTTER THAN HELL.

Another billboard was even wordier: NO GENTLEMAN, NOT TO MENTION A CHRISTIAN WOULD BREAK INTO A CHURCH SETTLEMENT AND ATTEMPT TO HOLD MEETINGS, OR TO ESTABLISH A COUNTER-ORGANIZATION. THOSE WHO DO ARE NOTHING MORE THAN RELIGIOUS BUMS, WITH LESS HONOUR THAN A GANG OF HIGHWAY ROBBERS AND THUGS. GET OUT OF THIS COMMUNITY IF YOU HAVE A DROP OF HONEST BLOOD AND GO ESTABLISH A SETTLEMENT OF YOUR OWN. IF THEY WANT TO KNOW WHO IS BOSS AROUND HERE, LET THEM START SOMETHING ELSE.

The signs, stunningly, did not bring peace upon the city. In 1912, a few years before he began forcing Flat Earth belief on the Zion school system, Voliva led a crusade against the local Cook Electrical company, which employed independents, many of them smokers. He ordered the construction of an anti-smoking billboard across from the company, despite a court injunction against the sign. To add a human element of heckling, he built a wire enclosure nearby, in which hundreds of Christian Catholic Apostolic Church members could safely loiter and chant anti-smoking slogans. Cook Electrical workers burned down the billboard in mid-April, and days later they took up bats and attacked a group of two hundred chanting churchgoers near the factory. A riot ensued, with Zionites beating the workers with bricks, resulting in injuries on both sides. Eleven brawlers from Voliva's side were arrested for disturbing the peace but immediately released on bond "for fear that the Voliva faction would storm the jail," the city's police chief told the *Chicago Tribune*.

Undeterred, Voliva's side built a new billboard (text: "STINKPOTS!!! The Rev. John Alexander Dowie very appropriately called TOBACCO USERS STINKPOTS. He Established Zion City—A Clean City for a Clean People. You have no more right to smoke in other people's Atmosphere than you have to spit in their Drinking Water") and sent a man with a gun to guard it. But Zionites outsmarted themselves by making the billboard double-sided, with anti-smoking screeds on both sides and a narrow gap between the two back-to-back wooden signs. The following week, while church elders were overseeing the construction of a new organ in their tabernacle, Cook Electrical employees stuffed the gap with oil-soaked rags and set the second billboard on fire. They smoked and sang parodies of Zion's anti-smoking songs as the signs burned. A weary fire department responded in a "leisurely" fashion, the *Tribune* reported. Church elders vowed that they would build a third billboard, this one made of steel.

The violence renewed in June, when 150 Cook Electrical workers pelted Zionites with eggs outside the factory. "In a few moments the Zion elders resembled a huge omelette," the *Inter Ocean* reported. Voliva tried summoning a thousand churchgoers for a counterattack but seems to have canceled the plans when the sheriff asked him to please not do that.

Voliva appeared doomed to re-create the voter fraud he'd accused his opponents of in 1909. Their inevitable rematch in the city's 1911 elections was just as bitter as the first election, but this one fell in Voliva's favor. "Opposing factions almost came to a clash of arms to rule the city," the *Inter Ocean* reported. "It was charged against Voliva and his followers that they carried the election through ballot frauds and intimidation."

Though Voliva's Theocratic Party won the race and would indeed continue to control the town for another two decades, he, his mayor, his bodyguard, and one of his personal friends were indicted for conspiracy and perjury over their alleged cover-up of shady election dealings. Voliva managed to change the trial's venue to a more sympathetic county and was acquitted after a single member of the jury declared him not guilty. The case was one of many that would see the temperamental Voliva in and out of courtrooms for much of his life. He was briefly jailed after refusing to pay a $14,000 judgment stemming from a verbal attack on one of Dowie's pallbearers. He was also found guilty of criminally libeling a pastor who had abandoned the church, calling the man "a big old blatherskite," as well as "a tomcat," "a fool," "a wild man of Borneo," "a discredited windbag," and other insults.

Voliva first seized power in Zion by casting Dowie as a false prophet and a failed healer who drove the city to ruin. But over the decades of his rule, Voliva's own life took on echoes of the tragedies of his predecessor. In 1915, Voliva's wife, Molly, became sick. Just as Dowie had refused medical attention for his daughter, the Volivas, too, turned away doctors. Molly died, and Voliva married one of his congregants the next year. He also fell prey to Dowie's old pattern of obscene wealth followed by financial ruin. When Voliva bought the bankrupt town of Zion in 1910, he had appealed to his flock for money, and even children turned over their allowances to make payments on the $700,000 loan. When Voliva finished paying off the sum, which he'd taken in his name, he had sole dominion over city property. He then sold some city land to a Chicago real estate company for $1 million and continued Dowie's habit of aggressively tithing churchgoers. By 1927, as he set out on his first world tour, his radio channel booming, he was said to have more than $10 million across his personal savings and the industries he controlled. The fortune, adjusted for inflation, would come to around $150 million today, a treasure that would have made him the envy of wealthy televangelists and megachurch leaders in the twenty-first century.

When the Great Depression struck two years later, however, it obliterated his wealth and Zion's. The financial miracles he'd worked in the past were useless this time around. Not even mass prayer and publicity campaigns could persuade enough people to buy Zion's trademark lace and fig bars or pitch in to its tithe. The money was gone, and it was gone everywhere. Zion's industries returned to the state receivership from which Voliva had purchased them decades earlier. Helpless in front of a desperate congregation, Voliva appears to have succumbed to stress. "The year 1929 and the economic debacle brought about a metamorphosis which gives us a penetrating light on the facets of Wilbur Glenn Voliva's character," the *Chicago Tribune* wrote in 1934. "Plunged suddenly and unwillingly into increasing financial troubles, Voliva has aged rapidly in the last five years." Once black-haired and portly, he turned gray and gaunt. His political power ebbed away with his body, but his strange geographical beliefs remained resolute.

For years, Voliva's Flat Earth obsession had been a focus of independent campaigns attempting to retake the city. "Voliva teaches school children the earth is flat" became an independent political slogan. When in 1934, two of Voliva's preferred candidates lost their elections to the school board, it was the first independent victory since the chaos of the 1909 elections. Independents were so overjoyed at winning two of the six seats on the board that they held a parade. "Zion will no longer be ruled by one man," Rev. Paul Goodwin, the pastor of the city's Grace Missionary Church told the *Tribune*. (Goodwin was a longtime Christian Catholic Apostolic Church punching bag, with Voliva calling him "little Grinny Granny Goodwin" from the pulpit.) Voliva responded to the loss with less-than-subtle threats that he always carried two guns and was protected by armed guards. People who voted for the anti-Flat independents were "just a bunch of yellow cur dogs with their tails cut off" and their children would probably go to hell, he told the *Tribune*. He added that he was less worried about schoolchildren defecting from his curriculum, because he would require each to personally pledge allegiance to him before returning to class. "I learned that from Hitler," Voliva said, "and when I get through I'll have the best organization in the world. President Roosevelt could learn a lot about human nature from me."

But the school board election proved to be the long-awaited crack in Voliva's steely control of the city. The next year, a slate of independent candidates, including an independent mayor, won election and set about repealing Voliva's strict lifestyle laws. Tobacco, alcohol, and movies would all be allowed in Zion, the city's new leaders announced. With his standard legal bullishness, Voliva threatened to sue over the election results. "This new mayor and his commissioners are misfits," he told the *Tribune*. "I'll fight them 100 per cent, day and night continuously, and I'll get them sooner or later. I'm the only man in Zion that amounts to anything. If I were to withdraw my hand the city would disintegrate. I built Zion single handed and I alone can hold it. I have just begun to fight."

Voliva also told the *Tribune* that his diet of buttermilk and Brazil nuts would give him the strength to defeat his rivals. But by the time of his threats, he was a sixty-five-year-old man living on an extremely inadvisable diet, going blind and diabetic, and losing the religious flock that had followed him for so many years. His days of legal luck had run out.

He spent his last years in Zion with his power diminished, his focus turned to his church's annual Easter-time play, which became so successful that a version of it remains in production today. His acidic tongue jeopardized even the play, however. In April 1937, while delivering one of his typically caustic sermons, Voliva ridiculed a churchgoer so aggressively that her teenage son burned down the tabernacle where the play was being held. This marked the end of another era, too: the WCBD radio station, where Voliva had broadcast Flat Earth theory to the world, was also damaged by the flames. Voliva sold off WCBD to a more mainstream broadcaster, who relocated the station to a site with a taller tower. It was soon struck by a plane, killing two people.

Bankrupt and dying of heart and kidney diseases, Voliva spent many of his final years in Florida. Like Dowie on his sickbed visits to Mexico, Voliva dreamed of establishing a new paradise in these warmer climes. But those plans were little more than fantasies. Zion, the city where he had been powerful enough to undo the earth's shape, was quickly secularizing. In 1938, when the city's new leaders needed to design a new vehicle-tax sticker to be displayed on every resident's car, they chose a globe. When Voliva died in Zion in 1942, the city had moved on without him. Two years earlier, the city's new schools had opened with a Globe Earth curriculum.

"The fact that the world is round, not flat, will be official Friday evening when Zion City will dedicate its new $300,000 air conditioned high school," the *Chicago Tribune* wrote. The building, which would teach independents and children of the Christian Catholic Apostolic Church together for the first time in decades, "is equipped with a geography globe in almost every room."

3 | The Joke

....

I'VE BEEN CONDUCTING an unscientific survey. Every time I find myself discussing Flat Earth—something I've done compulsively for years, with strangers and at Christmas dinners and once, to my horror, in a live television interview on an unrelated topic—I make note of what my interlocutor has to say about the theory. Nearly without fail, as if playing a word-association game, the other person starts and stops with the Flat Earth Society.

This, I suppose, is a normal, nonobsessive limit to one's Flat Earth knowledge, and for a long time it was mine, too. Before I knew the first thing about Flat Earth theory, I'd heard of the Flat Earth Society. Like most other people I meet, I'd assumed the society was a joke.

Despite decades of mockery, however, the Flat Earth Society began as the very serious vision of one soft-spoken, bespectacled Englishman named Samuel Shenton, who was a sign painter by trade. Born in 1903, he was the successor to the several generations of Flat Earth evangelists before him, though he had neither Samuel Rowbotham's natural grifting abilities nor Lady Elizabeth Blount's musical whimsy nor Wilbur Voliva's fire-and-brimstone spirit. But in the end, he needed none of their flair—only a willingness to endure decades of Globe Earthers' jokes at his expense. As new space-exploration programs delivered ever more photographic evidence of the globe, and Flat Earth became even more obviously ludicrous, Shenton became one of the only members of his movement to keep the faith. In doing so, he saw his Flat Earth Society become a laughingstock in the public eye, but also nearly synonymous with the Flat Earth movement, surviving through multiple American successors even fifty years after Shenton's death.

Shenton's disillusionment with the globe, and with the scientific community that supported it, began in his teens. While working as an apprentice for a sign maker in 1919, Shenton dreamed up a device that could solve the world's transportation problems. The planet spun on its axis, Shenton reasoned. Rather than waste fuel flying planes from one destination to another, why not send an aircraft into the sky and let it hover in place while the world spun below it? In Shenton's imagination, the aircraft could land across the Atlantic hours later, when the rotating Earth caught up to it. This, of course, is not how air travel works. Earth's atmosphere—and all the birds, planes, and fanciful aircraft inside it— are spinning along with the ground. If Shenton's proposed spacecraft really did hover for five hours before landing, it would find itself exactly where it took off.

Sixteen years old, with little formal education, Shenton could be forgiven for his patchwork understanding of the planet. But he never fully forgave how people responded to his invention. When he showed his designs for the craft to teachers and clergymen, they gave him a "sloppy push-off," he told the *Guardian*. Their dismissive response left him with a sour opinion of scientific society and a lingering hunger to challenge what he saw as its dogmas. Shenton soon became convinced his doubters had ulterior motives: the gatekeepers of knowledge were engaged in some shadowy conspiracy against him. He began conduct-ing his own scientific research in libraries, where he discovered a simi-lar, doomed airship design by a zetetically inclined archbishop (a friend of Lady Blount's). Vindicated by this sketch, Shenton ordered every zetetic text he could get his hands on. Inevitably, he came across the Flat Earth masterwork: Rowbotham's *Zetetic Astronomy*. Shenton made a full conversion to Flat Earth belief several days later. Like Rowbotham and Voliva before him, Shenton alleged that the Globe Earth model was part of a plot to deny God, although Shenton was less dogmatic in his Christianity than his forebears and made Flat Earth overtures to people of other faiths. He also accused the globe-making industry of being involved in the conspiracy, although he admitted confusion as to why the United States and the Soviet Union were knowingly wasting millions on fake space programs. He eventually abandoned his airship—temporarily, at first, because he believed it would be put to gruesome use in war, and then conclusively in 1939, when he realized the concept would not work on a flat, stationary planet. Besides, the invention paled in importance next to the great truth he believed he'd discovered.

Rowbotham's work inspired Shenton's, but by no means dictated it. Shenton played looser with his cosmology and offered his own descriptions of the planet's makeup. Rowbotham had claimed that Earth floated on primordial oceans, and his main text, *Zetetic Astronomy*, never explicitly mentioned the planet being enclosed in a dome, instead referring to a vague sky-like "firmament." Voliva had abandoned Rowbotham's ideas about Earth floating on a "great deep," and was more convinced of an enclosing dome. Shenton went all in on the dome model. He believed the dome was surrounded by water, and that the Great Flood of the Bible occurred when that giant shell cracked, allowing waves to pour down until God or some celestial carpenter fixed the leaky roof. Above the dome and the waters were the heavens, which looked like a series of six or seven stacked planes, each protected by its own dome. (Modern Flat Earthers still cite Rowbotham's and Voliva's models, but most have politely backed away from Shenton's description of watery skies and stacked heavens.)

By the end of the Second World War, Flat Earthers like Shenton were mostly isolated in their theories. Decades earlier, Lady Blount's Universal Zetetic Society would have provided him a clique of Flat Earth comrades. But the organization and most of its members had died early in the twentieth century, leaving stray Flat Earthers to the ridicule of the round world. Still, by August 1956, Shenton was willing to go public with his ideas, even if it meant mockery. That month, the *Daily Mirror* newspaper jokingly asked "if some people still believe that the Earth is flat." They published two responses: one pro-Flat testimony from a London man, and another from Shenton, in Kent. "I have studied this subject for some twenty years and have collected what I believe to be original matter in support of the 'flat Earth theory,'" Shenton wrote in a letter published next to the comics section. "There must be many people working on the same lines as myself who are unknown to each other. Perhaps contacts could be arranged."

The *Mirror* gleefully suggested he and the London man start a club. "Well, you laddies (and several more like you) seem pretty keen. Would anyone like to volunteer to be President of a new Flat Earth Club?" the paper offered. "We'll be delighted to put you in touch with would-be members—and that's flat! How about it, you folk who like to think for yourselves?"

The *Mirror* was kidding. Shenton was not. Four months later, in December 1956, he launched the International Flat Earth Research Society. The group's cofounder, William Mills (not the Flat Earther who'd written into the *Mirror*), had Flat Earth lineage of his own. Mills had married into the family of Frederick Cook, an old Universal Zetetic Society member and author of the books *The Terrestrial Plane: The True Figure of the Earth* and *Our Earth Flat, Not Spherical*. After a publicity blitz, Shenton and Mills hosted the first IFERS meeting at Mills's house. Reporters, curious onlookers, and some genuine Flat Earthers jostled for space in the living room as Shenton laid out his theory. Even the unconvinced would recall the meeting for years. Among them was astronomer Patrick Moore, who would go on to host the BBC astronomy show *The Sky at Night*. Moore may have attended for fun, but he remembered Shenton years later and invited him onto his show in 1969 to explain Flat Earth.

Laughingstock or not, Shenton's society made headlines. Most newspapers regarded him as a joke, although Chicago papers, whose veteran

reporters had covered the city of Zion's Flat Earth mania, were more suspicious of him. SHADES OF VOLIVA; IT'S BRITON'S THEORY NOW, read a
Chicago Tribune headline in 1959. The paper noted that "the idea of a flat
earth society raised eyebrows even in Britain, where there are organizations for almost everything," including a "League for the Welfare of French
Animals" and, as if anticipating what would become a major conspiracy
movement in the twenty-first century, "the Anti-Vaccination league."

The spike in headlines led to a trend of Britons using "Flat Earther"
as a derogatory term for a stupid person. Flat Earthers, predictably, did
not appreciate the insult. "I must protest at [the] derogatory reference
to 'flat-earthers,'" a man called H. W. Huttle-Glank wrote in a 1962 com-
plaint to the *Guardian*. "The International Flat Earth Society is a thriving
scientific body, and it would be a pity for it to be derided by those who
have not really studied the subject." (IFERS was not thriving, at least in
terms of its paltry membership numbers, and H. W. Huttle-Glank was
his own mystery within the British conspiracy world. "Professor H. W.
Huttle-Glank" was one of several ridiculous, likely fake names to appear
multiple times in *Cosmic Voice*, a magazine put out by an alien-worship-
ping group called the Aetherius Society. The magazine quoted Huttle-
Glank as an expert in an article on taking hallucinogenic drugs and
seeing flying saucers. Even if the Huttle-Glank persona were a hoax, he
boosted real Flat Earthers' profiles; at least two *Guardian* letters to the
editor referenced him and IFERS.)

Even the nation's leaders started treating the theory's name as a
put-down. Politician Enoch Powell used "Flat Earther" as an insult in
Parliament in 1964, and then prime minister Harold Wilson hurled the
epithet back at him. Shenton thought the Parliament fight could be a
chance to educate the public about his group. In an issue of his pamphlet, *The Plane Truth*, Shenton gave a summary of Flat Earth theory
and announced that "we trust that no more gibes about 'Flat Earthers'
will be occasioned from Prime Minister Wilson of the Socialist Party
and Enoch Powell of the Conservative Party." He trusted wrong, and

Powell was insulted with the term "Flat Earther" a second time in 1968, after delivering a famously racist speech.

Shenton was a gentle-mannered, serious man. "He is straightforward in argument and eager to explain. He does not try to make a mystery of his beliefs," the *Guardian* wrote of him. Shenton's idea of teaching Flat Earth theory usually involved presenting a series of charts and diagrams, all drawn in his steady sign-painter's hand. He appreciated an open ear, and early in his IFERS leadership, he grew angry when he felt the media was making fun of his ideology. "It was obvious from the start that [the] BBC didn't intend to take us seriously," he told the Associated Press of a television segment that he thought deliberately ridiculed his movement. "I wasn't allowed to explain our beliefs in detail." Unbeknownst to Shenton, his earnest demeanor might have only encouraged the mockery. "Perhaps the fault lies in the lack of eccentricity with which he preaches his eccentric beliefs," the *Observer* speculated in 1966. Previous Flat Earthers, like Rowbotham, who argued for sport, or Voliva, who ruled his city like a feudal lord, "were never guilty of such a failing."

Shenton's approachable everyman appearance made him a popular target for letters. He received approximately 150 per week, he told the *Birmingham Daily Post* in 1966. Both of the letters he showed the newspaper were from Americans, who appeared to be poking fun at him. One, who lived near the Kennedy Space Center in Florida, said: "I shall be able materially to further the work of the society from within the enemy's lines, as it were." Another, who worked for a US missile company, asked for more information on Flat Earth theories "to help subdue the panic in the event they should be revealed as fact."

Another letter, which Shenton shared proudly with the Associated Press in 1967, came from an American student who might have also been toying with Shenton's hopes. "Our entire physics class of 14 and our instructor at Eldorado, Iowa, are seriously worried about the prevailing scientific attitude towards the shape of the earth. The nature of our concern lies with the unscientific explanation of the earth's spherical shape," the letter read. "We support your society's attempts to show the true flat shape of the earth. We agree so heartily with your organization that we wish to become connected with it, if not through actual membership, perhaps through associate membership."

Membership in IFERS was a nebulous concept. In 1960, Shenton charged five shillings (approximately seven modern-day US dollars) in annual membership dues. He later abandoned the paid model. "He does not feel he can give a proper service to members," one paper reported. Once enrollment became free, trolls might have artificially swelled IFERS's lightly vetted membership rolls. In 1959, three years after the society's launch, the group had only twenty-five members, all of whom lived in England, although Shenton noted in an interview that the group had "contacts all over the world." As IFERS grew more notorious, however, pranksters' requests for membership poured in. A *Daily Mirror* columnist bragged in 1961 of joining the group as a joke, after an Australian man (who had also presumably signed up on a lark) invited him. Three American television producers who worked near the Manned Space Center in Houston wrote Shenton in 1965, asking permission to start an IFERS branch of their own. "Perhaps with the home of the astronauts so geographically close to our studios, we can even determine the type of plate the Earth resembles," the trio wrote.

Even if he didn't grant them IFERS membership, Shenton was happy to give speeches to nearly anyone who asked. Before IFERS gained international fame, Shenton made a local lecture circuit in his home county of Kent, dropping in on social clubs, where he was generally regarded as a passing amusement. Attendees "tried in vain to disprove his theories," but only became confused about their own arguments, the *East Kent Gazette* reported after a 1961 lecture. "But whether his world is round or flat, it was entertaining to hear a man who had a belief of his own and was not afraid to admit it."

Shenton was in particular demand at British universities and youth clubs. Warring branches of Young Conservatives and Young Socialists would sometimes compete to book Shenton, and Young Scientists' Clubs also made bids for his attention. Shenton repeatedly stated that his main goal was to rescue children from Globe Earth brainwashing, and for a time he gave many lectures to young people. But over the years, he became jaded to constant requests from insincere college students. "He knows from previous experience that half of them would be larking about," the *Guardian* wrote after Shenton turned down an invitation from the Bexleyheath Young Conservatives in 1969.

As it was for Rowbotham's movement, frequent, mocking media attention was one of IFERS's unlikely allies. The other was the space race between the United States and the Soviet Union. In August 1955, one year before the *Daily Mirror* made its surprisingly consequential call for Flat Earthers to start a club, the two countries announced competing plans to launch satellites into orbit around the earth. The rivalry was fueled by nationalist pride, as well as a keen anxiety about nuclear annihilation. A rocket powerful enough to launch satellites into space was likely capable of dropping nuclear warheads half a world away, a possibility that seemed all too plausible as the Cold War grew increasingly bitter. The world followed the twin space programs' development with fascination—some of it eager, some of it marked by dread.

IFERS was one of the only organizations immune from the nervous spectacle. Rather than grapple with the space age and all its associated fears and possibilities, Shenton's organization simply maintained that no one could orbit Earth because no one could find their way out of the planet's sturdy domed ceiling. The strength of that conviction was tested in spring 1961, when the United States and the Soviet Union both managed to send men into space. British journalists who remembered the initial commotion over the first IFERS meetings called Shenton for his opinion on the launches. He held firm. "It would not have been possible to put a man in Space if the world was round, because if the world was revolving the man could not be recovered," he told the *Daily Mirror* after the first American breached the planet's boundaries that May. The reporter noted sarcastically that he would pass Shenton's advice on to US president John Kennedy and Soviet premier Nikita Khrushchev.

Shenton's explanation for the spaceflights was simple. Yuri Gagarin, the Soviet cosmonaut who first orbited the earth in April 1961, "may have thought he went in a circle around the earth, but actually he was traveling in an ellipse parallel to earth," Shenton told a wire service. Interviews about space travel often served as an outlet for Shenton to rail against science. "Humanity has been brainwashed by science into the round earth theory," Shenton said during the same interview. (Later in his career, he would refuse to call Flat Earth a "theory," insisting that he knew it to be fact). "Science cannot shout us down. Take the moon, for example. It's transparent you know," he said, adding that his group believed so because they thought they'd seen stars shining through it. "I don't believe man will ever get there," Shenton said of the moon, "but if he does he'd better be ready to come right back. There isn't anything much to land on."

Astrophysicists begged to differ. Five years after Shenton's interview about the transparent moon, NASA sent the unmanned space probe Lunar Orbiter 1 to orbit the moon. On August 23, 1966, the probe sent back the first picture of Earth from the lunar orbit. The black-and-white photo shows the curved edge of the moon, and beyond it our decidedly round planet. What inspired awe in some viewers—the fullest view of Earth to date, the sweeping view of our home wreathed in cloud and shadow—nearly prompted an existential crisis for Flat Earthers. "I confess," Shenton told the *Observer* days after the photograph was released, "that it really knocked me. It was a terrible shock." But he quickly recovered himself and suggested a reasonable explanation for the picture. "It is probably one of the non-luminous bodies between us and the moon," he said. After subsequent space missions took pictures of the round planet, Shenton started alleging an outright cover-up. "That's where those Americans and Russians are so damned cunning," he told a reporter a few months before the first moon landing in 1969. "For some reason or other they obviously want us to think the world is round. Some of the pictures have been blatantly doctored. Studio shots, probably."

Shenton's talk of staged photographs was an echo from the future. Although moon-landing truthers are among some of the twenty-first century's most famous skeptics, the conspiracy theory was nearly as obscure as Flat Earthism when the Apollo 11 crew landed on the moon for the first time in July 1969. In fact, one of the first groups to question the moon landing did it in jest. The six-hundred-member Man Will Never Fly Memorial Society launched three years after the International Flat Earth Research Society and parodied the Flat Earth group at annual meetings, in which members got drunk and pretended to believe air travel was impossible. Their 1969 annual meeting, in Kitty Hawk, North Carolina, was a party of special proportions.

"Any event worth a line in the history books invites skepticism. The Flat Earth Society of London still has its doubts about Columbus," a *New York Times* article on the meeting began. "So it was only natural that at its first meeting here since man's 'alleged' moon landings, the Man Will Never Fly Memorial Society should cast a critical eye on the purported exploits of Apollo astronauts." One of the group's founding members, Julian Scheer, was an assistant administrator for public affairs at NASA. He entertained the whiskey-fueled meeting by adopting the persona of a conspiracy theorist and narrating clips of NASA training footage to show the members "how to make a case against the moon flights if they wanted to."

It is unclear whether the group knew of Shenton's moon-landing truther arguments from three years earlier, and even if they were aware, Man Will Never Fly members considered moon-landing truthers as ridiculous as Flat Earthers. Yet both conspiracy movements were real. By about a year after the moon landing, skepticism was taking hold. In 1970, the United Press International wire service polled 1,721 Americans and discovered "wide support for a theory that the government and the news media conspired to hoodwink the public with a fake telecast of a Moon landing." Among the respondents were a Philadelphia grandmother and a young woman from Charlotte, North Carolina, who both repeated rumors they'd heard about the moon landing being filmed in a studio on Earth. Meanwhile, a North Carolina man offered a religious explanation that would have made Shenton, and indeed many modern conspiracy theorists, proud. If God had intended humanity to walk on the moon "he'd put it closer by," the man said—sounding like the conspiracy theorists of 2020 who refused to wear protective face masks during a deadly pandemic because doing so would "throw God's wonderful breathing system out the door."

But aside from these assorted American truthers, Shenton and IFERS were largely alone in their stated skepticism for space programs. Moon-landing truthers wouldn't receive their next champion until 1976, when Bill Kaysing, a freelance writer who had worked on technical manuals for a rocket company decades earlier, self-published his book, *We Never Went to the Moon: America's Thirty Billion Dollar Swindle*. If early Flat Earth efforts were an attempt to grapple with a world increasingly independent of religion, Kaysing's thesis might be viewed as an attempt to reckon with the horrors of the United States' recently lost Vietnam War. Kaysing accused the US government of staging the moon landings as a means of distracting from the war and claiming superiority over the Soviet Union after an embarrassing defeat in Vietnam by communist forces. Americans were already primed to believe wild claims relating to the Cold War and communism. Although anti-communist conspiracy theories flourished in the 1950s (the second Red Scare saw a government crackdown on Americans with supposed communist sympathies), by the 1960s many of the more popular theories took a critical eye of US wartime activities. Conspiracy theorists accused the United States of concealing atrocities during the Vietnam War, sometimes rightly. Kaysing's book, which played on these paranoias, popularized the moon-landing conspiracy theory, although Shenton never lived to see its publication.

By 1969, Shenton and his organization were on the decline. "We've lost a lot of members because of this absurd Apollo trip," he told the *Daily*

Mirror. "It's the same with every new space probe. I should think we're down to fewer than 100 members now. But if their opinion can be swayed by such flimsy evidence, then they're no use to me or the Society."

Despite Shenton's explanations for the decade's discoveries—Gagarin had merely flown a circle over Earth, pictures of the planet from lunar orbit were faked in a photo studio—the space race was outrunning him. In 1966, he told the *Observer* that his neighbors had bullied him for his beliefs ("At one time I used to be afraid to go down the street") and that many IFERS members had quit as the space programs advanced. Those who remained were elderly, he said. And he was experiencing serious heart trouble, which he sometimes attributed to the stresses of running his group for so many years. William Mills, IFERS's cofounder, had died in 1960, leaving Shenton to manage the group alone. At sixty-three in 1966, he was "a king without an heir," the *Observer* observed. By January 1969, he wasn't even sure he'd convinced his spouse of the earth's flatness.

"There's my wife," he told the *Guardian* when a reporter asked him whether he'd ever personally converted anyone to his theory. "She's coming round."

"But apart from your wife, have you ever convinced anyone?" the *Guardian* reporter asked.

"No."

"No one at all? Never?"

"No, never," Shenton said.

He added that, for all his pleas for donations beyond simple membership fees, he had only ever received one, which was modest. His society had one last hope, however: Americans.

While IFERS was falling out of fame in Britain, the media in the United States was just beginning to fall in love with the group. "Much of [Shenton's] post still comes from America, where he and his society are near-legendary," the *Observer* wrote in 1966. "Many visiting foreign journalists call him. In Britain, ironically, many think his organisation does not exist, that it is just a music-hall joke."

"America is especially interested," the *Birmingham Daily Post* wrote that same year. Although many of those American news reports were written in humor, they found a serious reader in Charles K. Johnson, an airplane mechanic twenty-one years Shenton's junior. Like Rowbotham, Johnson would later describe himself as a lifelong Flat Earther who felt himself repulsed at the first globe he encountered. He recalled that it was at school in Texas, when he was in second or third grade in the early 1930s.

"It wasn't like today," Johnson told Robert Schadewald, a science writer who specialized in the study of pseudoscience. "They didn't have globes everywhere, and people didn't say globe every few minutes. They put out this globe, and started the propaganda on it. I didn't accept it from the start." His teacher didn't help matters. When Johnson asked how water stuck to a round planet, the teacher told him to fill a bucket of water and swing it around his head. The water stayed in the bucket, but Johnson (correctly) noted that the experiment did nothing to prove the planet's shape.

An avid reader, but never much of a student, Johnson quit school without graduating. Left to continue his education on his own, he scoured public libraries for evidence that would debunk the globe. His quest led him to Shenton and Voliva. A magazine article about the Zion theocrat introduced Johnson to Flat Earth "proofs." Just eighteen years old, he wrote a letter to Voliva. Voliva, who was within a year of death and had been largely abandoned by his former followers, wrote back, confirming everything Johnson had suspected about the flat planet.

The letter was one of Johnson's only contacts with Flat Earthers for decades, save for a notable exception: in 1959, Johnson entered a San Francisco record store and met a woman who happened to be purchasing the same album he was. She was Marjory Waugh, an Australian Flat Earther. Both were vegetarians and both had looked at the globe and concluded that, in order for it to be real, Australians would have to live their lives hanging from their feet like bats. Marjory, who lived in Australia until 1944, had "never hung by her feet," Johnson later clarified to the media. (Australia, where I've traveled repeatedly to visit family, remains a sore point among Flat Earthers. I've had a Flat Earther tell me my usual Los Angeles-to-Melbourne flight can't possibly exist. Australia's own recent attempts to muster a Flat Earth scene have ended poorly, with a 2018 Flat Earth convention organizer getting arrested ahead of the inaugural event for trying to burn down a Masonic lodge.) For Charles and Marjory, however, their strange shared opinions on Australia seemed too good to be true. It was as if some benevolent conspiracy had arranged for them to meet. The Johnsons married in 1962.

During that decade, Johnson also made contact with Shenton. Until then, he and Marjory had been relatively solitary in their Flat Earth beliefs. They moved to a quiet home in the Mojave Desert in California, twenty miles from the nearest small city. It was the perfect place to ruminate on flatness and aerospace conspiracy. In one direction, the red desert stretched out like an endless plane. In the other direction was the Edwards Air Force Base, where NASA worked on its space shuttles (all part of a bunk Globe Earth propaganda program, the Johnsons believed). But even in their isolation, the Johnsons managed to learn of Shenton and IFERS, and Johnson struck up a correspondence with the British man during the 1960s.

The friendship came at a fortunate time for Shenton. Ailing fast, he was searching for a successor to take over IFERS, but he couldn't find an inspiring leader among the aging conspiracy theorists who populated his club in its later years. For a while, he thought he had found his man in Ellis Hillman, an environmental studies lecturer at North East London Polytechnic, who had become a friend—if not an earnest member—of IFERS. Hillman was not a Flat Earther, but he was interested in alternative theories about the planet's shape and admired the group from a philosophical standpoint.

When Shenton died, his wife, Lillian, was left to oversee the transfer of leadership from her husband to Hillman. Charles Johnson, however, claimed that Shenton, in his dying days, willed IFERS leadership to him. Lillian remained dubious that the earth was flat, and she was even less convinced about entrusting her husband's beloved society to someone like Hillman, who viewed the group as a mere curiosity. She eventually worked out a power-sharing agreement between Hillman (who was lukewarm about leading IFERS, anyway) and Johnson (who urgently wanted the role). Hillman received some of Shenton's papers, archived them with his university's science-fiction foundation, and adopted the title of IFERS president, to give a few joking lectures about the subject. Johnson, meanwhile, received the rest of Shenton's writings and took up the IFERS presidency with solemn pride in 1972, the year after Shenton died of heart complications.

From his solitude in the desert, Johnson made for a model conspiracy theorist. Now forty-eight years old, with a stately silver beard, he spoke with a folksy Texan wit and cut a striking figure when reporters came to photograph him and Marjory outside their remote home. "Johnson conveys nothing but charm, coherence and sincerity," a Long Beach, California, reporter wrote in 1973. Like Shenton and Voliva before him, Johnson believed Earth was surrounded by a ring of ice, which Globe Earthers represented as Antarctica. But Johnson was looser in his particulars than some of his predecessors. "We don't know how far that ice extends," he told the Boston Globe. "Nobody has ever attempted to find out." "It is reasonable to suppose that the world is without end, is infinite in size," he said on another occasion. He was ambivalent on Shenton's idea of six or seven heavens stacked above the dome that supposedly encloses Earth, although he and Marjory remained Christian literalists.

Johnson was also more aggressive than Shenton in his membership drive. In 1973, one year into his leadership, he estimated membership in IFERS at around one hundred people, more than the couple dozen at the end of Shenton's reign. By 1975, he claimed IFERS had boomed to more than one thousand members. He publicly mulled a Flat Earth conference in New York, Chicago, or Boston, where many of his letter writers lived. But as with the British version of IFERS, there was good reason to be skeptical of Johnson's membership claims. "Not all of them have paid their dues," he told the *Globe*. "Some people don't want it known they're in the society. They're afraid people will think they're crazy for believing that the world is flat." In 1978, Johnson wrote in his newsletter, *Flat Earth News*, that "we have over 1600 'Members,' but don't think they are keeping up with their dues; they are not. We don't have any system of keeping at members, prod[d]ing them, etc., etc., so there is just a Hard Core of Stalwarts who make it possible for FLAT EARTH NEWS to go forth."

Johnson's squishy statistics might have been based on the circulation of *Flat Earth News* or on the letters he published therein, which often expressed support for IFERS but fell short of including the group's $7 membership fee. *Flat Earth News* didn't follow any regular publishing schedule. Newsletters sometimes concluded with a promise to send out the next edition "around December 1." Still, the Johnsons were able to crank out multiple editions each year, totaling eighty-nine issues by the end of the publication's run in 1994. It was more polished than Shenton's *The Plane Truth*, which sometimes included handwritten captions, and less religiously focused than Voliva's *Leaves of Healing* or *Battle Axe*, which generally focused more on fundamentalist Christianity than on Flat Earth. Editions of *Flat Earth News* usually opened with an attempted Flat Earth proof (often something to do with perspective or water level) and a picture of the Johnsons, before diving off the conspiratorial deep end—further than any of his predecessors dared to go. Rowbotham and Voliva had been straightforward in their theories about the supposed Flat Earth cover-up. Both men, who witnessed the fields of natural sciences and evolution gaining strength and offering alternatives to biblical theories, claimed Globe Earth theory was an attempt by scientists to deny God and hide the truth of the world. Shenton, who had a similar religious bent, had updated the theory to suggest certain industries like globe makers were advancing the conspiracy for profit.

But Charles Johnson put forth an even broader conspiracy theory: the global domination plot. Going further even than Kaysing's geopolitical paranoia about the moon landing as a cover-up of US military failures, Johnson alleged that Russia and Rome were about to unite, with England's backing. "Word has come to us from where the Double Cross Flag flies—Newton's Spinning Ball England says that Moscow and Rome are about to Unite! I wonder if it will be a 3 way marriage?" he wrote in his July 1978 newsletter. "The three Balls, or three Spheres system was fully established on a Globe. That's the Plan, anyway."

Johnson's wording might have been muddled, but it echoed a growing body of conspiratorial language about a New World Order or a One World Government that hoped to bring the planet under its sole control. Fears of secretive ruling groups had been latent in the West since the late 1700s, when popular conspiracy texts had blamed the Illuminati for the French Revolution. By the time conspiracy theorists latched on to the now-familiar term "New World Order" in the 1950s, they had a solid basis for suspicion. World leaders had spent the peacetime years of the early twentieth century advocating for intergovernmental organizations like the League of Nations and the United Nations, sometimes using the term "new world order" to describe their hopes for an idealistic new system of peace and cooperation. In the hands of paranoid groups like the far-right John Birch Society, the term became something deeply sinister. Spurred by a fierce Christian nationalism, militant anti-leftism, and no small measure of racism and antisemitism, this crowd alleged a worldwide conspiracy to strip the United States of its sovereignty and place it under control of a shadowy world government. These theories often blamed a combination of communist and Jewish interests, in the latter case building off centuries of antisemitic hoaxes that accused Jews of pulling the strings of world power.

Compared to the well-financed political savvy of the John Birch Society and its associates, the Johnsons were small-time conspiracy theorists. Self-educated and self-exiled in the desert, they were more interested in publishing their newsletter than with this polished clique. Yet, perhaps unconsciously, Charles Johnson absorbed some of these other conspiracy theories into his, lacing Flat Earth theory with what would become its long-term suspicion of world governments. The current United Nations, Johnson contended, was a perversion of its original design, which was supposed to reveal the world as flat.

"Uncle Joe [Stalin], Churchill, and Roosevelt laid the master plan to bring in the New Age under the United Nations," Johnson told *Science Digest* in 1980. "The world ruling power was to be right here in this country. After the war, the world would be declared flat and Roosevelt would be elected first president of the world. When the UN Charter was drafted in San Francisco, they took the flat-earth map as their symbol."

Johnson reasoned that because Roosevelt died before he could become president of the world, the United Nations knowingly concealed the truth of Flat Earth. To support his case, he presented the UN insignia: a circular, top-down map of the world similar to the models sketched by Flat Earthers.

Johnson also continued Shenton's spirited battle against the reality of space travel, galvanizing the moon-landing truther movement in the process. Where Shenton merely suggested that pictures from the moon had been staged in a studio, Johnson gave specifics: NASA had hired some of the top minds in Hollywood, he claimed, including Arthur C. Clarke, a science-fiction author who cowrote the screenplay for Stanley Kubrick's groundbreaking 1968 film *2001: A Space Odyssey*. Johnson was among the earliest to detail the Kubrick conspiracy in the media, where it flourished and remains in circulation to this day. "The space program is in the entertainment field," Johnson told a reporter many years later, in 1994. "We're not mad about it. We're not wringing our hands over it. It's entertainment for the masses, like a perpetual Star Trek going on. But there's not reality in it."

And in a limited way, Johnson was winning his space battle. By then, Kaysing's *We Never Went to the Moon* and Johnson's own theory about

Kubrick had inspired a genre of imitators, all adding their own flourishes to the conspiracy theory that claimed the moon landing was an elaborate hoax. The 1978 film *Capricorn One* had brought the theory to a wider audience, with the story of astronauts who were forced to fake a Mars landing. Although the O. J. Simpson–starring movie was a work of futuristic fiction, its tagline—"Would you be shocked to find out that the greatest moment of our recent history may not have happened at all?"—was hard not to read as a shoutout to Johnson's theory. By 1994, Johnson-variety moon-landing trutherism was thriving so heartily that people who had once treated it as a joke now invested serious effort in combating it. Julian Scheer, the NASA public affairs official who cofounded the Man Will Never Fly Memorial Society and who, in 1969, had led the group in pretending to doubt space travel, was frequently called upon to argue the other side.

"Despite all that we tried to do and to tell the full story, there were those who maintained—either half seriously or not—that we faked the whole thing," Scheer said of early moon-landing conspiracy theorists in the same 1994 article that quoted Johnson. "That was not a widespread feeling, but there were skeptics."

The growing visibility of conspiracy theories about the moon made Johnson a semiregular feature of headlines and trash-TV interviews for the rest of his life. He pursued those headlines in the face of remarkable bad luck (twice his car broke down en route to much-anticipated speaking engagements, forcing him to cancel), and open scorn. During a 1986 interview on the combative talk show *Hot Seat*, the audience chanted "flathead" at Johnson and "USA" when he called the moon landing a hoax. Elderly and unrattled in front of the show's braying audience, Johnson appeared dignified, even comparatively sane. Some of Johnson's modern Flat Earth contemporaries have uploaded clips of the interview to the internet, where they immortalize the old society leader as a warrior for the cause.

Still, Johnson and his wife rarely found the serious audience they craved. Every edition of their *Flat Earth News* was stamped with the slogan "Restoring the world to sanity," but it was the rest of the world that considered the Johnsons and their modest movement insane.

"We're two witnesses against the whole world," Charles Johnson told Schadewald, the science writer, who forged an unlikely friendship with the Flat Earth movement. "We've chosen that path, but it isolates us from everyone. We're not complaining; it has to be done. But it does kind of get to you sometimes." (Schadewald was awarded IFERS membership at one point but later expelled for "spherical tendencies.")

For all their successful recruitments—Johnson claimed thousands of Flat Earth Society members, many times Shenton's strongest membership numbers—the Johnsons really were the society's two core believers. The couple who had met, as if fated, in a record store spent decades chronicling their devotion for each other in the pages of *Flat Earth News*. Those same pages would chart the couple's decline, and with it, the temporary end of the Flat Earth Society. The newsletter's March 1994 issue included a sign of what was to come.

"Sorry we didn't get the December issue out. But there was good reason!" the paper read. "The greatest woman of this century, Marjory Waugh Johnson was sick. So everything ground to a halt, no letters answered . . . Anyway Marjory had two trips to hospital, two weeks in each time, I of course never left her side day or night. So no December issue. She is better, will be OK, so full speed FORWARD."

The issue was *Flat Earth News*'s last. At the time of its publication, Marjory was seventy-three and sicker than the newsletter let on. Emphysema had left her dependent on an oxygen tank and robbed her of the freedom to wander the desert and keep up with the couple's ever-present pack of rescue animals. Emergency followed emergency. While Charles Johnson was watching television in September 1995, the couple's front porch burst into flame. Johnson carried Marjory and her oxygen tank to safety, but their home of twenty-three years (so remote the couple needed to transport all their water from a well at the bottom of a nearby hill) was beyond saving. Their records, including their membership lists and their prized writings from Shenton's personal archive, were lost to the ashes. "It's all gone," Johnson told the *Los Angeles Daily News*. "I don't know how we'll get all that information back. I hope people will write to us wondering what happened to us and we'll be able to get their names again. Right now we're really at a loss." The couple moved into a trailer on the property, where Marjory spent her final months before dying in May 1996. "When the house burned, with all her treasures, she gave up the will to live," Johnson told the *Boston Globe*, which, appropriately for its name, had always taken an interest in the couple. "It's very lonely without her, but Marjie wanted to keep the work going, so I'm forcing myself to go on."

He went on for several years, during which several hundred of the society's three-thousand-plus members wrote to reenlist. But like his old hero Voliva, who saw the last of his sputtering power destroyed by a church arson, Johnson was all but finished after the fire. Although he hired another IFERS secretary to fill Marjory's old role, the society rarely made public statements anymore, except to answer questions from the occasional journalist who came knocking. Johnson died in his home in March 2001, at the age of seventy-six.

The Johnsons' shared grave marker lists their dates of death as the dates they "ascended." The wording is not uncommon for tombstones, but for the Johnsons, this last word might have carried additional Flat Earth significance. One of Charles Johnson's favorite pieces of biblical Flat Earth evidence was the story of Jesus's rise into heaven—not his journey outward from a round planet, but his literal ascension "up" into the clouds and whatever lay beyond.

To Johnson, who believed he'd spent his life walking the surface of a two-dimensional world, the ascent to rejoin his wife was his first and final journey upward.

4 | The Reboot

I WANDERED THE labyrinthine halls of the hotel-slash-convention center feeling hypercaffeinated and distinctly unwell. I had just had coffee with a pleasant, thoughtful gentleman in his sixties who told me that NASA was lying about the existence of outer space so that when Jesus returned to Earth, we would mistake him for an alien and kill him. As I walked from the coffee cart, a child shone a laser pointer (useful for measuring the earth's curvature or lack thereof) almost directly into my retina.

On this miserable, sleeting weekend in November 2018, I'd flown to Denver, Colorado, to report on the second annual Flat Earth International Conference. I was not enjoying myself. All the clocks in the building were arbitrarily incorrect, compounding my jet-lagged sense of navigating a slightly wrong reality, and I'd already been reprimanded for misusing the hotel breakfast buffet wrong (yogurt dispute). By the event's second day, my draft consisted of a single unpunctuated observation: "probably going to go insane at the flat earth conference."

For nearly all of the seventeen years after Charles Johnson's death, the Flat Earth movement had been quiet—at times close to extinction. Then in 2015, the year Donald Trump launched a conspiracy-laden presidential campaign that many dismissed as a joke, Flat Earth began a much-mocked comeback. The joke was on the doubters. By November 2018, Trump had spent two years in the presidency shaping US policy after his paranoid impulses, and the Flat Earth movement was bigger than ever. Big enough for its diehard believers to fill Aurora's Crowne Plaza convention center for two days. Of the hundreds of people who packed the building, I was among the handful who subscribed to the globe model.

Maybe Flat Earthers know the sensation, but it was new for me: the disorienting knowledge that everyone around you subscribes to an interpretation of truth incompatible with your own. The feeling took root the first morning as a couple told me of the need for a Flat Earth–inspired "societal collapse," and it intensified as I watched the musician Flat Earth Man perform his song "Welcome to the Satellite Hoax" for a dancing crowd in a hotel ballroom.

"Welcome to the satellite hoax," the crowd around me sang, as if it were a Beatles concert and I were some shut-in who'd never heard of the Beatles. The song went on: "Just another one of them NASA jokes. You can't find me a picture of a satellite without bringing up a bunch of that CGI."

It was as if our realities had become atomized and we lived on slightly different planets. On the main stage one night, I watched a Flat Earther debate a Globe Earther who believed that the earth—not the sun—was the center of the solar system. After a couple beers with Flat Earthers at the hotel bar, I found myself in a regrettable argument about flight patterns. (You can't fly nonstop from the United States to Australia or South Africa, said a woman who was unmoved by my increasingly high-pitched insistences that I'd taken both those flights within the past two years.)

The in-person disputes felt as futile as arguing with a stranger online. I ate breakfast with a Flat Earth family who told me about evil druids while a nearby television aired a segment about Trump's tweets. Perhaps, I thought, as the conversation turned to conspiracy theories about school shootings, we were experiencing a disconnect on a level that simply could not have happened during the Johnsons' lifetime. This six-hundred-person Flat Earth festival, this president who doled out fictions via his Twitter account, this whole choose-your-own-reality moment, was a product of the internet.

Depending on your degree of techno-pessimism, the advent of the internet was somewhere between a triumph and the clear start of civilizational decline.

Early users predicted that the internet would democratize knowledge and lead to radical equality across the globe. What they got instead was a World Wide Web as flawed and brilliant as the spectrum of grifters and do-gooders and trolls who inhabit it. The internet made it easier than ever to look up facts about golden retrievers, or organize a grassroots movement against an oppressive regime, or order a pizza without having to hold a conversation with an actual person. It also made it easier than ever to sow the seeds of a hoax or find like-minded individuals who share your suspicions. Just as the newspaper boom in Samuel Rowbotham's time and the rise of radio in Voliva's enabled the spread of the Flat Earth sentiment, the sudden surge in available information online gave rise to a rich conspiracy culture.

The end of the Johnsons' lives overlapped briefly with the beginning of mass internet use. But with their love of self-published newsletters and off-the-grid living, the Johnsons were resolutely off-line. A Flat Earth email newsletter—or, God forbid, an internet discussion forum—was out of the question for them. Their Flat Earth Society membership registry, printed out and stored in their home until their catastrophic house fire, was one of the last social networks that could go up in flames.

Flat Earth's internet renaissance would come long after the couple's passing. In those intervening years, other conspiracy theorists became experts in exploiting the web, breaking the internet in ways that shaped how we use it today. These pioneers laid the conspiratorial groundwork for Flat Earth online. So when the theory finally made its digital debut, its path had been primed by decades of wingnuts and their websites.

The internet has always been at least partially cesspit. Decades before many Americans logged on, some of the country's worst actors were already figuring out how to exploit it for their own ends. That included violent white supremacists, who built some of the earliest internet networks and used them to push conspiratorial propaganda about other races. In 1983, neo-Nazi (and former regular Nazi) George Dietz launched a message board for antisemitic conspiracy theories and Holocaust denial. Dietz, a former Hitler Youth member who pinned all the world's problems on the Jews and openly yearned for genocide, saw the internet as a recruitment tool—particularly for young people. "All I want to do is get the thinking processes going," Dietz told the *Washington Post* in 1985, in an eerily prescient article about online extremism. "I'm not interested in reaching old people whose minds are already set in concrete, who know people who were killed or maimed in World War II. It's the young people I'm interested in." He claimed approximately 90 percent of visitors to his message board were children or young adults. The previous year, a coalition of racists associated with the Ku Klux Klan and a white-supremacist terrorist group called the Order had pooled their resources to launch Liberty Net, an online network that let users transmit racist conspiracy theories into Canada, bypassing laws against international transmission of hate literature (the international link was something of a technological feat at the time, as it preceded the creation of the World Wide Web). Liberty Net also acted as a community hub, hosting everything from white-supremacist dating advertisements to calls for assassinations.

Conspiratorial cults also used the internet for recruiting. In 1996, a set of rambling essays about an alien religion began appearing on off-beat discussion boards, like those for militias and libertarians. The posts directed readers to a website for Heaven's Gate, a California-based cult that would achieve infamy the following year when thirty-nine of its forty-one members put on matching tracksuits, placed $5.75 in their pockets, then died together in a chillingly tidy suicide ritual. The group theorized that an alien spaceship was hiding behind the approaching Comet Hale-Bopp, and that, by ingesting lethal doses of phenobarbital and vodka, they could leave their earthly bodies and hitch a ride on the alien ship. The only other thing they left behind was a rainbow-hued website, with instructions for the cult's surviving members to keep the site alive. The group believed its internet legacy was more important than letting all its members board the spaceship to salvation.

Heaven's Gate was cosmically wrong about everything else but correct about the internet's ability to spread a message. Its website remains online decades later, and its posts on militia forums suggest the group deliberately targeted semifringe ideologies, with the hope that those readers would be into far more extreme ideas, like apocalyptic warnings about alien gods. (Heaven's Gate was notably internet-savvy for its time, buying alien abduction insurance online and paying with money earned by Higher Source, a web design company the cult ran. After the mass suicide, Higher Source customers said they'd noticed the company's employees dressed strangely, but wrote it off as a quirk of computer geeks.)

The early internet wasn't all white supremacists and alien cults. But its subculture status meant conspiracy theories flourished online. By the mid-1990s, the internet was "a fertile garden for conspiracy theories because of the hidden nature of it," Jessie Daniels, a City University of New York professor of sociology focusing on inequality on the internet, told me. "You had a sense of being a hobbyist, someone who was privy to this sort of secret world that other people didn't know about, an alternate world of knowledge that other people didn't have access to. That's like the enriched soil environment in which conspiracy theories grow: the idea that you have special knowledge, that you know things other people don't, and that if people would just pay attention to the signs, then they would make sense of it."

The Flat Earth Society and the early, conspiratorial internet could have been a love match. But the society's only apparent online presence was a sparse web page set up by pranksters associated with a parody news site. "The Flat Earth Society is not in any way responsible for the failure of the French to repel the Germans at the Maginot Line during WWII," read a disclaimer at the bottom of the fake Flat Earth Society page when it launched in 1998. "Nor is the Flat Earth Society responsible for the recent yeti sightings outside the Vatican, or for the unfortunate enslavement of the Nabisco Inc. factory employees by a rogue hamster insurrectionist group."

This grab bag of groan-inducing 1990s humor still exists unchanged, like a specimen in amber, on a hidden web page for an otherwise serious site about Alaska tourism. (I have no idea how it got there or whether the site's current owners even know the page exists.) The *Miami Herald* referenced the page in a running 2003 column about "particularly interesting and/or revolting websites," but in the following years, the internet (and even the page's creators) appeared to forget about it. The real Flat Earth Society remained an off-line affair, and the club effectively disintegrated in the digital era after Charles Johnson's death in 2001.

Instead, a new school of truthers took up the mantle of the internet's most outrageous. This new conspiratorial clique was typified by two men: Mike Adams and Alex Jones. Though neither was a Flat Earther, both would help build an internet that rewarded the most outlandish movements—especially Flat Earth.

In 1999, conspiracy theorist Mike Adams helped usher the world into a revolution in paranoia: At the turn of the millennium, aircraft were going to fall from the sky, he implied, with the exception of military Blackhawk helicopters, which would be armed and ready for the rollout of martial law. Your children would be swept away into "government-run re-education centers." Police were stockpiling guns and probably coming to seize yours, and the power grid would fail, and your flimsy paper money would be useless except as kindling, should you need to boil some of the freeze-dried mangoes you bought in bulk from a doomsday preparation wholesaler. And that was if you were an optimist. There was always a chance you'd get vaporized in a nuclear apocalypse the moment the clock ticked over into the year 2000.

This was the world according to Adams's panic-mongering website Y2K Newswire, which, in the final months of 1999, promoted headlines about the so-called Y2K bug, a mythic computer error that would allegedly send the world into meltdown when the new millennium began.

Adams was a computer pioneer first, and a conspiracy theorist second. In 1993, he founded a tech firm that helped large companies manage mass-email marketing lists. His real legacy, however, would be the mass emails he sent outside of corporate life. Before social media giants like Twitter and Facebook made it easy to trumpet your opinions to the world, email chains were the best way to FW: FW: FW: your fears to a wide circle of acquaintances. As Y2K neared, Adams used his spam-mail savviness to convince strangers that they should really start panicking now. One of his most notorious emails, "Thirty-Nine Unanswered Questions About Y2K," spread fast enough to become a well-known headache for skeptics.

"Adams' 'Thirty-Nine Unanswered Questions About Y2K' have arrived in my mailbox about 50 times today," a technology blogger wrote in a December 1999 article in which he addressed all thirty-nine of the hand-wringing hypotheticals. The blogger also revealed that Adams, who often raged against supposed "censorship," had threatened to sue him.

The Flat Earth Society was inactive when Adams's emails blanketed the internet. Yet when some columnists confronted the mounting wave of spam, they anticipated the technology falling into the hands of groups like the society. "Who will be next?" one journalist wrote of obnoxious mass-email campaigns. "The Democrats? The pro-life lobby? . . . The Flat Earth Society?" Other columnists rhetorically dismissed their most annoying emails as coming from Flat Earthers.

Adams's emails, though, were more than annoying; they were profitable. The mass messages contained links to Y2K Newswire, where readers could feast on fear and, conveniently for him, waste thousands of dollars on Y2K preparedness in a single sitting. The website featured

$99 subscriptions for Y2K information ("much of it too sensitive for public release"), dehydrated foods in bulk, and overpriced gold coins. A yearlong digital subscription to Y2K Newswire with a "one year basic food unit" cost $569. It was a shameless cash grab, making what Adams claimed was more than $400,000 in six months as part of an experimental internet sales blitz.

Adams also boasted on Y2K Newswire of developing "patents on search engine ranking improvement technology"—effectively, tricks to make a website appear higher in search results. Although he was vague, we can guess how he might have hacked conspiratorial content to the top of a search. One of the easiest ways to make a website appear prominently is to link to that website from other pages. These frequent cross-references trick search engines into assuming a website is authoritative and credible, even if it's actually the paranoid screed of a doomsday prophet. Already in the late 1990s, Adams had registered a number of websites. His "search engine ranking improvement technology" was likely a strategy of linking those sites together, propelling their conspiratorial contents to the top of search results.

At least that's what he went on to do when Y2K passed without catastrophe. When the new millennium arrived without financial collapse or martial law, Adams replaced Y2K Newswire with a single page defending his actions. (On it he claimed the site "never made a dime from product sales or recommendations," an impressively brazen reversal of his recent claims of making almost half a million dollars off the site.) Then he went on to register a series of new websites, with titles like News Target, TruthWiki, Health Ranger, and Natural News. Not all the sites were particularly active. Some even hosted identical articles, but by linking them together, like he'd alluded to on Y2K Newswire, Adams was able to land his websites high in the Google results for innocent searches on topics like health foods and alternative medicine.

While Adams was using conspiracy theories to warp the inner workings of the internet, his sometimes colleague Alex Jones was using the internet to turn them into a formidable political force. Since 1999, Jones has presided over Infowars, one of the web's premier conspiracy sites. Infowars' two decades online have seen—and shaped—an increasingly conspiratorial internet.

Previously a shock jock on public-access television and radio stations in Austin, Texas, Jones made wild claims almost reflexively; after losing a fistfight to a local oddity known as SpaceHitler in 1997, Jones told police he'd been attacked by a man with "eyes that look like a goat's . . . and pasty white green skin" who was armed with "a double edged military type killing knife." His first posts on Infowars were equally incredible: gun-grabbing government forces were establishing "concentration camps" in preparation for a massive crackdown on civil liberties. "Military helicopters 'invading' our neighborhoods are real and are the strike force for the new world order," one typical article read.

Jones got lucky. In July 2001, amid ramblings about the New World Order, he claimed the US government would orchestrate a terror attack as a pretense to enslave the masses. The White House would probably blame Osama bin Laden, leader of the terror group al-Qaeda, Jones speculated. Two months later, al-Qaeda militants crashed planes into the World Trade Center, the Pentagon, and a Pennsylvania field on September 11, 2001, in one of the most paranoia-provoking events in US history. Jones cried vindication. "I'll tell you the bottom line," Jones told listeners to his show after the attack. "98 percent chance this was a government-orchestrated controlled bombing."

The 9/11 attacks would popularize a new strain of conspiracy culture, with Infowars at the forefront. Here, Jones was both a skilled messenger for American paranoia and largely blind to the true plots unfolding before him. The month after the attacks, President George W. Bush signed into law the Patriot Act, enabling sweeping surveillance measures against Americans in the name of preventing future acts of terror. Other post-9/11 programs were more transparent in their targeted surveillance of Muslim Americans: a joint program by the CIA and the New York City

Police Department established spy networks in Muslim communities. The National Security Entry-Exit Registration System, which launched in 2002, oversaw intrusive data collection from noncitizen men and teen-agers from twenty-five countries, twenty-four of which were predominantly Muslim. Any of these programs should have been enough to rattle Americans' sense of security when it came to civil liberties.

But Jones, who'd made his name selling the most occult and sci-fi visions of dystopia, missed the point. His subsequent documentaries claimed 9/11 was a government ruse to justify repressive regimes still to come. When he did reference the crisis facing Muslims in the United States and abroad, it was secondary, as part of a greater plot to incon-venience people like him. During a 2005 documentary, in a segment about the US torture of Iraqis in the notorious Abu Ghraib prison, Jones claimed that "the only reason the elite is selling us on torture is they want to condition us to where we will accept its use on us," as if the "us" of his audience were the torture's true victims.

Myopic and rambling, Jones's brand of 9/11 trutherism would take years to become popular. "The statistics on trutherism show that the numbers of believers were initially low, but they grew in the years fol-lowing the attacks," journalist Anna Merlan writes in her book *Republic of Lies*. "This echoes the way the official story of the Kennedy assassi-nation was increasingly questioned in the decades after, according to many polls, as the initial shock of the president's murder faded and peo-ple began looking, as we often do, for deeper meaning." In May 2002, fewer than one in ten Americans believed a conspiracy theory about the attacks, Merlan notes. By September 2006, one in three Americans believed it was "likely" the US government had orchestrated the attacks or knowingly allowed them to happen.

Among those one in three were many of the people who would later join the Flat Earth revival. Robbie Davidson, founder of the Flat Earth International Conference, described 9/11 trutherism as the on-ramp to conspiracism for many conference attendees. 9/11 "was pretty pivotal for sure," he told me at the 2019 conference. "Most people didn't come to that awakening until two, three years after [the attacks]. It wasn't, like, instantly like, 'Oh, I'm skeptical.' Everyone believed it at first."

Some of those soon-to-be Flat Earthers viewed Alex Jones's online empire as a place to find—or recruit—conspiratorial kin. While waiting for the 2018 Flat Earth International Conference to kick off, I found myself shooting the breeze with Scott and Julie Simons, a Flat Earth couple who'd driven in from Utah. Scott was clutching their car's ITS-FLAT license plate, on which he was collecting Flat Earth autographs, and telling me that in five years, Flat Earth would be accepted as fact worldwide. The Simonses were old-school Flat Earthers, some of the only I've met who converted before the 2010s. They went Flat in 2008 for "for religious reasons," Scott told me. Since then, they'd been trying to find like-minded peers on forums for fringe theologians and Alex Jones fans, but they kept getting banned for their views.

"We've been kicked off more forums than I can count. Christian theology, Infowars, [Alex Jones'] Prison Planet," Scott said. He had lost count of how many forum usernames he'd registered.

Forums for big-name conspiracy sites were the increasingly obvious go-to for new conspiracy theorists like the Simonses. In their enthusiasm, however, they had missed the most obvious site for kindred spirits: the Flat Earth Society, which had recently relaunched online, under new management.

From Charles Johnson's death in 2001 "until 2005 or so, the society existed in name only," Pete Svarrior, a Flat Earth Society spokesperson, told me in a phone interview. (The name Svarrior, I'm sure, is an alias. No one of that name appears to have an internet presence outside the Flat Earth Society character and, though he speaks with what I'd cautiously identify as an Irish accent, he declines to say where he's from.) "There was nobody to take it on as it was collapsing in the '90s to early 2000s," he said. "The society died because there wasn't a clear line of succession and interest was kind of falling."

Then in 2004, for the second time in a century, a man calling himself Shenton dragged Flat Earth theory from the garbage heap of forgotten conspiracy theories and polished it into a vibrant movement. This man was not Samuel Shenton, the English eccentric who launched the International Flat Earth Research Society in 1956. He went by Daniel Shenton—a pseudonym, Svarrior told me.

Everything I know about Daniel Shenton I've learned from his acquaintances or his old interviews. The pseudonymous man's internet activity dried up in the mid-2010s and not even his Flat Earth Society acquaintances were able to arrange an interview. So, most unzetetically, we have to learn about him from secondhand accounts.

By his own telling, Shenton found his way to Flat Earth theory when he was listening to English musician Thomas Dolby's 1984 album *The Flat Earth*.

"I'm sure he didn't plan it this way, but Thomas Dolby is responsible for the Society's existence now," Shenton wrote in a 2009 forum post. He had listened to Dolby's album in the late 1990s. "I'd found a copy on vinyl at a used record store and figured, 'hey, I liked that big song of his . . . so why not?'" he added. "At that time, I had some vague idea that there was (or had been) something called the Flat Earth Society but I didn't really know anything about it. But I loved the album (particularly the title track) and listened to it often . . . and it got me thinking."

A Virginia man who relocated to the United Kingdom, Shenton said he replicated the founding Brits' Flat Earth experiments. He traveled to the Bedford Canal, where Samuel Rowbotham first claimed to measure the earth's lack of curvature. Shenton, of course, had come to the same conclusions.

"I started doing research and learning more about the Society and Flat Earth theory and gradually I came around to the Society's way of thinking," Shenton wrote online. "In 2001, I was saddened to learn that Charles K. Johnson, then president, had passed away and the Society had essentially died with him. I decided then that I would resurrect the Society. And here we are today. I still regret that I never contacted Charles when he was alive, but the new Society is my tribute to him and all of the other Flat Earther leaders who came before him."

Initially, the new society was little more than an online discussion forum, which Shenton launched in 2004. The page drew a mix of earnest conspiracy theorists and Globe Earthers who were just there to argue. Often, the pro-globe contingent was so large its members doubted whether any genuine Flat Earthers used the forum.

"There are about five real FEcrs on this site and perhaps a few dozen worldwide, but for all intents and purposes there are no longer any real Flat-Earthers," one skeptic wrote in response to a 2006 thread asking for Flat Earthers' conversion stories.

"Five liars, you mean," another Globe Earther replied.

The globe fans might have accidentally gotten the ball rolling on the movement's relaunch. Shenton's forum, full of argumentative Globe Earthers, ballooned to host more than sixteen thousand members in its first five years online, according to the society's own figures. The scene's revival also stirred new interest among journalists. As forum membership snowballed, major media outlets like the BBC and Fox News ran features on Flat Earth.

In 2007, historian Christine Garwood published the book *Flat Earth: The History of an Infamous Idea*, which traced the movement from Rowbotham to the Johnsons. Daniel Shenton cited Garwood, the BBC, and Fox in his decision to launch a new Flat Earth Society website and begin accepting new members in 2009. The digital launch would take the movement further than its analog ancestors had ever gone, the society announced in a press release: "The official launch of the website marks an important transition for the Flat Earth Society."

"Traditionally, the Flat Earth Society has communicated with its members through printed newsletters such as the *Earth Not A Globe Review* and the *Flat Earth News*," the release continued. "'Technology has moved on and we're thrilled to be able to reach a much broader audience with our message,' Flat Earth Society president Daniel Shenton said. 'The Internet is an amazing tool for communication.'"

He and the society were charmingly, wildly late to the game. I was a teen in 2009, but I'd already used the web to hack Neopets accounts, and my rural school district had undergone a regional scandal when some kids made a web page threatening to murder fans of a niche punk-rock scene. Alex Jones, meanwhile, had been pumping out 9/11 trutherism online for years, and Mike Adams had broken the internet god knows how many ways while jamming his conspiracy theories to the top of web searches and email inboxes. In the face of this digital melee, the relaunched Flat Earth Society's communiqués about the "amazing tool" of the internet seemed almost quaint.

In fact, Shenton took almost the opposite approach to Adams and Jones in his conspiracy mongering. Adams and Jones appeared in videos and talked about themselves on their websites with almost messianic fervor. I have no idea what Shenton even looks like. Occasionally, he'd upload a guy in a Flat Earth Society T-shirt on Facebook—at the beach in Tanzania, on safari in Kenya, at the Pyongyang Marathon in North Korea—but he always cropped out most of his face. Jones and Adams kept their websites lively with a constant churn of freshly imagined theories, but Shenton appeared much more interested in acting as a public historian. He and his society digitized the Johnsons' old newsletters. They also scanned old event posters from Samuel Shenton's era and uploaded them to the internet.

"I thought it was a shame that all these documents would go unseen forever," Daniel Shenton told the *Guardian* in 2010. In that interview, he revealed another striking difference between him and the Alex Joneses of the internet: he believed in climate change and in modern medicine, and did not believe that the US government had orchestrated the 9/11 attacks. He had "resolutely mainstream views on most issues" except Flat Earth, the *Guardian* wrote.

Dare I advance a conspiracy theory about a conspiracy theorist? I'm skeptical, at times, of this pseudonymous Flat Earther's belief. Not outwardly religious like many of the movement's founders or current believers, not especially fixated on making money, apparently uninterested in other conspiracy theories, "Daniel Shenton" has none of the obvious motivations. He often strikes me as something of a jokester historian, doing a legitimate public service by archiving a little-respected movement's sacred texts. But what do I know? I've never met the guy.

I put the question to Pete Svarrior, the Flat Earth Society's spokesperson, who described Shenton as mysterious even to society members.

"He almost certainly does believe Earth is flat," Svarrior told me. "It's not always one hundred percent possible to tell. He is quite hands-off and doesn't talk much about his beliefs. Save for a few historical interviews in which he speaks quite openly about it. Whether or not he currently does, I don't know, but I would assume so."

The line between skeptic and believer can be porous. Svarrior said he himself was a globe believer when he clicked on the forum on a whim in 2010 or 2011.

"My immediate reaction was, 'No way. That thing can't actually exist. What are they on about?'" he told me. "So I joined out of curiosity, just to kind of find out what's going on. That's how I got hooked. Originally, I came in to try to have a conversation and have a debate. Eventually—it was a very long process—I started to realize that I am perhaps getting convinced."

The new, digital Flat Earth Society put the conspiracy theory back on the internet's map, but its actual membership numbers are trivial. As of 2016, the last time it was updated, the society's public membership list stood at 555 people. By early 2021, the society's forums hosted a modest 25,200 users—approximately 0.007 percent of Reddit's active membership at that time—with a male-to-female ratio of 15.8 to 1, according to the organization's own statistics. The small, relatively polite square of cyberspace they'd staked out was of little interest to other conspiracy theorists, including some who would go on to become the loudest voices in the Flat Earth movement.

One of them, Eric Dubay, didn't bother much with Daniel Shenton's clique. Instead, he tried taking Flat Earth theory straight to Alex Jones.

Dubay, a minor-league conspiracy peddler, ran a truther blog infused with antisemitic posts that read like a buffet of the internet's worst offerings. His first self-published book, a muddled 2009 rant about the New World Order, cited Jones's 9/11 conspiracy content liberally. It also documented Dubay as being on the cusp of Flat Earth belief. While not yet committed to the movement, he did claim Earth was a stationary object at the center of a universe that revolved around it. "Why can I feel the slightest Westward breeze but not the Earth's 1,000 mile per hour Eastward spin?" he asked, in a zetetic argument that would have made Rowbotham proud. He even inadvertently reinvented the stationary aircraft Samuel Shenton had devised and abandoned as a teenager in 1919: "If the Earth is spinning beneath us, why can't I just hover in a helicopter, wait until my destination reaches me, and then land when it comes?" Dubay wrote. (As Samuel Shenton should have learned from his own machine, the earth's atmosphere orbits alongside it, which is why you can't just hover in a helicopter and wait for your destination to wheel into place below.)

Dubay's writings were undoubtedly influenced by Flat Earthers. "At the time I had already read Samuel Rowbotham and William Carpenter's old 19th century flat Earth books," Dubay later wrote in a blog post about the book, "and though personally still on the fence regarding the shape of the Earth, I was confident they were correct about the location (or Geocentricity) of Earth, so I wrote about it." He also cited Charles Johnson in the book itself while addressing the moon landing (a hoax, of course).

He'd made the full leap to Flat Earth by the end of 2009, when he sent Alex Jones a link to Rowbotham's writing, imploring the conspiracy superstar to convert. Jones made fun of him on air by name. Undeterred, Dubay kept preaching Flat Earth, and started making YouTube videos on the topic. Jones's mockery didn't stop Dubay from borrowing his style, and eventually accusing him of being a fake conspiracy theorist, due to what he claimed was Jones's insufficient antisemitism.

Battle lines were beginning to solidify across the conspiratorial internet. Allyships emerged: some fringe websites borrowed the techniques Mike Adams had pioneered years earlier, promoting their theories across a network of websites by aggressively hyperlinking to each other or allowing partner sites to republish their articles in full.

This strategy would persist for years to come. A 2018 study by researchers at the University of Washington and Harvard University revealed a coalition of conspiracy-pumping websites using a similar tactic to Adams. Although these sites had different owners, they repeatedly linked to each other and sometimes copied each other's articles verbatim, amplifying their messages across the internet. The tactic saw semilegitimate-looking news sites network with more fringe websites like the notorious hoax site YourNewsWire and the blatantly antisemitic JewWorldOrder.

Flat Earth rode, and continues to ride, the wave of shady web traffic. JewWorldOrder, for instance, has repeatedly run pro–Flat Earth theory over the past five years, ringing in 2021 with a New Year's Day post titled "Best Flat Earth Video 1000% Proof The Earth Is Flat." On one of my recent trips to the site, a Flat Earth article was flanked on one side by an ad for a luridly antisemitic book by an author who wrote one of the most popular Flat Earth books on the market, and on the other side by a picture of neo-Nazi who had famously been kicked off an extremist social media network for suggesting that Jewish children be taken from their parents and raised for continual torture. Not great.

Conspiracy theorists who couldn't keep up with the scene's most bombastic personalities found themselves getting trampled. In 2005, a young man named Dylan Avery struck internet gold when he released

Loose Change, an amateurish documentary claiming the US government had arranged the 9/11 attacks as a pretext for the Iraq War. *Loose Change* became perhaps "the first Internet blockbuster," *Vanity Fair* wrote the following year. ("We beat the woman getting punched in the face," Avery told *Vanity Fair* after *Loose Change* earned more views than a popular video of a woman getting punched in the face.) Experts quickly debunked large chunks of the documentary, leading Avery to release new versions of the film, sidestepping those issues and raising new ones. Alex Jones got involved with the *Loose Change* "final cut," released in 2007, which lists him as an executive producer.

Jones would go on to apply *Loose Change* logic to virtually every traumatic event. He accused an escalating series of horrors of being "false flags," a conspiracy term for a staged event designed to further some nefarious aim. Jones slapped the label on everything from the murder of children at Sandy Hook Elementary School in 2012 to a deadly white-supremacist rally in Charlottesville, Virginia, in 2017, by which point milder conspiracy theorists like Avery wanted nothing to do with him.

"Before when you said you believed in 9/11 Truth, it meant the original investigation was shoddy, but you weren't a nutjob. Now, as soon as something happens, people say it's a false flag," Avery told the *Outline* in 2017. "To see what's happened with Alex Jones—he just said something about Charlottesville and actors, or whatever the hell? I don't know, man. Everything is just so goddamned weird right now."

The Flat Earth Society fared no better than Avery as its conspiratorial kin stepped on the accelerator. Though he had come to dismiss Alex Jones as a fraud, Eric Dubay continued to borrow Jones's style to create rambling, documentary-like videos. In a particularly Jonesian turn, he eventually accused the Flat Earth Society of being a fake group designed to discredit the movement, due to its more modest conspiratorial stances. Soon he was outpacing the society online. His YouTube videos had captured an audience that the older group had never managed to find.

When Dubay started making Flat Earth films in 2014, he helped push the theory over its tipping point and into the mainstream. One especially popular Dubay video, *200 Proofs Earth Is Not a Spinning Ball*, drew its inspiration from Rowbotham disciple William Carpenter's 1885 text *One Hundred Proofs That the Earth Is Not a Globe*. Along with Rowbotham-era "proofs" like the apparently flat horizon at ground level, Dubay mixed in more modern junk science, like false claims about space travel and experiments based on incorrect (and easily Google-able) measurements. Dubay even occasionally got Carpenter's name wrong, calling him John while describing him as the inspiration for *200 Proofs*.

Basic facts might have eluded him, but Dubay and his Jones-style paranoia helped finally sever the Flat Earth movement from the Flat Earth Society that birthed it.

"I think it started with Eric Dubay," Pete Svarrior told me. "When Eric appeared on the Flat Earth scene, he really wanted to make a move to become *the* big Flat Earth guy. There were a few other groups already in place. They had views other than his. He was really struggling to get some of his political stuff out there . . . Where he managed to find a little bit of traction was by decrying other groups to be psyops or government conspiracies or what have you. He got a niche of people who could go 'Not only are we being lied to, but also the government is now spawning these extraneous groups that are trying to detract people from the truth.'"

Globe Earthers took note of Dubay's *200 Proofs* video and made their own videos debunking Dubay's arguments—not that these fact-checks vanquished the theory. A growing cohort of conspiracy YouTubers began dabbling in Flat Earth in 2014 and 2015. They began organizing digital hangouts on Skype, then in person at localized meetups. And unlike the polite, anonymous debates on the Flat Earth Society forums, this crowd was less interested in arguing their points with nonbelievers and more focused on building a boots-on-the-ground movement with real faces and real money.

Zen Garcia, a writer who'd focused for decades on obscure Christian offshoots, turned his focus to Flat Earth in 2016, churning out book after book on the topic and opening a publishing house for other Flat Earth writers. Musicians like Flat Earth Man carved out their own niches in the burgeoning community. A British man who performs songs like "Don't Believe In Gravity" in character as a gruff, conspiratorial cowboy with a deep Texas accent, Flat Earth Man has tens of thousands of YouTube followers.

I met both men at what was perhaps the movement's greatest commercial success to date: the 2018 Flat Earth International Conference. There, the Flat Earth Society was not just absent; members of this new scene viewed the Flat Earth Society as too moderate. Suspiciously moderate. Maybe even, as Dubay had suggested, a conspiracy in itself.

The website for the conference included a disclaimer: "FEIC is not in any way affiliated with the Flat Earth Society." The message was bolded. The conference organizers were sick of people assuming they had anything to do with that grandfather of Flat Earth social clubs. At the conference, speakers publicly disavowed the society.

Rob Skiba, a popular YouTuber in the Flat Earth scene, began a speech by addressing what he said were harmful media misrepresentations of the Flat Earth movement. "None of us belong to the Flat Earth Society. Media, please take note of that," he shouted with visible frustration. The audience broke into applause and wolf whistles. "Most of us consider that website to be either controlled opposition [a term for a government-run operation aimed at discrediting a movement] or a joke."

Conference organizer Robbie Davidson was of a similar mind. "I think it just got infiltrated real fast. I think something moved in there," he told me the following year, in a different hotel-slash-convention center, for the third annual conference. "I don't know. I just say we're not affiliated in any way. I've never even met one of them. I've never even met someone from the Flat Earth Society. They've never come to this conference. Any of my conferences."

Part of Davidson's suspicions stemmed from the Flat Earth Society's understated internet presence, which appeared almost freakishly mild amid the growing noise of hard-core Flat Earth evangelism online. "They just do funny little things on social media," he said.

Even Svarrior, who runs the Flat Earth Society's Twitter account and writes the tweets Davidson distrusts, acknowledged the rift. "This is a momentum we initially had pretty much complete control over, and we've lost it since other groups have spawned and taken their own direction," he told me. Independent of the Flat Earth Society, Flat Earth had hit the big time online.

So had other conspiracy theories and their promoters. By 2018, Alex Jones had an audience of millions, and all the influence that came with it. When in 2012 he falsely accused Sandy Hook parents of faking their first graders' deaths as part of a shadowy plot to ban guns, legions of Infowars fans harassed the grieving parents until some went into hiding. Jones's expansive Sandy Hook–era audience included not just up-and-coming Flat Earthers like Eric Dubay, but also Donald Trump. Months after launching his presidential campaign on a platform of anti-Muslim and anti-immigrant paranoia in 2015, Trump appeared on Jones's Infowars show. "Your reputation is amazing," Trump told the Sandy Hook truther. "I will not let you down."

As large social media platforms came to dominate the internet, Mike Adams hitched his news empire to Facebook. Between 2015 and 2019, his website Natural News's Facebook page erupted from 1.5 million followers to more than 2.9 million—far more than other leading US conspiracy pages. In some countries, Natural News became one of the biggest promoters of an anti-vaccination movement that sent immunization rates plummeting and measles outbreaks soaring. In the United States, Natural News's Facebook page was one of just seven pages that accounted for a combined total of 20 percent of the most viewed anti-vaccination posts from January 2016 to February 2019.

At this point, I published an article in the *Daily Beast* detailing Mike Adams's past work. Facebook banned Natural News the day after my article's publication. A Facebook spokesperson told me the ban had nothing to do with my article, and that it was actually because the Natural News page had violated a Facebook policy against "spam." Adams, by all accounts an architect of internet spam, meanwhile accused Facebook of commissioning the article from me so they could justify banning Natural News. In a nearly hour-long video rant about the ban, Adams, who once worried about martial law, urged Trump to "unleash the military police" against large tech companies. "We need a new D-Day against the tech giants," he said. (I did not, in fact, collaborate with Facebook, and do not think my reporting merits a raid by the military police.)

Adams, who'd kicked off the century by selling dehydrated foodstuffs for the Y2K apocalypse, had also pioneered another facet of the Flat Earth movement: the conspiracy theory wanted its believers' money. FEIC founder Robbie Davidson told me he lost money on the 2017 conference, which was sponsored by an obscure wood-burning stove company and a brand of "energy pills" that contained two coffee cups' worth of caffeine per capsule. (Davidson's previous employment seems to have been a get-rich-quick scheme in which he raised awareness for the cryptocurrency Bitcoin by driving a Kia Soul covered in Bitcoin decals around the country, trying to get people to buy raffle tickets for the car.) He said he broke even on the 2018 conference, which hosted a large hall of vendors selling conspiracy goods and attracted some six hundred believers, all of whom paid between $199 and $349 for tickets to the two-day extravaganza. In 2019, Davidson told me, the FEIC turned a profit.

But even in 2018, the conference was more than just a financial null. When I arrived at the Colorado event, I found believers greeting each other by their internet usernames around the breakfast buffet, or showing one another Flat Earth videos on their phones while they mingled in the convention center's hallways. Some had been up half the night talking with friends they'd never met in person. A guy who had brought a pan flute hit it off with a guy who had brought an acoustic guitar, and they sat around the hotel lobby playing pan-flute jams.

The vibe was like "summer camp," Flat Earther Rick Hummer said in his opening remarks on the main stage—that is, a summer camp where everyone already knows everyone else's Twitter handles.

Flat Earthers had built their own world in the virtual reality of the internet. They'd borrowed the momentum of code-jamming grifters like Mike Adams, who'd learned to warp the internet to his financial favor. They'd borrowed the militancy of conspiratorial grand marshals like Alex Jones, making a firm break from the civil chatter of the Flat Earth Society forums and marching into the meatspace to preach their gospel anew. Now, with the presidency occupied by someone who'd endorsed Alex Jones on the campaign trail, and hundreds of Flat Earthers surrounding me in that Colorado hotel, it was clear that the conspiratorial internet was leaking into the real world.

Someone, mistaking me for a Flat Earther, handed me a flyer for an upcoming day of off-line Flat Earth activism.

"We shall all come together and walk proudly in public on the streets of our individual towns and cities across our beautiful plane to inform our sleeping brothers and sisters about the truth of our physical reality," the flyer read.

It ended with a plea for readers to follow a series of YouTube channels.

5 | The Rabbit Hole

THE SUN SET pink above the beaches, and the jungle birds sang into the coming dark and the Hawaiian tide rolled onto the sand like something out of a movie. In the depths of this paradise, every night, two couples sat in a hotel hot tub, fixated on a small screen that they held studiously above the frothy water.

"I didn't care about Maui," Ginny, a Northern California woman told me. "All I wanted to do was share with them about Flat Earth. Every evening, we watched two or three *Flat Earth Clues* [a Flat Earth video series], the whole time on Maui, and before they came back, they were convinced."

Just months earlier, Ginny had been a Globe Earther. She hadn't even believed a close friend who confided that she was second-guessing the planet's shape. "She told me, 'Ginny, I think the earth is flat.' I said, 'What? That is the most wackadoodle thing I have ever heard.'"

The friend told Ginny to search for Flat Earth videos on YouTube. And while Ginny had doubted her longtime friend, strangers on the internet soon changed her mind. She watched hours of Flat Earth videos over the course of several days and converted before the week was up.

"I spent like three nights wide awake and then I was hooked," she said. "I told my husband, 'You won't believe what I've been watching.'" He watched the videos and became a convert, too.

Like her friend before her, Ginny couldn't wait to share the YouTube gospel with more friends. When she and her husband took their vacation with two friends soon after, all Ginny could think about was when she would be able to show Flat Earth videos to the other couple, who were still unwinding from a previous leg of their vacation.

"We had to wait two days, because I knew they were exhausted from their trip," she said. "I was like, 'You guys, I'm dying, I'm dying.'" I later met both women at a Flat Earth conference. Neither was public yet about their beliefs.

Serious Flat Earthers spend money on their belief. They buy books, conference tickets, and T-shirts that earn them strange looks in the grocery store. But the real money in Flat Earth doesn't stay in the movement—it gets siphoned off to Silicon Valley. Every time a Flat Earther watches a video in a Hawaiian hot tub or joins a Facebook group to meet other believers, they're helping support a sprawling, multitrillion-dollar technology industry that knows conspiracy is good for business. Every minute spent on internet platforms like Facebook or YouTube is more money (often in the form of ad revenue) in those companies' coffers. In order to squeeze the most value from each user, these tech giants developed algorithms that serve up an addictive combination of comforting and titillating content. Conspiracy theories—endlessly intriguing, and tailored to our worst suspicions—became one of the best-performing products in the attention economy. The truth became less profitable than fiction. So Facebook and YouTube, two of the internet's largest empires, let their reality-warping algorithms run for years, flattening the world around them.

In hundreds of conversations with Flat Earthers, I've met only three who converted before 2014. This wasn't because 2014 was some significant year for pro-Flat scientific discovery; no great experiments cast doubt on the globe that year. The basic principles of Flat Earth theory have remained the same since the 1800s. But the old theory got new life in 2014 because Eric Dubay and other truthers started uploading Flat Earth videos to YouTube and establishing Flat Earth Facebook pages that drew in a motley assortment of paranoiacs from across the conspiratorial internet. On those websites, finally, after 150 years of ridicule, Flat Earth found itself in an environment that embraced it—even depended on it.

Much of YouTube, the Google-owned website that has become virtually synonymous with "online video," has been unwatchable garbage from the beginning. I know because I was one of the site's earliest contributors of unwatchable garbage. When I was in middle school, I became one of the first YouTubers when my friend and I used an unattended basement computer to upload stop-motion videos of Beanie Babies reenacting scenes from young adult novels. Really mortifying stuff. But it was 2005, months after YouTube's launch, and the website was a wasteland of cat videos and poorly lit webcam monologues. YouTube democratized video, letting kids broadcast themselves into a public space that was once reserved for professional news outlets. Quality was no barrier to participation. If anything, no-budget videos became YouTube's hallmark. The site's apparently unfiltered clips contrasted with traditional media, and gave its videos an air of gritty reality.

"YouTube positioned itself very early on as alternative media," Kevin Roose, a *New York Times* technology columnist, told me. "It was not just different from TV in the sense that it was lower-budget, mostly amateur, and not as centralized. It was also seen as more real, more authentic."

Conspiracy theorists frequently accuse the media of plotting to withhold truths and keep the public in the dark. Believers in QAnon, a far-right conspiracy theory that falsely accuses former president Donald Trump's rivals of satanic pedophilia and cannibalism, sometimes claim that journalists rise at four in the morning to receive orders from the government. QAnon is extreme, but a broad swath of Americans echo its mistrust in the media. Sixty-one percent of respondents to a December 2018 Pew poll said the media deliberately withholds important stories.

There's no pleasing everyone; no nightly news broadcast will perfectly mirror every viewer's perception of the world. But this broad skepticism of journalism suggests that at one or more points—whether due to institutional biases baked into corporate media companies, lack of racial and economic diversity on newspaper mastheads, budget cuts that bleed local newsrooms dry, or something else entirely—somehow my profession has failed its audience. When most Americans watch the news, they do not see the world they believe to be true.

For that disillusioned 61 percent, YouTube videos offer an alternative information source, one that eschews the glossy authority of TV news in favor of relatability. Far from being discrediting, YouTubers' lack of official media titles can serve as a form of conspiratorial street cred. These are real people willing to say what the media won't, the reasoning goes. Their amateur explanations can override expertise, especially for the many people who make YouTube their primary news source. "YouTube, itself, has cultivated an ecosystem of distrust in official narratives," Roose said.

There's big money in distrust. YouTube makes billions annually by selling advertisements on its site. The longer a person watches YouTube videos, the more ads YouTube can show them, and the more money YouTube can wring from them. The most valuable YouTube consumer isn't the viewer who logs on, watches a short cooking tutorial, and logs off to continue the rest of their day. The ideal YouTuber is an obsessive (and likely unwell) person who mainlines videos morning to night, their viewing habits providing YouTube with an increasingly detailed personality profile that the company can use to deliver ever more targeted content. To transform you, the casual cooking-tutorial watcher, into someone more closely resembling the obsessive viewer, YouTube devised an algorithm that recommends videos based on those you already watched. If you watch a cooking tutorial about blueberry muffins, YouTube reasons, you might also enjoy a video about chocolate chip pancakes. YouTube will recommend the pancake video in a little sidebar to the right of the muffin video you're already watching. Often, YouTube will automatically play the recommended video, letting you passively bask in a stream of baking content.

The tactic works in theory. Maybe you'll watch the pancake video, sitting through a pre-video advertisement that drums up a little more revenue for the Silicon Valley megacorp. But after watching a muffin video and a pancake video, you're probably bored of breakfast. Videos about crepes and croissants will be of diminishing interest to you. Viewers don't want exactly what they have already seen, YouTube has realized—they want novelty, tailored to them.

Guillaume Chaslot is a former YouTube employee who helped devise the company's recommendation algorithm when he worked there, starting in 2010. During that time, YouTube veered away from recommending videos based on their relevance to someone's previous viewing habits and started recommending videos that viewers were likely to spend more time watching.

"It's not trying to optimize for relevance," Chaslot told me. "It's trying to optimize for watch time, or at least it was when I was working there."

Which videos kept people on the website the longest? "Extreme videos are extremely good for watch time," he said. The bizarre, the fringe, and the impossible lured in the most viewers. So YouTube's recommendation algorithm, at least before a major overhaul in 2019, prioritized the strange. The recommendations often had a tenuous link to whatever a person was already watching. The blueberry muffin tutorial could lead you to a video on survivalist food preparation; a video on stargazing could lead you to moon-landing conspiracy theories, which could lead you to a Flat Earth clip.

"There's a spectrum on YouTube between the calm section—the Walter Cronkite, Carl Sagan part—and Crazytown, where the extreme stuff is," Tristan Harris, a former design ethicist at Google told the *New York Times* in 2019. "If I'm YouTube and I want you to watch more, I'm always going to steer you toward Crazytown."

Flat Earth, the world's most ludicrous theory, is a monument to the extreme. Fittingly, the theory became Chaslot's go-to case study when explaining the "structural problem" with YouTube's recommendation algorithm. In 2017, Chaslot did an experiment. "Is Earth flat or round?" he typed into Google. Of the first twenty results in the search, 20 percent favored Flat Earth theory, he found. Those results already offered a massively warped reality: far fewer than 20 percent of people are Flat Earthers, and 0 percent of facts support the theory. But those results were mild compared to YouTube's, where 35 percent of search results presented Flat Earth theory as true. And both of those figures paled compared to the videos YouTube recommended for someone who was *already* watching a video about Flat Earth. Ninety percent of the recommended videos in Chaslot's experiment promoted Flat Earth as reality.

Those recommendations were YouTube's real gift to Flat Earth theory, serving up the movement's videos to anyone who seemed even vaguely interested. The theory's shock value kept viewers watching—and generating ad revenue for YouTube. Some never clicked away.

Joshua Swift didn't go searching for Flat Earth. He describes the theory as something that happened to him. "It came on Autoplay," he told me. "So I didn't actively search for Flat Earth. Even months before, I was listening to Alex Jones." He said this last bit with derision.

The 2018 FEIC, where I first met Swift, had three types of attendees: there were hundreds of Flat Earthers, all there for a good time. There were reporters like me, although our ranks thinned by the hour as journalists collected their sound bites, said good riddance, and got the hell out of there. The third faction were academics who came to observe this largest-ever gathering of the strangest-ever conspiracy community. Among them was Alex Olshansky, a researcher on a Texas Tech University study about YouTube's role in the spread of Flat Earth. In interviews with thirty Flat Earthers across two conferences, Olshansky and his team met only one who hadn't converted based on information they saw on YouTube.

Many described their Flat Earth discovery in the same passive terms as Swift. "They would say it 'popped up' on YouTube or something like that. Generally, what that means is that YouTube is recommending it to them," Olshansky told me.

They were correct, in a sense. YouTube's profitable tendency toward the extreme led many to Flat Earth after they'd watched slightly less obscure videos. "The majority of them were already watching some other conspiracy videos on YouTube, like 9/11 Truth or Sandy Hook," Olshansky said. Alex Jones's Infowars was a popular entry point for proto–Flat Earthers. For most of them, Olshansky said, YouTube "would recommend Flat Earth into their feeds. They'd usually see it and dismiss it. And then, for some reason, they'd get curious enough to click on it. A lot of them would be dismissive and would try to debunk it." After they failed to do so, he added, they would "start questioning everything they thought they knew and then they go into the rabbit hole of finding more YouTube videos."

The rabbit hole goes deep. In 2018, one of the most popular Flat Earth videos was uploaded by the Brazilian group Dakila Research. On its face a scientific group, Dakila was actually the latest venture from Urandir Fernandes de Oliveira, an infamous alien conspiracy theorist who often goes by his convenient initials, UFO. He claims in interviews that when he was thirteen, aliens abducted him and microchipped him and gave him supernatural energy-manipulation powers. For decades since, he's been trying to build a city in rural Brazil, where his followers will commune with aliens. Although the plot got him in legal trouble in 2000 (land dispute), UFO reemerged triumphant in the YouTube era, bolstered by his embrace of Flat Earth. His organization successfully built a conspiracy-driven compound in the middle of the Brazilian plains, where fans from around the world came to live in huts to be near fellow Flat Earth and pro-alien "knowledge seekers." (The humble city's finest home is empty, reserved for an alien deity.) Flat Earth is big in Brazil; in a 2019 study of thousands of Brazilians, 7 percent said they thought Earth was flat. Those believers look a lot like their

US counterparts: primarily Christian literalists and heavy social media users. But some of the residents of the Brazilian Flat Earth compound include converted members of Dakila's international YouTube audience. Sixty-year-old Amanda Riveros said she left the United States to live in UFO's UFO city, which he advertised as the best place to ride out the imminent apocalypse.

"My life took a turn. I lost family, friends, work," she told the Brazilian news site *Epoca* in 2019. "They called me crazy, but today I wouldn't exchange [the city] for anything. If I could start my life over by knowing this, I would be someone else. When you come here, you know yourself. I found a family here. We end up thinking the same way, wanting things the same way."

Flat Earth's YouTube converts don't need to run away to a Brazilian doomsday compound to find community. They can find it on YouTube. For Ginny and her friends in the Hawaiian hot tub, that YouTube trail led to *Flat Earth Clues*, created by scene superstar Mark Sargent. But even Sargent's conversion began with a YouTube binge in 2014. After years of watching conspiratorial content—skeptically, he says—he went looking for information on Flat Earth, which he considered "more of a joke than a conspiracy."

At the time, information was limited. He found himself "watching a German video about flight paths in the Southern Hemisphere, and how they only worked on a flat, dinner plate type world. I didn't know German, but the animations seemed clear enough," he wrote in his self-published 2019 book. "Maybe I would just watch one more video, and one more after that."

YouTube's then-sparse Flat Earth offerings were enough to convince him to join the Flat Earth Society, and in 2015 he launched his own YouTube channel. Unlike some of the lengthy, rambling Flat Earth videos that preceded them, videos in Sargent's *Flat Earth Clues* series average only around ten minutes long—digestible, low-commitment clips for watchers like Ginny whose interest started off casual.

Other YouTubers, some with large followings of their own, were also sucked in. Rob Skiba, a fringe Christian internet personality who for years preached Bible-flavored conspiracy theories about supernatural beings, added Flat Earth to his portfolio of weird theories after he invited Sargent onto his podcast in 2015. Skiba's conversion was a big win for Flat Earth. With hundreds of thousands of YouTube followers, his channel often served as a bridge between various conspiratorial and religious communities, hosting them together in sermon-like livestreams. When Skiba started making his own videos about Flat Earth theory, he converted many of the digital congregation that had begun following him for his theories about biblical creatures having sex with humans.

Skiba is now an annual fixture at the Flat Earth International Conference, which wouldn't exist without YouTube, either. FEIC's founder, Robbie Davidson, started his Flat Earth journey when he fell for a joke about the theory on YouTube.

"In 2015, I came across a video that was uploaded in 2007, and it was an atheist making fun of the literal interpretation of Genesis," Davidson told me. "As a creationist, I looked at it and I said, 'Wait a minute, if I'm a literal creationist, I have to be one hundred percent, right?' He brought up a couple things in humor, but I said to myself, 'Wait a minute, that's what the Bible says.' He had mentioned Flat Earth, and I said, 'That's strange.' So I typed in 'Flat Earth' and I found Mark Sargent's *Flat Earth Clues.*"

The videos sent Davidson "down the rabbit hole," he said. "One thing led to the next, and all of a sudden . . . That was April or May of 2015. I created my YouTube channel in August 2015."

Three months between converting to Flat Earth and becoming one of its leading YouTube voices is not an especially long time. But Flat Earth encourages active participation. "I created my YouTube channel, and it grew very, very quick. I have over five hundred videos. I've done six documentaries, and I have close to twenty million views on my channel," Davidson told me in November 2019. He'd churned out approximately ten videos per month, every month, since starting his channel, in addition to participating in video chats with other emergent Flat Earth YouTubers.

YouTube's community-driven culture is ripe for conspiracy movements, said Becca Lewis, a Stanford University researcher focusing on the politics of technology.

"YouTube gives the opportunity for broadcasters and their audiences to build communities with each other," she told me. Unlike television or radio presenters, YouTubers are in close dialogue with their viewers, who can voice their approval or displeasure by upvoting the video or writing something absurdly cruel in the comments section. (Viewer feedback is so baked into YouTube's business model that parents have reported their young children chirping "Don't forget to like and subscribe!" instead of "Goodbye" at the end of conversations. The catchphrase is a common sign-off for YouTubers, whose financial existence depends on a steady subscriber base and well-liked videos that perform well in YouTube's recommendation algorithm.)

Some serious YouTube fans develop "parasocial" relationships with their favorite stars, in which they invest genuine emotional energy into a one-sided fixation on a video maker, who likely does not know the fan exists. The viewer's relationship with YouTubers, imagined or not, can be a "powerful force when it comes to propaganda and belief systems— ways of understanding the world," Lewis said. "Conspiracy theories and extremist belief systems can draw in people who are feeling lost and confused, and who want to find a world where they feel they belong. If they can stumble into a community that's actively trying to recruit people, that can be really powerful."

With what seems like half the movement producing their own YouTube videos, Flat Earth is overflowing with microcelebrities, all jockeying for views on their videos or collaborations with better-known video makers. The most popular of those YouTubers have around one hundred thousand followers. When I left a Flat Earth lecture to use the bathroom at a 2018 conference, I returned to find multiple business cards for Flat Earth YouTube channels on my empty chair. While walking from one room to another, someone pushed a CD full of a Flat Earth YouTuber's music into my hands.

While earnest Flat Earthers were handing out business cards and CDs, other opportunists were circling the scene. YouTube's algorithmic bias toward Flat Earth has led Globe Earth YouTubers to make Flat Earth films and leech off the movement's growing notoriety.

"There was a whisper that was being passed around content creators—not just ours but other people—that if you made a Flat Earth video, you would get more hits and you would get five hundred percent more comments, which track into the YouTube algorithm," Sargent told me. "When that happened, people started making more Flat Earth videos."

In other words, Flat Earth was algorithm gold. That meant celebrity YouTubers were coming for the theory, whether they believed it or not.

The first morning of the 2018 FEIC, I stepped outside for a sanity break and was immediately overcome with the blind animal terror of an adult realizing she's in the background of a video that will soon be dissected by critical teenagers. A small crew trailed a blond man, who wore a shirt advertising his own YouTube-based clothing line. It was Logan Paul, a YouTube megastar, who was still recovering from the scandal of uploading a video of a suicide victim in a Japanese forest. Paul had millions of YouTube followers, many of them young people. In Denver, he was posing as a Flat Earther for an upcoming mockumentary on the movement.

No good could come of this. But given that I was at the FEIC as a reporter for the *Daily Beast*, I felt contractually obligated to wade into this shit. I asked Paul why he thought Earth was flat. What were the pros and cons for the theory?

"Well, the pros are that Earth is flat and that the earth is basically, like, flat," he answered before breaking off into laughter.

He tried again: "Don't you think if the earth was round, our shoes would have a curve in them?"

Logan Paul is not a Flat Earther, and wasn't trying particularly hard to pass as one. But Robbie Davidson hadn't caught on. He had invited Paul to give a keynote address at the conference as guest of honor. Gesticulating excitedly on the main stage, Davidson emphasized "the magnitude of what Logan Paul represents. He has eighteen million subscribers on YouTube." The crowd gasped. "He has over four billion views on his videos." People clapped and cheered, even louder than they had for the conference's next-biggest celebrity, the musician who sang "Welcome to the Satellite Hoax."

Paul took the stage. "I consider myself a man of truth, someone who hates being ignorant," he said, going on to recite conspiratorial talking points about the moon landing as if reading them off a grocery list. "I guess I'm not ashamed to say my name is Logan Paul, and I think I'm coming out of the Flat Earth closet."

Davidson came back onstage, speaking with near-revolutionary zeal.

"This is the first step: someone with a very big following putting their name on the line and saying 'You know what, I'm almost there. There's a lot of compelling evidence,'" Davidson told the crowd. Earlier that day, he'd given Paul a long interview for what he thought would be Paul's explosive documentary on the subject. "I have a very good feeling he's genuine," Davidson told me.

For someone who believes all the world's governments are conspiring to hide the shape of the planet, Davidson is a trusting man. But while he was hyping Paul as a potential Flat Earth icon, the YouTube star's presence was tearing the FEIC apart. The first morning of the conference, Davidson announced that Mark Sargent had abandoned his scheduled presentation to attend to a family emergency. That wasn't true, Sargent emailed me after Paul's speech.

"Even the conference speakers didn't know he was coming until the night before, and when I got confirmation Thursday morning, I immediately withdrew my presentations from the conference and flew back to Seattle," Sargent told me.

"Logan's team swore the conference promoter to secrecy, and when it was revealed, it caused some major ripples. There were over twenty speakers at this event, and only Robbie Davidson officially endorsed him," Sargent added. "My reasons for leaving were simple. His stunt at the Japanese suicide forest was unforgivable, and should be a social-media life sentence. Having him try to use the Flat Earth members as part of a comeback is beyond insulting."

The Flat Earth Society, ever the opponents of the FEIC crowd, also distrusted Logan Paul and used his appearance to twist the knife in their rivals.

"It would be needlessly heavy-handed of us to accuse him of lying," a representative of the Flat Earth Society told me after news of Paul's speech went viral. "However, to our knowledge, Logan had not shown any interest in the Flat Earth Movement prior to his surprise announcement, and he has shown himself not to be very knowledgeable on the subject during the conference. We wouldn't want to tell anyone whether or not true Flat Earthers put sugar on their porridge, but personally we'd rather reserve any endorsements until Logan shows himself to be a contributing member of the FE community."

Paul, of course, did not become a contributing member of the Flat Earth community. Months later, he released a mockumentary denouncing Flat Earth and making fun of the conference-goers who had been so eager to embrace him as the movement's first big celebrity. Paul's team printed out a picture of Davidson's face and taped it to a Flat Earth "shrine," where an actor pretended to worship. Davidson, who had been so optimistic about the film, watched the YouTube video with growing horror.

"Oh man, it was bad for me. It was bad for me," Davidson told me after the movie was released. "To tell you the truth, with Logan Paul, I thought [the movie] was going to be neutral. It was never going to be good, but it was going to be neutral . . . Yeah, the community was not so grateful to me. I feel like this year I'll probably redeem myself a little bit, but my intentions were pure, and again, it was one of those things."

Davidson was embarrassed. But maybe he should have been triumphant. Paul's video received millions of views, many of them from youthful fans who wouldn't have given Flat Earth a second thought without the movie. Mainstream attention, even negative, can draw curious recruits into the Flat Earth scene. It was true of Flat Earth pioneers like Samuel Rowbotham, whose critically panned lectures still drew crowds—and it is true of the movement in the internet age, claimed Nathan Thompson, moderator of what was then Facebook's largest Flat Earth group.

"All the stuff they do to make Flat Earth look stupid or spread disinformation about the leaders in the movement, all it does is add fuel to the fire,'" he told me. His group saw its largest membership surges after Netflix released a Flat Earth documentary in 2018, he said. "It actually has the opposite effect of what they want, which is more people waking up."

Conspiracy theorists like Thompson may have distrust for companies like Netflix or YouTube (which he has accused of censoring his videos), but not enough to abandon those companies, whose algorithms have boosted their theories through the noise of the internet.

"It's popular—that's the only reason I use it," Thompson told me of YouTube. "If people will let me put content on their websites, I'm going to do it."

Google's products are so popular that even the most powerful people in the world have trafficked in bogus conspiracy theories about the search engine's algorithm. In August 2018, an unscientific study posted on a right-wing blog snowballed its way through the conservative media ecosystem until it reached then president Donald Trump's Twitter feed.

"Google search results for 'Trump News' shows only the viewing/reporting of Fake New Media," Trump tweeted very early on a weekday morning. "In other words, they have it RIGGED, for me & others, so that almost all stories & news is BAD. Fake CNN is prominent. Republican/

Conservative & Fair Media is shut out. Illegal? 96% of results on 'Trump News' are from National Left-Wing Media, very dangerous."

Trump's tweet, grounded in longstanding and largely unfounded grievances about the supposed censoring of conservative voices in the mainstream media, began with a post on a conservative blog called *PJ Media*, in which the author said she searched for "Trump" under Google's news tab and was dismayed to find two articles from CNN, plus more from "CBS, *The Atlantic*, CNBC, *The New Yorker*, Politico, Reuters, and *USA Today*."

"Is Google manipulating its algorithm to prioritize left-leaning news outlets in their coverage of President Trump?" the author asked. "It sure looks that way based on recent search results for news on the president."

Never mind that outlets like CNBC or Reuters can hardly be called bastions of pinko commie media, or that when I tried to replicate *PJ Media*'s experiment hours later, I found plenty of results from conservative outlets, like Fox News. The *PJ Media* post caught the attention of programmers at Fox News, who ran a segment on the censorship conspiracy theory starring Diamond and Silk, a pair of pro-Trump sycophants who began their broadcast careers as YouTube personalities, and who would lose their Fox News gigs two years later after falsely claiming that the COVID-19 pandemic was a hoax. In their segment, Diamond and Silk claimed that big tech censorship of conservatives was real, because Facebook had deleted some of their posts without warning. (In fact, internal emails revealed that Facebook repeatedly contacted the duo about posts that violated site rules.)

Trump, a fan of Diamond and Silk, completed the cycle of fact-free outrage with his tweets, which prompted his economic advisor, Larry Kudlow, to suggest government action against Google. Trump's Twitter screed, based on a conspiratorial blog post, was close to becoming public policy.

But William Douglas, a Flat Earther from Oregon who made similar claims of censorship that month, didn't fare as well as the president.

"Return my channel, you lowlife assholes, before someone else comes and shoots more of your employees, you fucks," he tweeted in a typo-ridden screed that I've edited for legibility. "Fuck you, @YouTube, I'm a few hours away and if you are just going to ignore me, try ignoring my gun, you fucks." He added, "I would kill 100 YouTube employees if given the chance." And, "No more warnings, expect massive casualties."

He carried on like this for a while. Eventually a YouTube employee called the feds. Douglas, a small-time conspiracy video maker, was protesting what he said were restrictions on his YouTube account. If YouTube was censoring him, however, they were doing a poor job of it. By September 2018, he had more than four hundred thousand views of his videos, which spanned conspiratorial topics from Flat Earth to government mind control to QAnon. "YouTube Is Censoring This Video Sound Analysis," he titled a video about an organ-theft conspiracy theory, posted not long before his Twitter rant. The supposedly censored video had earned nearly thirty thousand views by the time he was arrested for his threats.

Douglas wasn't even the first YouTuber that year to consider a mass shooting over censorship fears. In April 2018, San Diego internet personality Nasim Aghdam packed a semiautomatic pistol in her car, drove overnight to YouTube's San Bruno, California, headquarters, and fired her way into the company's lobby, where she shot three YouTube employees (nonfatally) and herself (fatally). Although she ran a popular YouTube channel for fitness videos and vegan activism, Aghdam had become convinced YouTube was targeting her videos for suppression.

"Youtube filtered my channels to keep them from getting views!" she posted on her website. "There is no free speech in real world & you will be suppressed for telling the truth that is not supported by the system. Videos of targeted users are filtered & merely relegated, so that people can hardly see their videos!" She also waged bizarre protests against the company, like standing on the side of a highway waving a sign about YouTube censorship.

Although YouTube was not censoring her videos, there was a kernel of emotional truth behind Aghdam's claims. Her father told NBC News that Aghdam felt cheated after her income from her videos suddenly evaporated, likely the result of a YouTube policy change that upended the way ad revenue was distributed across channels.

Conspiracy or not, Aghdam's feelings of victimization by YouTube cost her her life. Unlike Aghdam, Douglas kept his, but saw it drastically changed; he was sentenced to sixteen months in jail for threats he'd made while under the influence of a conspiracy theory about his conspiracy videos. In February 2020, when he pleaded guilty to extortion, Douglas said he'd made the threats during a mental health crisis. He'd since sought counseling and medication, he said, and was feeling much better.

Though Douglas was wrong about YouTube's targeting of his channel in 2018, he was presciently correct about the company's changing stance on conspiracy theories. In January 2019, YouTube announced that it would tweak its algorithm to recommend fewer harmfully incorrect videos. The announcement cited three conspiracy theories by name: counterscientific miracle cures, 9/11 trutherism, and Flat Earth. Although those videos remained on the site, they became harder to find.

The new policy was a gut punch to Flat Earthers who made their names and livelihoods on YouTube.

"My [subscriber] numbers have literally dropped," Robbie Davidson told me ten months after the algorithm change. "I was at a point where I was doing four hundred to five hundred new subscribers per day. Now I'm lucky if I get one hundred new subscribers in four months."

Davidson was reluctant, however, to implicate YouTube. "The weird thing is, I don't think YouTube is evil. I think they're getting so much pressure. Everyone's blaming YouTube," for conspiracy theories, he said. "All the media is pointing to YouTube."

Though it won me no love from my Flat Earth friends, I was certainly among "the media" in this instance. YouTube's algorithm change came after a series of reports from me and other journalists highlighting the role of YouTube recommendations in luring people to fringe beliefs. But while YouTube faced mounting pressure to give recommendations that more closely reflected reality, another social media giant was evading similar scrutiny for the profit-driven, algorithmic havoc it was wreaking on truth.

Facebook knew it had a problem in 2016. That year, a sociologist in the company's employ conducted a study of extremist content in German political Facebook groups. Certain groups were teeming with racist and conspiratorial material, according to a *Wall Street Journal* report that revealed the study's existence in May 2020.

The issue wasn't just that people were being racist online (a problem as old as the internet). It was that Facebook's own recommendation algorithm was driving users to those groups. "64% of all extremist group joins are due to our recommendation tools," an internal Facebook presentation on the study said, namely the "Groups You Should Join" and "Discover" algorithms. "Our recommendation systems grow the problem."

Facebook's recommendations actively cross-pollinated the conspiracy world, luring truthers over the lines that once demarcated their individual theories. The result was a conspiratorial melting pot: QAnon followers preaching their gospel on pages for people who believed airplanes were spraying mind-control drugs, bogus miracle cures being sold in anti-vaccination groups, and nearly every popular conspiracy theory finding its way onto Flat Earth pages, which saw skeptics of all stripes gather to share notes.

Facebook ignored the warning in 2016, the *Journal* reported. "We've learned a lot since 2016 and are not the same company today," a Facebook spokesperson said after the study came to light in 2020. "We've built a robust integrity team, strengthened our policies and practices to limit harmful content, and used research to understand our platform's impact on society so we continue to improve."

Try telling that to Beth. Technically, Beth isn't a real person—she's my alter ego, my middle name, under which I registered a dummy Facebook account that I use to research Facebook's algorithmic recommendations for conspiracy theorists. When I created Beth's Facebook account in 2018, two years after Facebook's internal report, I was deliberately light on details. She shared a few conservative-leaning posts: a clip of an American flag; a video of Trump speaking at a White House press conference. Beth also joined some of the better-known conspiracy groups on Facebook: the big pages for Flat Earth and QAnon and, for the sake of character development, some politically neutral groups for people who like hunting for bargain furniture. Then I let Facebook recommend pages it thought Beth would like. Immediately, I was staring down the barrel of conspiracy theories I'd never even heard of. After I joined Flat Earth groups, I received recommendations for a bevy of alternative planetary models, including one (which predicted Earth was on a collision course with a dark twin planet) that had apparently grown so fed up with incursion from Flat Earthers that it explicitly banned all Flat Earth posts. After I joined QAnon groups, Facebook recommended a fan group for a pseudonymous paramedic who had achieved almost prophet-level status among followers of the QAnon theory. After I joined that group, Facebook's algorithmically generated recommendations suggested I join two "prophesy" groups that required me to click a box certifying that I thought Trump was God's divine choice for president.

When it comes to recruiting newbie conspiracy theorists like Beth, Facebook can be Flat Earth's best advocate. Facebook's "Groups" tab recommends pages based on users' possible interests. Beth's suggested groups include Flat Earth Soldiers, Flat Earth Academy, J's Flat Earth Academy (unrelated to the previous group), Flat Line, League of Extraordinary Flat Earthers, and for reasons I cannot deduce at all, a half dozen pages about St. Clair, Michigan. I likely wouldn't have discovered any of them without Facebook's guidance.

Like YouTube, Facebook makes its colossal fortune by displaying advertisements, which are tailored to individual users based on their Facebook activity. Although I gave Beth a birth date that would put her in her midforties, Facebook consistently filled her feed with advertisements for senior living facilities and the American Association of Retired Persons, presumably because the fringe groups she joined are largely populated with older people. (When I dug into Beth's targeted advertising profile, I learned that Facebook had labeled the account's political leanings as "very conservative," with an interest in "Earth," "Planet," a QAnon slogan, and "Potato.") Other reporters have run similar experiments. In 2017, *BuzzFeed News*'s Ryan Broderick made a new, blank Facebook account and hit "Like" on the page for the Republican National Committee. He then liked the recommended pages and the subsequent recommendations. The result was a rapidly radicalizing news feed, which quickly veered from mainstream conservatism into far-right racism, conspiracy theories, and eventually soft-core porn and hard-core neo-Nazism.

Facebook's polarizing potential is so well known that multiple nations have used the platform to sow political discord in rival countries. Facebook's internal study of German extremist groups in 2016 found the pages rife with pro-Russian propaganda. A similar propaganda blitz that same year on US-based Facebook pages, led by a Saint Petersburg–based troll farm called the Internet Research Agency, stoked political tensions in the United States through widely shared posts that played up both the left and right ends of the political spectrum, including right-wing posts that lauded Trump's presidential campaign and left-wing posts that highlighted Hillary Clinton's shortcomings and discouraged Black Americans from voting.

The Russian troll farm also used Twitter to promote anti-vaccination conspiracy theories, which falsely claim vaccines are unsafe or that vaccines cause autism. The IRA used the hashtag #VaccinateUS to feign an authentic internet trend, according to researchers who discovered the disinformation campaign. "Like other antivaccine tweets, antivaccine messages with #VaccinateUS often reference conspiracy theories," the researchers found. "However, whereas conspiracy theories tend to target a variety of culprits (e.g., specific government agencies, individual philanthropists, or secret organizations), the #VaccinateUS messages are almost singularly focused on the US government (e.g., 'At first our government creates diseases then it creates #vaccines.what's next?! #VaccinateUS')."

The Twitter campaign—maddeningly, a real conspiracy to spread conspiracy theories—coincided with a larger social media–driven surge in vaccine refusal. In 2019, as preventable measles outbreaks swept the world, the World Health Organization named "vaccine hesitancy" one of the top ten global health threats. Much of that hesitancy stems from a single study in 1998 that incorrectly linked vaccines to autism. Not only was the original study's research faulty, failing to demonstrate a causal link between vaccines and autism, but it used cherry-picked test subjects instead of a randomized sample, and received funding from lawyers who represented parents hoping to sue vaccine manufacturers. Britain's General Medical Council subsequently barred the study's lead scientist, Andrew Wakefield, from practicing medicine, citing his "callous disregard" for his patients and "multiple separate instances of professional misconduct" throughout the study. (In turn, Wakefield alleged a conspiracy to "discredit and silence" him.)

Wakefield's study, though scientists had dismissed its claims for years, was officially retracted in 2010. By that point, though, social media had grown powerful enough to give the anti-vaccination movement its own life online, independent of the study that spawned it. A May 2020 study in the journal *Nature* analyzed pro- and anti-vaccination sentiment in a network of more than thirteen hundred Facebook pages and nearly one hundred million Facebook users. Its results spelled an ominous warning for science. The pro-vaccination pages had more combined followers, due in part to popular pages like that of the Bill and Melinda Gates Foundation. But those massive pro-vax pages had limited reach; their millions of followers seldom shared their posts. Anti-vax pages, while smaller, had mastered the viral meme, the study found. Their conversational, sensational posts spread far and wide across Facebook groups and pages that took no official stance on vaccinations. They completely overwhelmed the factual pro-vaccination campaigns.

"It's like we as a public health community still have the old IBM model and not the startup Silicon Valley approach," one scientist told *Science* magazine. The deliberately scientific pages were siloed, while the deliberately counterscientific pages were mingling with the masses. What's more, Facebook hyperlinks posts to their original sources, which means all the anti-vax posts shared on vax neutral pages, like Breastfeeding Moms in KY, gave readers a direct pathway back to anti-vax Facebook pages.

Although Wakefield's original anti-vax conspiratorial claims centered around moneymaking schemes by pharmaceutical companies, the theory has since interacted and morphed with other truther movements online. In Flat Earth Facebook groups, which often act as a catchall for extreme beliefs, vaccines stand accused of everything from causing mass deaths to being a way for the Illuminati to control our minds. "Most flat Earthers are against the vaccine and 1 world order," read one typical post in the largest Flat Earth Facebook group in April 2020. "Most Atheists and sheep want the 1 world order." Nathan Thompson, the Facebook group's founder, has filmed himself badgering a doctor about vaccines in public and heckling him when he could not name vaccine ingredients while Thompson pursued him around a parking lot.

Facebook's recommendation algorithms might lure a previously undecided person into an anti-vax group, and an anti-vaxxer into a Flat Earth community—or worse. Anti-vaccination is a popular cause in some far-right and white-supremacist movements, with fringe websites churning out anti-vaccine content. For years, Natural News, Mike Adams's organic food information repository/far-right primal scream, pumped out anti-vax content alongside its calls to unleash the military against the left. By February 2019 (several months before Facebook banned Natural News and Adams publicly blamed me for it), the site was responsible for some of the top-performing anti-vaccine posts on Facebook. Even more explicitly fringe websites, like the white-supremacist site Red Ice, have also made a bid for anti-vax readers, publishing anti-vax content that downplays the website's overt racism in an apparent effort to attract those with less extreme views. One such Red Ice article, about vaccine laws in Sweden, has appeared frequently in massive anti-vaccination Facebook groups with hundreds of thousands of members.

George Washington University researchers found similar ties to the far right when they traced web-based conspiracy theories about the COVID-19 virus in spring 2020. Misinformation about the virus was spreading quickly, creating a public health risk and drumming up anti-Asian sentiment in online hate groups. Facebook in particular was a hotbed, with pre-COVID conspiracy groups pivoting toward actively harmful paranoia. Flat Earth groups temporarily sidelined their spherical cause to proclaim the virus a hoax, or the result of a depopulation plot, or—in a synthesis with the anti-vax movement—part of an elaborate plot by Bill Gates to secretly inject people with microchips under the guise of vaccination.

The sheer scale of the pandemic and its associated lockdowns sent the conspiratorial internet into new modes of collaboration. *Plandemic*, a COVID-19 conspiracy documentary featuring discredited virologist Judy Mikovits, spread like a plague across social media in early May 2020. Mikovits is a former research scientist who turned anti-vax after her main medical discovery was retracted because it appeared to have originated from a laboratory error. In *Plandemic*, she falsely claimed that COVID-19 was a government plot and that wearing a protective face mask only increased the risk of contracting the illness. Some of the film's initial success stemmed from early efforts by a prominent QAnon supporter who collaborated with Mikovits to set up a Twitter account and an online fundraiser ahead of the movie's release, generating buzz and networking her with the conspiratorial internet. But the slickly produced video—made with professional-looking camerawork—duped an army of otherwise nonconspiratorial internet users, including several celebrities, athletes, and Instagram influencers with millions of followers. (In a particular blow to my morale, indie rock darling Angel Olsen shared the video on Instagram before deleting it and offering an apology.) Facebook and YouTube banned the video, calling it an imminent health concern, but users on both platforms kept the clip online by reuploading it under different names and sharing links to the new uploads on Facebook. And because of Facebook's algorithmic rabbit hole, COVID-19 misinformation sucked some *Plandemic* viewers into more extreme beliefs. Ann-Marie, a newly converted QAnon follower, told me she'd only learned about the far-right theory after binge-watching online videos about COVID-19 hoaxes. "If it wasn't for COVID19, I would have been just continuing to tell my kids about the 'stuff' I was finding," Ann-Marie told me of her tentative pre-COVID ventures on the conspiracy internet. Without the virus, she said she "wouldn't have found out about QAnon."

One COVID-19 hoax popular in Flat Earth Facebook circles wrongly claimed that truthers could exempt themselves from wearing protective face masks if they lied about having a disability. Flat Earth YouTuber Shelley Lewis closed the circle of Facebook, YouTube, and real-world disinformation when she tested the theory by livestreaming video at a California supermarket that required shoppers to wear face masks.

"Hi, I have a medical condition that I'm not allowed to wear a mask and I'm not required by HIPAA rules and regulations to disclose that," Lewis filmed herself telling a supermarket manager who had asked her to wear protective gear. HIPAA, the Health Insurance Portability and Accountability Act, prohibits doctors from sharing patients' medical information, and comes nowhere near Lewis's mangled interpretation. Nevertheless, Lewis leaned into the theory when the manager refused her entry.

"You're discriminating against me now, do you know that? You're discriminating against me," she told him. The clip went so viral online, with one mocking tweet racking up nearly ten million views, that Lewis deleted her social media accounts.

Ironically, Lewis was among those in greatest need of protection from COVID-19. She had lupus, an autoimmune disease that places people at heightened risk of serious COVID-19 complications. Lewis's battle with lupus had helped lead her to Flat Earth, she told me in late 2019, shortly before COVID-19's outbreak. As a child, she'd longed to be an astronaut. She wanted to be the first woman to walk on the moon. Her dream led her to enroll in the prestigious US Military Academy in West Point, New York. But lupus changed that, she said.

"I got a medical discharge. Everything I wanted came to this screeching halt, where, now what am I going to do with my life?" she told me. "I was diagnosed with lupus. I was thrown into the civilian world where I had no game plan of what I wanted to do. I jumped from job to job and doctor to doctor. No doctor could really help me."

Disillusionment with doctors, who couldn't provide her with a permanent cure, led her to abandon the medical system and seek healing in herbs and vegan food. She claims that the alternative treatment worked, leaving her in doubt about the veracity of modern medicine. When Flat Earth YouTubers became a breakout genre in 2015, Lewis was conspiracy-adjacent enough to watch, but not enough to believe yet.

"I went down this whole rabbit hole of 'These guys are crazy, this is stupid,'" she said of her process flicking from video to video. Then her internet friend Rob Skiba, the fringe Christian personality who converted after hosting Mark Sargent on his podcast, started posting about Flat Earth on Facebook. Begrudgingly, she took another look at the conspiracy theory.

"All the pieces started coming together. I thought, 'This is absolutely insane. But the earth is flat,'" she said. Within a couple years of converting, she was a Flat Earth YouTuber, too.

6 | Alone in a Flat World

SOMETHING WAS WRONG, and Nate Wolfe had a pretty good idea what. His sermon wasn't until Sunday, but early on a Friday morning, he received a text summoning him to church. Immediately, please.

Wolfe, a pastor, lived only a mile from his church in the suburbs of Toledo, Ohio. He'd moved his whole family cross-country for the job seven years earlier. The insular church community was his world—his "fishbowl," he described it. But minutes after arriving that Friday morning, Wolfe became a fish out of water. Church elders sat him down and summarily fired him.

"They didn't want any discussion," he told me. "They just slid a piece of paper across the table to me and said, 'We can't have a member with this kind of association.'"

That embarrassing association was Wolfe's Flat Earth belief, which he'd kept under wraps in order to avoid this kind of situation. He'd been full-on Flat for a year, ever since he went to YouTube to research a sermon on the Great Flood and stumbled across YouTube videos promoting a "biblical" Flat Earth model. YouTube recommendations led him to Robbie Davidson's channel, and eventually, in 2018, to Take On The World, a Christian Flat Earth conference an hour from Wolfe's home. Wolfe left the conference with a new cohort of Flat Earth friends and a new conviction to live publicly as a Flat Earther. He made plans to broach the topic during an upcoming church leadership meeting. He was going to do it delicately, making a biblical argument for Flat Earth, in terms his fellow church leaders could understand, beginning with Genesis 1.

He never had a chance to perform his practiced lines. Church leadership discovered his Flat Earth belief when they learned he'd attended Take On The World.

A pastor giving an unexpected Flat Earth sermon would, without doubt, harm a congregation. The deeply polarizing theory has a way of setting people at odds with each other and drawing them into other fringe beliefs—no good for a house of worship. But often, as in Wolfe's case, Flat Earthers are the biggest victims of their beliefs.

Wolfe's sudden firing, he told me, was "traumatic."

"My kids have grown up here," he said. "The church was most of our family and close friends. When I got fired, there was only a handful, like literally four or five people out of two hundred, that reached out to us. Most of the other people, even those who didn't reach out, had been our close friends at the church. It was just like, all of a sudden, we didn't exist."

Flat Earthers have divisions among themselves. Flat Earth Society members and the movement's YouTube vanguard are at odds not just over outreach methods but also over differences in alternative gravitational theory. Some Flat Earthers believe the planet ends at an ice wall, while a smaller faction preaches an "infinite plane" model. Some Christian Flat Earthers will make antisemitic remarks about Jewish Flat Earthers completely unprompted. But almost universal in this community—more binding even than belief in a flat planet—is the experience of ridicule and social rejection. Old acquaintances unfriend Flat Earthers on Facebook, and in real life, after seeing one too many posts calling NASA a satanic psyop. Employers question their sanity. Family members find somewhere else to spend Thanksgiving. It's a loss that foregrounds every conversation at Flat Earth meetups, so common that some Flat Earthers describe themselves with the language of persecuted minorities: announcing one's belief in the theory is referred to as "coming out," a term most commonly associated with the LGBTQ community.

In their own way, Flat Earthers really do live in an enclosed dome of a world. For so many, the conspiracy theory becomes the wall of a social snow globe, parting them from loved ones and trapping them inside with the only other people who will believe them.

On both mornings of the 2018 Flat Earth International Conference, emcee Rick Hummer engaged the audience in a call-and-response game, asking them to yell out insults they'd heard since coming out Flat.

The shouts from the audience sounded like a collective scream of catharsis.

"Crazy," came one popular response. "Retard," someone shouted. "Flat-tard!"

Cindy Gruender, a Colorado woman, didn't need to shout. She wore her favorite insult, "Miss Flat Earth," on a sash across her chest, like a pageant queen. She was reclaiming the title after it was given to her as an insult at a church that she later quit, she said.

Flat Earthers often wear rejection as a badge of honor, although not all do it as literally as Gruender. In a YouTube video that plunged me into a weeklong depression, an upbeat girl in her early teens performs skits about the ostracization her family faced after going Flat. One skit shows the family "nicely, but not so nicely, being ousted from the church," as reenacted by a young boy in a pastor's outfit taping a NO FLAT EARTHERS sign to a church door.

"But at the end of the day, you always have Jesus, the online Flat Earth community, and your family," the girl says. "Unless your family has disowned you. Then you just have Jesus and the online Flat Earth community."

Depressing or not, the girl was probably correct. Flat Earth and other conspiracy theories are community affairs, driven by a push-pull phenomenon of rejection from mainstream society and affirmation by a small cohort of fellow believers. In a 2018 paper, researchers at the

University of Kent and Vrije Universiteit Amsterdam identified conspiracy theories as "a social phenomenon in that they reflect the basic structure of intergroup conflict." The theories, in other words, thrive on antagonism.

By definition, conspiracy theories imply a coordinated plot by a hostile group. But the most successful conspiracy theories also imply the existence of another group: victims. Theorists become more devout when they identify as part of population under attack, the researchers noted. The more a person identifies with a persecuted "ingroup," the more likely they are to suspect evil deeds by a threatening "outgroup" with which they do not identify. In a 2015 study, for example, Indonesian students were more likely to believe conspiracy theories about Western countries staging terror attacks if researchers first emphasized the students' Muslim faith and described the West as a threat to Muslims.

Americans are no more immune than Indonesians. In the 1980s, the Soviet Union's KGB spread rumors throughout the United States that the CIA had engineered the HIV virus to wipe out the country's Black and gay populations. Often, groups that have been dealt a bad hand can be more likely to perceive the world in a conspiratorial light due to past suffering, be it the result of a deliberate conspiracy or passive societal failings. So while the anti-Black HIV rumors were false, the theory took off with some Black Americans who remembered the country's history of documented medical plots against people of color. For instance, J. Marion Sims, the pioneer of modern gynecology, experimented on enslaved Black women without consent or anesthesia. And from the 1930s to the 1970s, the US Public Health Service ran a deceptive syphilis experiment on Black men in Tuskegee, Alabama.

In their book *American Conspiracy Theories*, which compiles decades of data, researchers Joseph Uscinski and Joseph Parent found a trend of conspiratorial thinking among the disenfranchised (minorities, the poor, and people without a college education) and among groups fearful of losing status. "Conspiracy theories are essentially alarm systems and coping mechanisms to help deal with threats," the Josephs write. "Consequently, they tend to resonate when groups are suffering from loss, weakness, or disunity."

Joining a conspiracy movement is only a short-term hack for feeling safer. Once committed to a conspiracy theory, people find themselves even likelier to be socially ostracized. This can lead to a vicious cycle of alienation and acceptance, pulling a person away from society at large and further into a conspiratorial movement. The Kent and Amsterdam researchers found that conspiracy theorists learn to brace themselves for backlash. "Consistently, expressing conspiracy theories increases expectations of negative evaluations, and fear of being socially excluded," the researchers noted.

Nate Wolfe, the Ohio pastor, told me he hadn't met "a single Flat Earther that hasn't lost someone" to their disagreements about the earth's shape. "There are some that have been completely disowned from their family. There are some whose best friends of twenty, thirty years, forty years won't talk to them." One of his Facebook friends, a father of young children, died by suicide in 2019, he said. "It was due to a lot of the pressures, and it was due to persecution that he was getting from his family. He may have had some other emotional struggles and things, but he had made a post about how rough things were, and then . . ."

The phenomenon of alienation extends to other conspiratorial groups, like the QAnon community, the delirious and alarmingly bloodthirsty right-wing movement that accuses Trump's foes of occult horrors, among a sea of shifting allegations. QAnon burst onto the scene in late 2017 when someone on the anonymous message board 4chan claimed to be a high-level military intelligence source, code-named Q. The person promised the imminent arrest of members of Hillary Clinton's inner circle. Though the prophesied crackdowns never happened, the theory has morphed to accommodate different upsetting branches of conspiratorial thinking, like denialism of mass shootings and belief in secret government-run depopulation plots. Jockeying for position as the most absurd conspiracy theory of the moment, QAnon and Flat Earth frequently overlap in membership, to the chagrin of some QAnon believers who think Flat Earth is a step too far. (Q himself denounced Flat Earth in 2018 after a fan pleaded with him to "shut the Flat Earthers up," but not even the movement's prophet could separate the conspiratorial cousins.)

With its baffling insistence that Hillary Clinton has literally eaten children and its lust for mass executions, the QAnon theory can understandably put some believers at odds with family members, who are often bewildered or upset by their loved ones' convictions. "She's isolated herself," the son of one QAnon believer told the *HuffPost*. He'd cut ties with his mother after shouting matches over her beliefs, among which was her insistence that Clinton had ripped off and worn a child's face. "She has no relationship with me or my kids."

A Reddit board for people who've lost friends or family to the theory called QAnonCasualties had more than 150,000 members by April 2021. "Brainwashing our kids," read the subject line of one post, in which a mother alleged that her husband had begun inundating their young children with Flat Earth theory and conspiracies about child trafficking. "This is not the man I married," she wrote.

Kimberly, a QAnon follower from California, told me the theory was tearing apart the small apartment she shared with her boyfriend. "He does not think this QAnon thing is anything except nonsense. I drastically disagree," she told me when I contacted her in 2018 for an article about conspiracy theorists' isolation during the holiday season.

"It's just been difficult because we live in an apartment and it's very small," she said. Without a fellow Q supporter in the house, she turned to YouTube videos about the theory, which she watched in secrecy. "I have to listen with my headphones. I live in headphones now."

QAnon Facebook groups double as pity parties. "Happy Thanksgiving everyone!" one member wrote in a popular QAnon group on Thanksgiving 2018. "My children have chosen to not include me in festivities this year bc their minds are not open to the truth, but I am Thankful for PRESIDENT TRUMP and the WW1WGA [a QAnon slogan] family!! If anyone else is spending today by themselvs I would be happy to exchange photos of our meals."

Other believers commiserated in the comments. "My older boy has been 20 miles away for 5 years!! Havent seen him and I'm not chasin! Happy Thanksgiving!" Another posted an image that has devastated and haunted me ever since, of a bologna-and-Dorito sandwich on white bread with the caption "Thanksgiving dinner, it was delicious I just had seconds about ten minutes ago."

Some consoled each other with the thought that their hero, Donald Trump, was shouldering an even greater burden. "To al of you, so sorry, but think what trump goes through everyday, including holidays," one wrote.

"That is true!" another replied. "His burden is much greater than mine is."

Rachel Bernstein is a psychologist who has spent decades helping people exit cults and alternative belief movements. Conspiracy theories and cults rely on similar information systems, closing believers into an ideological echo chamber, she told me.

"There's a closed loop of logic and communication. You're not supposed to go to other sources of information," Bernstein said. "In fact, you're taught that other sources are automatically going to be wrong."

Even before hopping on the Q train, Kimberly had distanced herself from much of the news media. As part of a personal mission to never see or hear "any more advertising, ever," she had given up cable news, the radio, and newspapers. "I stopped watching TV and started getting my news from Twitter," she said. By the time we spoke in late 2018, she was a prolific pro-Q Twitter personality, and tweeted about feeling removed from family at Thanksgiving.

Robert Foertsch, a Flat Earth internet personality who drives a car covered in YouTube decals, has felt similarly. "I'm gonna be driving separate to Thanksgiving," he told an interviewer in 2019. "There's family tension. They're all excited about living on the globe, and I say I know that's a lie."

The chronic isolation is enough to make some Flat Earthers worry about members of their movement. Noel Hadley is one of the Flat Earth movement's best in-house historians. His YouTube channel is full of archival footage of early Flat Earthers like Samuel Shenton and Charles Johnson calmly explaining their theory to bewildered news crews. But unlike those elder statesmen of the Flat Earth movement, some new truthers are anything but calm.

"A lot of people in this movement get disenfranchised," Hadley told me of the new converts he sees in video comments sections. "Here's why: We have people coming in here feeling like they don't have a voice. They're questioning a lot of reality. Their families pushed them aside, they've lost their friends, their spouses have left them over this. So people get angry. They lash out. They feel like they don't have control, and this is how they control their lives."

Those Flat Earthers are a minority, any Flat Earther will assure you. To hear a Hadley or a Nate Wolfe (both perfectly nice guys in conversation) tell it, there's a fringe within the fringe, tarring the Flat Earth movement's otherwise good name.

"In fairness, I will say there are some Flat Earthers—just like anybody who believes any out-of-the-mainstream thing—who are very pushy," Wolfe told me at the 2019 Flat Earth International Conference. "I'm under no illusion that all Flat Earthers are these wonderfully kind people and they're all so smooth and gentle in their presentation. No, some are very aggressive, and they probably get some of what they deserve."

Fifteen minutes after speaking with Wolfe, I watched the first fight of the first day of the third annual FEIC break out in the cafeteria of a hotel-slash-convention center in suburban Dallas. First some agitated voices, then the scraping of chairs, then a bearded man gesticulating violently and bellowing across the crowded food area. The shouting man was Nathan Thompson, the previously mentioned proprietor of the largest Flat Earth group on Facebook, and though details remained in dispute throughout the conference, the fight seemed to have begun when someone touched Thompson's hat (a custom red ball cap with a Flat Earth map on it). Several hours later, while I sat talking with conference organizer Robbie Davidson in the lobby, Thompson came shouting through the room again, chasing someone out of the building and into the cold Texas night.

Davidson had invited Thompson to the conference as a speaker, so I tried to broach the topic gently: Wasn't this kind of behavior a little, you know, *unchill*? Apparently not.

"I've had some good talks with him, and I've seen some good stuff. So I believe in him. He's a young guy and stuff," Davidson told me. Thompson was thirty-four at the time. "I think there's a lot of potential there. I'm not saying that I'm anything special, but you know, I'm almost fifty. I can impart certain things . . . As you're representing yourself to the media and to the world, remember that it's different than just being yourself. You've got to kind of tone it down sometimes."

Toning it down is not really Thompson's thing. Thompson promotes "flat-smacking," an aggressive brand of Flat Earth evangelism that involves confronting strangers in public. This usually consists of heckling someone in a parking lot or at an airport baggage claim, and is about as unpersuasive as you'd imagine. But the real victories are the videos: Thompson and his crowd often record their confrontations, in the hopes of upsetting someone so dramatically that the video goes viral.

That's exactly what happened in spring 2017, when Thompson encountered a NASA employee in a Starbucks. We'll never know exactly how the conversation began. Thompson claims to have asked the stranger some questions about space suits, but the video begins later, with Thompson cutting in front of a line of customers to harangue the NASA employee as he orders a coffee.

"Come on, you won't even chat with me?" Thompson asks the man. "You hate Americans. Is that it?"

"Excuse me?" the stranger counters. "How the hell did you get that? Don't ever accuse me of that again." The beleaguered barista behind the cash register asks Thompson to leave. Ranting and raving in the parking lot, Thompson describes his expulsion as anti-Flat persecution, further proof that everyone from NASA to Starbucks is helping to perpetuate the great globe lie.

"Well, I just got kicked out of Starbucks for asking a NASA employee questions, because he's *lying*," Thompson snarls into his phone's front-facing camera. "He's a *blatant liar*. What a joke that was. Now we're outside. Beautiful America. Man, that was ridicul—I got NASA freaking stickers from the NASA employee, guys! And then I started asking him questions and he tells me to go outside of Starbucks. I'm freaking shaking! I am shaking."

If the media really was intent on burying the Flat Earth movement, as Thompson and his peers suggested, it wasn't doing a very good job. Thompson's video of the Starbucks spat broke out of Flat Earth circles and hit the mainstream, with write-ups in tabloids like the *Daily Mail*. Thompson continued to be a nuisance and brag about the resulting expulsions, as if they were the result of a conspiracy and not the consequences of being weird in public.

"I just got kicked out of John Wayne Airport for sharing Flat Earth. Great success," he posted on Facebook in September 2019. Moments later, he followed up with a video of himself yelling at a bewildered-looking man wearing a neck pillow. The video caption read, "This crybaby glober at John wayne Airport ran away from the debate at baggage claim and told me to meet him outside. So I met him outside, and he called over security."

When I called Thompson two days after the airport incident, I wanted to confirm a suspicion: Did Thompson speak to any Globe Earthers anymore, or was his social circle limited to Flat friends?

"Pretty much, yeah," he told me. "I wouldn't waste time talking to people who don't know where they live. It's pretty basic. As far as being friends and stuff, you're a reporter, you need information, I'll deliver it to you. But if you wanted to go get a drink, I probably wouldn't want to hang out with you, to be honest. You believe in cartoon globes. Like, I'm sorry, but that's like an adult believing in Santa Claus."

Flat-smackers have some firsthand experience with Santa Claus. In a 2018 video that swept through their circles, a Flat Earth YouTuber dressed as Santa and went to a mall at Christmastime, where he distributed Flat Earth literature to children from a bag labeled FREE GIFT until mall security guards asked him to please cut that out. Though the video's title, "Flat Earth Santa Kicked Out Of Mall!" suggests a dramatic expulsion at the hands of a jackbooted police force, Flat Earth Santa's exit was so leisurely that on his way out, mall security allowed him to hassle a food court employee who was distributing free samples.

This current of overplayed indignation runs through the conspiracy movement at large. Suffering for one's belief can be a form of street cred among truthers, even among less confrontational Flat Earthers like Wolfe. After being fired from his pastor job and withdrawing deeper into the Flat Earth movement, Wolfe wrote a book about his experience. The cover depicts a shadowy group of men gazing at him with sinister intent. But unfortunately for Wolfe's book sales, the title—*Fired for Truth*—was already associated with a different brand of conspiracy theorist.

In August 2017, a Google engineer named James Damore circulated a memo accusing the company of hiring too many women even though, he claimed, women were biologically less suited to work at tech companies than men. The document, debunked by actual neuroscientists, relied on cherry-picked data and was built on a framework of misogynist tropes that flourish in right-wing conspiratorial scenes. (During the 2019 Flat Earth International Conference, while I was seven months pregnant, I excused myself from a conversation with a man who was listing all the movies I was not allowed to watch while gestating, only to escape straight into a presentation about the evils of mothers in the workplace.) Damore's memo spread widely among Google employees before the company fired him. Rather than reflect on possible errors in his work, Damore launched a website titled Fired For Truth and made the rounds on conservative and conspiratorial media channels, which cast him as a figure of Christlike suffering.

Occasionally, Flat Earthers' suspected persecution becomes very real *pro*secution. In February 2020, Thompson took his flat-smacking act to an elementary school playground where he yelled at students who were playing at recess.

"I'm gonna flat-smack them. Guys! You don't live on a ball! The earth is flat! I've got flyers for you right here. You can check out my YouTube," he announced on a livestreamed video, while a teacher quickly herded children away from him and the dog he was walking on an extra-long leash. He dropped Flat Earth leaflets over the playground fence as students hurried back into the school.

"I've been wanting to flat-smack this school for a while," he told the camera. "You know, I might come back when they're out of school and they're all waiting for the bus and walking home and stuff, because I just feel calm." Minutes later, he revealed that he was carrying pepper spray, because he'd been "just waiting for a dog to . . ." He trailed off when he saw some women walking nearby. "Ladies! Ladies! Can I chat with you?" The women declined. "They, like, ran away. I think they were scared of my dog. But you know what, I'm gonna get their car. You best believe it," he said, attempting to shove a flyer under the car's gas cap.

Two days later, police arrested him on a disorderly conduct charge for yelling at the children. Thompson claimed he was reported by Globe Earth "trolls" who had posed as parents from the school. "All these Globe Earthers stalk me like I'm Kim Kardashian," he told me. "They just called police and made false claims because they're liars and have nothing better to do."

I asked Thompson if he understood why his critics were upset. I mean, I have a young kid, I told him, and I'd be worried if a stranger on a playground started yelling—

"I didn't start yelling at anyone," he said. "I just asked to give them a flyer, and the teachers acted like the flyers were a bomb and pulled the kids away, so I raised the tone of my voice because the kids were farther away. That's what you do when you're outside. You don't whisper outside when people are far away. That would look freaking stupid. You wanna say it's weird to yell at kids? No, it's weird to whisper if you're outside. That's weird."

Mike Hughes, the notorious Flat Earth stuntman hoping to take a picture of the flat planet from a homemade rocket ship, also got himself into legal trouble. Hughes subscribed to conspiracy theories about the legal system and frequently filed lawsuits against famous people's names under the mistaken belief that he could claim them as legal "entities." Hughes was such a familiar figure in his local California court that he came to regard some court officers as friends.

"Most these courts in San Bernardino know who I am, and they've researched me," he told me. "In fact, a couple of judges have asked me how my back's doing, when my next [rocket] launch is, so they know who I am. Some of the bailiffs wave hi to me, because they follow me on Facebook and see my launch. People know who I am."

The judges, in fact, were not his friends. The courts were so annoyed with him that they tried to take their own legal action. They reached out to two Flat Earth YouTubers, Patricia Steere and Mark Sargent, who were in Hughes's bad books. Sargent later told me that San Bernardino police tried to enlist him and Steere in an attempt to put Hughes behind bars.

"San Bernardino said basically, 'We're looking for ways to go after Mike because he's wasting legal resources and court resources. You have no idea how many people he's filed against,'" Sargent told me. (He and Steere had accidentally been unhelpful. They had mistaken the police for identity-theft scammers and told them to "get bent," he said.)

Ultimately, though, the law didn't need help. Hughes was charged with nine felony counts of unlawful use of identifying information, seven felony counts of attempted extortion, and three misdemeanor counts of filing false business statements. He pleaded not guilty and bonded out of jail.

Sargent thought the charges, which were dropped when Hughes died soon thereafter, were only meant to scare Hughes straight. "I think they hit him with a small thing and put him in jail for two weeks as a warning, like 'If you keep pursuing this, we are going to destroy you,'" he told me.

But for all their mistrust of the law, conspiracy theorists often destroy each other. Suspicious by trade, truthers like Hughes often accuse peers like Sargent of being "controlled opposition." (Sargent was a "disinformation agent," Hughes once claimed to me. He believed he owned Sargent's "legal entity," and in May 2019, he filed a lawsuit demanding that Sargent stop using the name and surrender all his possessions.) I've heard similar allegations lobbied against Hughes by Flat Earthers who accused him of leeching off the movement to fund rocket launches, his real passion.

Rise high enough in these ranks, and charges of subversion are a near inevitability, Noel Hadley, the Flat Earth history chronicler, told me.

"There is a lot of fear of infiltration. Everyone's looking over their shoulder," Hadley said. His wife is a software engineer who has done contract work for the government, prompting fellow truthers to create their own conspiracy theories about the couple. "People think that I'm an MK-Ultra," he said, referring to a now-defunct but very real government program that attempted to study mind control, "but that I don't know it, and that my wife is a trained government handler, that our marriage was arranged." He and his wife have been together since high school—a fact, he noted sarcastically, that would mean the government had plotted to pair them together since childhood.

Robbie Davidson said he'd seen so many conspiracy theories about himself that someone had actually printed his face on a deck of Illuminati-branded trading cards. "I think it's playing into a very paranoid-type mindset," he told me, less than two minutes before accusing the Flat Earth Society of being untrustworthy. "I think that there's a lot of paranoia. Conspiracy, healthy conspiracy, I think, is good. But it can get a little crazy."

There's "a little crazy" and then there's "international, intra-movement, transphobic harassment rings that upend a person's life." YouTuber Patricia Steere experienced the latter.

Steere was an unassuming 9/11 truther until 2015, she said, when 9/11 videos on YouTube led her to moon-landing truther videos, which led her to Sargent's *Flat Earth Clues* series. "It immediately rang true, and then later I proved it to myself," she said during a panel at the 2018 FEIC. She launched her own Flat Earth YouTube channel within months. A former radio host with vivid red hair, Steere quickly became one of the movement's most recognizable personas. Flat Earth channels can be as dry as dirt, populated with pseudoscientific rants and hours of equations that never add up right. Steere's broadcasts were more like a mellow coffeehouse where she and other truthers gathered to gossip. If Flat Earth had an Oprah Winfrey figure, it was Steere.

Sure, she lost some Globe Earth friends along the way. "If they're going to judge you for it, it's probably not going to work out. They're not loving you for who you are," she said at the conference. After going public on Facebook, she added, "I had a lot of people unfriend and block me."

Still, she said, "Flat Earth has brought me a sense of purpose I didn't have before." But it didn't bring nicer friends. From the beginning, she battled trolls in the comments of her videos, many of them members of her own community. Some accused her of not being fully committed to the conspiratorial cause. Eric Dubay, one of the first Flat Earthers on YouTube, started making videos calling her a "shill" (a fraud looking to

cash in on the movement) and stylizing her name as "PatriCIA," as if
to imply that she was secretly working for the US government. Steere
also had the misfortune of being one of just a few prominent women
in a field of mostly male Flat Earth YouTubers. (Just three of twenty-six
speakers listed for the 2018 FEIC were women. In 2019, it was three out
of twenty-seven.) Dubay made videos dressing as Steere in drag and
photoshopping her to appear overweight.

The vitriol took Steere by surprise. "She literally asked me, verbatim,
'Why are some people so mean?'" Sargent told me. "It's like, have you
not been on the internet? You could make a video about kittens playing
with children in a cancer ward, and within a hundred hits, you're gonna
have thumbs down, people unsubscribing."

He advised Steere of the internet's cardinal rule: never read the comments section. "I said, 'You're gonna snap,'" he recalled. "'Maybe not
now, not next year, but you're gonna snap. There are gonna be too many
comments. No one can do it. If you read enough bad things, you start
losing it.'"

Sargent and Steere were close friends at the time, and even mulled
a romantic relationship before a weekend together revealed them to be
incompatible. ("There just wasn't chemistry there," she told Hadley in
an interview.) She wasn't going back to dating Globe Earthers, though.
At fifty-six in 2019, she was looking for her true love, her soul mate, she
said in a video that has since been removed from YouTube. And she
thought she'd found him. Antonio Subirats was a small-time Flat Earth
YouTuber, a bit player on the scene until Steere invited him to Skype into
her show, she said in the video. They had the chemistry that was missing from Steere's relationship with Sargent. Their webcam conversations
continued long after they stopped recording.

"We went from talking about ideas to talking about each other and
the things we valued in love. I thought he was a very deep person, a very
wise person, and a very kind person," Steere said in the video. Subirats
told her he was falling in love with her and asked her to move in with

him. They'd get married, he'd said. He'd hand-forge their gold wedding rings, and they'd make Flat Earth videos together in holy matrimony. They'd never met in person—he lived in the United Kingdom, and she lived in Texas—but they were used to overcoming world maps. Steere loaded her life into suitcases and made what she thought would be a permanent trip across the pond.

Their relationship was fraught from the moment he picked her up at the airport in a ragged hoodie, Steere said. Irritations, small at first, began to nag at her from their earliest weeks together: Subirats would spend late nights listening to ASMR *Lord of the Rings* videos on YouTube, which consisted of people reciting lines from the Tolkien trilogy in a breathy voice. Red flags piled up: Subirats told her he'd been institutionalized for taking too much ecstasy; gatherings with his family devolved into arguments, during which he raged at them about chemtrails and vaccines. Steere, who'd inherited wealth, said she gave Subirats £3,000 (about $4,000) to help move them out of his small apartment, but he wouldn't agree to a new place. Every time they toured a nice home, she claimed in the video, "He'd bring out a radiation detector, hold it up, and say 'Nope, radiation. Can't live here.' This happened fifty times, and it turned out nowhere was suitable."

Steere said she pushed her doubts to the side until one night two months into her stay. Until then, they'd been having consensual sex—gently, at Steere's request. That night began no differently. Then, she claimed, something changed in Subirats's demeanor. He became forceful, a change she described as almost demonic. "I said 'Stop, you're hurting me, stop!'" she alleged. "He said 'You can't tell me what to do,' and finished and fell asleep. I'm raw, bleeding."

She wasn't sure, at the time, whether "rape" was the right word for what she'd just experienced. She wasn't focused on legal definitions at all. She was lying awake trying to figure out how to leave the country and the man for whom she'd upended her life. She later booked an airport hotel and a flight home. One of Subirats's sisters, whom he'd berated about chemtrails, helped Steere pack her bags and make a speedy exit in a taxi.

But she hadn't escaped Subirats on the long arm of the internet. During a private video chat with some Flat Earth friends months after returning to Texas, Steere gave her account of the breakup. Word got back to Subirats. Not only did he deny the allegations, but the next conspiratorial videos he uploaded were about Steere. He claimed she was a transgender woman.

"He told people that I'd had my penis removed, that I had scars all over my body, and that my vagina was white like my skin," theoretically a sign that it had been surgically altered, Steere told viewers. "None of it was true."

The Flat Earth community can be quick to seize on a new conspiracy theory but slow to embrace LGBTQ rights. Blame the movement's latent conservatism and strong evangelical leanings. The transgender community is at a double disadvantage among truthers, due to decades of harmful and dangerous stereotypes that falsely cast transgender people as deceitful. Alex Jones and other right-wing figures spent years accusing Michelle Obama of being transgender (which she is not). An entire rabbit hole of YouTube videos accuses transgender people of being part of an Illuminati plot. QAnon supporters wrongly link the transgender rights movement with the sexualization of children, whom they believe are being abused and/or eaten by Democrats. At the 2019 FEIC, YouTuber Rob Skiba went on a tangent about transgender people, ostensibly to prove a point about political correctness gone awry: if a journalist describes a transgender woman as a woman, he implied, how can you trust them when they say the earth is round? (Transgender women *are* women, and Earth *is* round.)

"There's a thing in the truth-seeking world called 'transvestigations,'" Steere said in her video, "where people who are self-appointed experts look at pictures of women in Hollywood and presidents' wives and famous singers and say, 'Shoulders are too wide, gotta be a man. Doesn't

have a waist, gotta be a man.' All those Victoria's Secret angels, according to transvestigators, are men. All your favorite actresses are men, but
Arnold Schwarzenegger is a woman. Bruce Lee, that's a woman, according to transvestigators."

Flat Earthers, "transvestigators," and their overlap watched Subirats's
videos and joined his crusade against Steere. Exasperated, she shared
pictures from her childhood, which clearly showed that she had been
born and raised as a cisgender girl. The new evidence didn't help her
case. Subirats told followers that, while the photos did show a girl named
Patricia Steere, that the girl had later died and that a boy who was in love
with her "decided to be her, and then got into the truth-seeking community and was sent by government agents to [Subirats]'s house to try to stop
him from truth-seeking because he's so damn important," Steere said.

Eventually, both halves of the former couple went dark on YouTube:
Subirats after the site banned him for violating its terms of service, and
Steere after the abusive comments became so frequent that she shut down
her channel herself. She'd finally snapped, like Sargent had warned. On
New Year's Eve 2019, Steere returned with a new channel, this one about
recognizing and surviving abusive relationships. But even as she tried
to build a public persona and form connections outside of conspiracy
circles, their politics continued to wall her off from the rest of the world.
With Flat Earth's reputation, she worried that new followers would flee
when they learned her opinions on the globe. Instead, she spoke vaguely
about abuse she'd suffered in the "truth-seeking" community.

"I'm using the word 'truth-seeking,'" she explained in her first video
on the new channel, "so people who find this video on narcissistic
abuse—and my whole channel—won't be put off by what I'm using it as
a euphemism for. I'm still FE."

With friends like these in the Flat Earth community, you don't want
to be their enemy. While embattled believers like Patricia Steere and
Robbie Davidson have decided to remain involved, other truthers have
departed the scene, only to find anguish on the other side.

Serena, a Florida woman, doesn't share her last name, and for good reason: she was among the first crowd of QAnon followers in November 2017. "From the beginning," she told me. "I was all in and so full of hope." That changed when Q started posting Bible verses. The daughter of a former CIA agent, Serena knew military intelligence wouldn't risk exposure just to spout off sermons. Disillusionment turned to disappointment turned to an urgent need to warn fellow Q followers of the fraud. But when she tried to preach against the movement's prophet, she found herself facing torrents of threats and abuse.

Undeterred, but now semianonymous, Serena joined #DenounceQ, an anti-QAnon movement composed of former believers and people trying to pry their loved ones from the conspiratorial clique. One man in her group lost both his parents to the conspiracy theory, she told me. "He's been trying to tell [QAnon followers] what we know: that Q's just a franchise for profit and entertainment, and it has estranged him from his mom and dad."

Leaving the QAnon community was a harsh break, one that left Serena so disenchanted with conservatives that she cut ties with the Republican party and got "out of politics" entirely. She also started reading about cults, and recognized too many uncomfortable similarities to the QAnon circles she used to frequent.

Cultists and the QAnon community both "isolate their followers and turn their followers against all other sources," she told me. "They also create apathy by telling people, 'Just trust me. Trust the plan. We've got this.' They've created a complete circle: no matter where you go, they have an answer. But all the answers are nonsensical."

Close-knit conspiracy circles like QAnon and Flat Earth can absolutely "fall under the rubric of cult definition," said Rachel Bernstein, the psychologist who focuses on cult exit. She typically helps people leave cults that promote "an us-versus-them mentality," which casts the rest of the world as either unenlightened or actively trying to steal something away from cult members. "It sets up a dichotomy," she said, "a division and distrust and isolationism that is very controlling."

When the rest of the world stands against them, some Flat Earthers turn to their conspiratorial community for reassurance.

In October 2018, a member of the largest Flat Earth Facebook group shared an email from her employer. "It is important that you attend this meeting tomorrow because we will be discussing information we received in regards to your public social media presence online," her boss had written.

Flat Earthers replied to the post saying that they were praying for her, that her employers were "Satanists," that her freedom of speech was under fire.

I clicked on her profile. Although she might not have recognized it as such, one of her most recent posts was an antisemitic caricature, showing a hook-nosed man labeled "banking elite" controlling other men on puppet strings—a version of a centuries-old conspiracy theory about Jews. Within days, her employer fired her.

"I express my freedom of speech and I lost my job, meaning I lost my housing, lost my compensation for all the work I've already put into this position," she wrote in another post on Facebook. "So. Please. Help me. I don't know what to do or where to go next because this is unjust . . . Somebody please give me advice."

Soon thereafter, she shared a meme from a Flat Earth page, of a person walking alone in the rain with the text "if you want to seek the truth, prepare to lose friends." Above the image, she added "but also prepare to gain real connections with complete 'strangers.'"

If I were this woman's Jewish colleague or client, should I have to work with someone who views my very existence as part of an evil plot? No, of course not. But did this young woman, who was not white, know that she was sharing memes that had emerged from white-supremacist internet circles, memes that incite real hate? Perhaps she didn't. In a perfect world, the meeting with her employers could have been an intervention. Someone could have explained the antisemitic connotations, the harm they did; she could have chosen to remove the posts and to speak up when she saw other conspiracy theorists pushing the same hoaxes. But this isn't what happened, and even if it had been, online conspiracy communities make the already difficult task of debunking much harder. Losing her job didn't seem to snap the woman out of Flat Earth belief. Instead, she appeared to turn further into the support of the fringe online community that told her she wasn't unkind or crazy.

For some Flat Earthers whose real-life friends ditch them over their faith, online acquaintances are the closest they'll come to a support group.

"Let's face it," said Nate Wolfe, the pastor who lost his job after attending a Flat Earth conference. "Truthers, because of the persecution that a lot of them have faced, can become very isolated. A lot of them will just pull down the blinds and be like, 'All I need is me, myself, and I, and my friends on the internet.'"

It's a disconnected way to live. Before Flat Earthers started organizing meetups, Robbie Davidson told me, the movement looked like "just some kooky, crazy conspiracy people online." Believers would host video hangouts, but the kinship they craved was fragmented by screens and laggy Skype connections. When "you sit down with someone, look them in the eyes, and see their mannerisms, it becomes real," Davidson said.

Meetups, many of which sell individual tickets for hundreds of dollars, are critical to the movement. "I always encourage people, go to a meetup, even if you have to drive two, three hours," Wolfe told me.

It's a plea I've heard across years of Flat Earth conferences. "Especially if you have family who ridicule you," Rick Hummer, the FEIC emcee, said during the 2018 conference, attendees should think of the event "as a big family reunion."

Two women in the crowd at that event had traveled from Northern California, where their homes were in the heart of a raging wildfire. One showed me pictures a first responder had just snapped of her neighbor-hood, which had been reduced to ash. The other woman was waiting to learn whether her home was still standing. Her mother, who lived in an area evacuated because of the fires, was missing. She felt "a little guilty" coming to the FEIC as her world burned, she told me, but the Flat Earth family she met at the conference was helping her keep her mind off things.

But soon the two-day conference would end, and the pair would return to what remained of their homes, and to the family and friend-ships they had already feared losing to Flat Earth. One of the women approached the microphone during a question-and-answer session with Patricia Steere. Already that day, I had heard conference attendees discuss a conspiracy about the wildfires, suggesting that they were the result of government ray guns. Her question, however, had nothing to do with forest-fire plots, or even the specifics of Flat Earth theory.

She wanted to know how she could "come out" as a Flat Earther on Facebook without losing friends.

7 | Mike

. . . .

THE ROCKET TOOK off like a punctured balloon, wobbly and erratic. A jagged trail of steam traced the ship's path across the sky, up thousands of feet above the California desert. For a moment, the rocket seemed to hover, oblivious to gravity.

Then the inevitable descent. To onlookers on the ground, the ship and the man inside it were a blur of black.

"Come on, parachute," one watcher murmured anxiously.

"Pull it, Mike," another man shouted. But the parachutes that had bloomed above Mike Hughes on his previous death-defying rocket launches were nowhere to be seen. "Pull it! Pull it! Oh God."

Hughes's rocket crashed into the dust with absolute finality. There was no need to call an ambulance.

Until that moment, Hughes had been one of the most famous living Flat Earthers. He had earned his fame by taking the theory to its logical conclusion. He was going to build a rocket ship, blast into Earth's upper reaches, and see for his own eyes whether the horizon was flat or curved. "This space launch is to prove or disprove the Flat Earth," he told me in spring 2019.

I thought it was a terrible idea. I suggested, much too gently, that it was a terrible idea. I thought it was such a terrible idea that I wrote a chapter about Hughes and the cadre of conspiracy theorists attempting dangerous stunts to prove their beliefs. I titled the chapter "Someone

Is Going to Die for No Reason." Then I dropped the matter and never raised it to him again. Hughes was sixty-four at the time and didn't need my advice, I reasoned. Besides, I doubted he'd really attempt the launch. For the past year, he'd notified me of various complications: parachute malfunctions and unforeseen weather that delayed his project. I began to suspect he was searching for excuses, avoiding a dangerous stunt that would force him to confront the curved horizon. I was wrong about his convictions. On February 22, 2020, in a gray stretch of desert, Hughes joined the growing ranks of conspiracy-theory casualties, and I've had to live with that scrapped chapter title on my conscience ever since.

In the mid-1840s, when Samuel Rowbotham popularized Flat Earth as a "zetetic" science, he preached that zetetics should believe only what they could personally observe. Rowbotham was a fraud, routinely borrowing and often misrepresenting real scientists' work when it suited him. But Hughes, with his insistence on seeing the world for himself, was one of the truest zetetics I've ever known.

He arrived at Flat Earth gradually, through decades of discounting the histories he'd learned in school. "It never starts with Flat Earth for anybody. It always starts with something else," Hughes told me. His starting point for skepticism was learning that the US Army had massacred hundreds of Native Americans at Wounded Knee, South Dakota, in 1890. "We're not taught the biggest mass shooting of all time was done by our government to an Indian tribe," he said.

Hughes never fully trusted the government again. While many Flat Earthers lean conservative (I spent much of a 2019 Flat Earth conference sitting next to a man wearing a Donald Trump hat indoors), Hughes always viewed Trump with distaste. It helped that Hughes didn't fully regard himself as subject to US laws. In various court filings before his death, he frequently used language and tactics ripped straight from the sovereign citizen movement, a bogus crusade that claims that people can skirt the legal system by declaring themselves "sovereign citizens," immune from most laws.

He told me, on multiple occasions and at great length, that he thought people's names were actually government-owned copyrights, and that he could file lawsuits to seize those names, the very thing that had annoyed the San Bernardino authorities so much that they eventually pursued his arrest. "Basically, I have claimed legal entities for very famous people. They can't even exist," he told me. "Barack Obama, Mark Zuckerberg, Elon Musk, Warren Edward Buffett. I own the legal entities they're operating under."

Once, he even tried roping me into a lawsuit he filed against YouTuber Logan Paul, over Paul's Flat Earth documentary, in which I'd had a fleeting appearance. I wrote a short article about the one-sided feud but otherwise avoided the matter.

All this might sound insane to the uninitiated. But unusual as his antics were, they made sense within his own ironclad system of justice, which preached suspicion of the powerful and honor for the underdog.

"All this stuff is hidden from us because it doesn't fit the agenda," he said, recalling learning about the massacre of Native Americans. "You start questioning this stuff, and then one day Flat Earth shows up and you go, 'Wow. That's even a lot for me.' And then you spend a few hours looking at it—or for me, several months—and it got to the point where I couldn't dismiss it."

Hughes had an advantage that most other would-be zetetic Flat Earthers lacked: he knew how to build a rocket and had no fear of dangerous stunts.

Born to a race-car hobbyist in 1956, Hughes spent much of his youth traveling the county-fair circuit, where his father competed in dirt-track races. Oklahoma City was home, but Hughes and his family spent so much time traveling from state to state, speedway to speedway, that life began to feel like a long racing circuit of its own. "It's just consuming. It consumes your life," Hughes wrote of his father's hobby in his self-published autobiography. "You got no time for anything else and it just eats at relationships like termites to wood."

But those who knew Hughes best thought his father might have shaped him into the record chaser he became.

"Since then, I have wondered, did he know he was enough?" Hughes's ex-wife, Faith Garber, told me a few months after Hughes's death. She said she had been wondering about Hughes's relationship with his father. "What's missing?" she wished she'd asked Hughes. "Is something missing? Is that why you feel like you need to do this?"

Garber and Hughes worked together at an Oklahoma City steak house. They fell in love fast and married young, in January of 1981. "We lived in a little one-bedroom apartment and didn't have anything but a bunch of plants and a twin-sized bed," Garber said. "But we were happy. We spent our time in the garage a lot. He has always been a daredevil. Always."

Hughes had been racing motorcycles professionally since his teens and hoped to turn his father's old hobby into a career. But the racing life didn't last, and neither did his marriage. He and Garber split early and amicably, and he turned to a job on the opposite side of the pit stop, working in NASCAR crews. It was there, turning wrenches and pumping high-octane fuel, that he started building his foundation as a Flat Earth stuntman. Hughes may have dropped out of high school, but fixing race cars was a crash course in rocket science.

"I was an aerodynamicist," he told me. "I've got cars in museums, I got a couple cars on the front row of Daytona, so I know how air moves around things. And I'm not afraid to test my theories."

When his pit-crew gigs dried up like his racing career, Hughes started driving a limousine, and chasing thrills as a freelance stuntman on the side. While trying to outdo a famous stunt by daredevil Evel Knievel, Hughes began tinkering with homemade rockets, which could propel him on long horizontal jumps off ramps. One stunt led to the next. If he could launch across a river, he thought, then perhaps he could break the record for vertical height in a homemade rocket. He toppled that record, then broke his own record on a subsequent launch, inching upward each time until his dreams became a list of altitudes.

"I don't believe in science," he told reporters in November 2017. "I know about aerodynamics and fluid dynamics and how things move through the air, about the certain size of rocket nozzles and thrust. But that's not science, that's just a formula. There's no difference between science and science fiction."

But there is a difference. A science-fiction author can save a character from certain death with a few twists of plot. Hughes was working with the indifferent mathematical fact of gravity. And as early as a March 2018 launch—Hughes's first after coming out as a Flat Earther— that difference very nearly killed him.

Hughes had intended the launch to take him only eighteen hundred feet in the air, much too low to observe the planet's curvature. Still, he managed to fundraise more than $7,000 online from Flat Earthers— and from people who thought his project was a big joke. They almost funded a tragedy. Short on cash, Hughes built the rocket in his garage and converted an old mobile home into a launch ramp. Then he hauled the whole thing to Amboy, a windswept California ghost town with a history of bad karma: stories of hauntings and occult rituals and bloody motel rooms. Other towns with legitimate governments had turned Hughes away, unwilling to deal with the headache of a potential rocket catastrophe. But Amboy, a popular filming location for horror movies, was virtually a theme park for destruction, and its owner welcomed Hughes for what was nearly another nightmare.

As he approached his rocket (emblazoned with RESEARCH FLAT EARTH), Hughes noticed a hissing noise, like an air mattress deflating. The noise was a vapor leak, but after the trip to Amboy and the make-shift launch-ramp assembly, no one knew how long the rocket had been compromised, which would determine how dangerous it would be. "We don't know if it's been going for five minutes or five hours," Hughes told me. A friend who had helped with his rocket construction urged him to wait, telling him they could fix the problem, if Hughes was willing to postpone.

"I said 'You know what, I'm not waiting any longer. I got in, and I did it," Hughes told me. His secondhand parachutes were twenty-three and twenty-one years old. "I didn't even know if they were going to work. They were all I could afford."

One of the chutes failed on the way down, and Hughes slammed into the earth, barely clinging to consciousness. "It was pretty ugly," he said. "I could have died."

When he recovered from the hard landing, Hughes announced his new plans to prove Flat Earth by flying to outer space in a "rockoon," a homemade rocket attached to weather balloons that would carry it upward after the rocket fuel burned out. He would build the rockoon in his garage, ride it sixty-eight miles above Earth's surface, and, before gravity reclaimed him and his parachutes deployed, take a photograph of the world.

It was a breathtakingly dangerous stunt, but everyone who knew Hughes said there was no talking him out of it.

"He had an IQ of 136. He's very smart," Waldo Stakes, Hughes's close friend who had helped him build his rockets, told me, "but he's very hardheaded . . . Once he's made his mind up about something, he'll just continue no matter what. He'll just do it."

Just do it, death be damned, is a popular sentiment among Flat Earth's most extreme zetetics. At the 2019 Flat Earth International Conference, I found myself seated behind a man named Bobby Hartley, who wore a T-shirt advertising a 2025 trip to fabled lands beyond Antarctica.

The frozen continent often conjures an air of foreboding among Flat Earthers. The most popular Flat Earth models, including Rowbotham's, argue that Antarctica extends like an icy ring around the pancake planet, keeping all its oceans in check. Common variations on this claim include a theory that Antarctica's most distant edge touches the base of a dome that encloses Earth and that the international treaties against colonizing Antarctica are actually part of a nefarious scheme to prevent people from seeing the dome. This subset of believers claims that Antarctica is highly militarized and that unauthorized explorers will eventually hit a kind of polar Area 51, defended by armies of the New World Order.

There are dissenters within the Flat Earth world, of course. A group called the Infinite Plane Society suggests that Antarctica extends out to eternity, a universe of ice to cradle our little blue oasis. Hartley told me he thought another world existed beyond the ice wall, and that other people likely already lived in this distant land.

"I just got into Flat Earth about a year ago, but I'm obsessed with this land beyond Antarctica. I want to go there so bad," Hartley told me. He seemed like a pleasant guy, and our conversation felt almost normal, until he divulged, laughingly, that the trip was something of a suicide mission. "Of course, we all might die. I'm not married. I have no kids."

It was a startling comment from someone I'd just met thirty seconds earlier, and I asked him whether he was serious. Apparently so.

"There is about a five percent chance of me making it. Out of that five percent chance of making it, I would say a one percent chance of ever coming back. It would almost be a one-way trip." Those odds would be worth it, even to spend twenty-four hours in the land beyond the ice, he said. I made some polite noises, with what I hoped was a neutral expression.

I'll probably never be any good talking death wishes with strangers, but a couple years in this scene had made me better at it. This was the second time that year, for example, that I'd spoken with a Flat Earther who had pitched me on a likely deadly trip to the lands beyond Antarctica. Months earlier, I'd spoken with Michael Marshalek, a friend of Mike Hughes, who was planning his own trip across the ice.

"Mad Mike is going up, and I'll be headed south," Marshalek told me. He was out to prove Flat Earth by trekking as far as Antarctica would take him. For Marshalek, all specifics of Earth's shape were under consideration until he reached its edge. "I think it's infinite until proven otherwise," he said. "If there's a dome, which many Flat Earthers believe in, I myself want to go out there and see that, take a chunk of the dome."

Like Hughes, Marshalek was making steady, even worrying progress toward setting off on his mission. A tech worker for a major New York City bank, he already had most of the funds saved for his planned expedition by the time we spoke in May 2019. He intended to reach the South Pole (or whatever's out there) by snowkiting, a technique that involves riding skis while clinging to a large kite or sail that captures the wind.

The plan had obvious challenges. Snowkiting is an extreme sport, one that leaves a rider at the mercy of sudden winds and rocky terrains—two conditions Antarctica has in frightening abundance. Snowkiting also prioritizes speed over distance. The world's longest and most challenging snowkite race is the Ragnarok, a scrupulously supervised hundred-kilometer race in Norway each year. Antarctica, meanwhile, is merciless and more than 2,381 miles (or 3,832 kilometers) across. Famed polar explorer Børge Ousland has used a kite and skis to cross parts of the continent, but he also offset them with grueling hikes in parts of the expedition where snowkiting would be, in his own words, "certain death."

And Ousland knew where he was going. He knew how much food to pack, how many days he could survive in the frozen wild before sending out an SOS. Marshalek, with his philosophy of "infinite until proven otherwise," would not be setting out with the same luxuries. If he planned to survive a journey that could be infinite, I asked him, wouldn't he eventually need to turn around and come home? How would he know when that was necessary? Marshalek promised to reveal his full itinerary in due time. When he did, he expected it would strike a blow against "edge-ophobes," his term for Flat Earthers who don't seek the planet's outer limits. He accused edge-ophobes of being afraid to explore, caught in a gridlock of excuses about why they can't simply traverse Antarctica. "They're stuck in debates all the time," he said. "They say, 'You can't burn fuel, there's treaties, it's too cold.' They're all excuses."

Here's another excuse, for any Flat Earthers reading: anyone trying to sell you a ticket for a Flat Earth–oriented Antarctic expedition is probably trying to scam you. I've stumbled upon two of these grifts without really trying.

In March 2017, someone who called himself John Bramha began registering social media accounts and buddying up with Flat Earthers online. Bramha claimed to be part of the elite group that enforced Antarctica's boundaries, protecting it from intruders. He and a handful of others from this secret police force had turned rogue after discovering the wonders that lay at the earth's edge, and now he was leading expeditions to the end of the world to share the truth of what lay beyond. For his trouble, of course, he needed funding. Specifically $1 million in hard-to-track Bitcoin payments. "You might think that's a lot of money, but it's just the cost of ten Tesla Model S cars," he told viewers in a YouTube clip. "People spend, collectively, way more than this on personal luxuries." He planned to earn his million by selling ten seats on his expedition for $100,000 each. He never showed his face in his videos, and the avatar he used on Facebook and Twitter had been stolen from a stock-image website.

By the way, Bramha said, the $100,000 trip would cure his customers of cancer. The dome surrounding Flat Earth was actually a wall of pure energy that "cures you instantly of anything you might be suffering from, medically," he claimed on YouTube. He shared a supposed picture of said energy wall, which looked like a pretty standard glacier.

For a group that doesn't believe in gravity or the moon, Flat Earthers were remarkably quick to support Bramha. At least one popular Flat Earth YouTube channel made a video vouching for the shadowy Antarctican, without ever meeting him. Flat Earthers tweeted that they'd filled out applications for Bramha's $100,000 excursion, and by summer 2017 Bramha claimed (albeit dubiously) that he'd sold six tickets. Of those alleged customers, two were counting on the trip to save their lives. "We have two persons on board who are suffering from Cancer and this expedition will heal them," Bramha wrote on Facebook.

The expedition was scheduled for November 2017, at which point (of course) Bramha vanished from the internet, taking with him whatever money he'd swindled from the desperate. The popular Flat Earth YouTube channel that had vouched for him uploaded a new video, this time claiming Bramha's scam was evidence of a conspiracy to make Flat Earthers look bad. As it turned out, the new video noted, Bramha's picture of the "pure energy" glacier had been taken by a professional photojournalist focused on the environment and climate change. The photojournalist had won grants from scientific institutions, including NASA. The connection to NASA, that great Flat Earth bogeyman, was enough for Flat Earthers to accuse Bramha of being a "big science" saboteur. To them, Flat Earth theory was still vindicated, in its way: someone wanted to suppress its believers.

Remarkably, the following year, someone else tried a similar stunt. A company called Over the Poles offered a onetime flight over part of Antarctica starting at $11,900. The trip is technically possible, although rarely attempted, due to the danger involved. One notorious 1979 Antarctic sightseeing flight left all 257 passengers and crew dead after it crashed into a mountain in whiteout conditions. Over the Poles said it was going much farther inland than that deadly crash site and, while it did not market exclusively to Flat Earthers, it acknowledged the conspiracy movement on its website.

Michael Marshalek told me he bought a ticket in the brief months that Over the Poles operated its website. Then, like Bramha's venture before it, the company and all its affiliates vanished from the internet, leaving people holding expensive tickets to nowhere.

Yet as vicious as the Antarctica scams were to their victims, the situation could have been worse: the ice-wall-curious crowd could have taken an ill-planned trip to the South Pole and died. They would have joined the growing ranks of conspiracy theorists committing real-world harm in an effort to prove their beliefs.

Chief among this dangerous crowd are adherents of QAnon and Pizzagate (a sort of QAnon predecessor that specifically accuses Trump's foes of participating in child sex trafficking under Comet Ping Pong, a Washington, DC, pizzeria and ping-pong arcade).

On December 4, 2016, a man named Edgar Maddison Welch drove six hours from his home in Salisbury, North Carolina, to Comet Ping Pong. He recorded himself during the interstate journey. "I can't let you grow up in a world that's so corrupt by evil. Gotta at least stand up for you. And for other children just like you," Welch said in a video addressed to his two young children. "Like I've always told you, we have a duty to protect people who can't protect themselves . . . I hope you understand that one day."

The video was the completion of a conspiratorial cycle. Earlier that day, Welch had mainlined YouTube videos on the Pizzagate conspiracy theory, which made him "sick," he later told investigators. Pizzagate had been thriving on YouTube, where far-right vloggers had uploaded hours-long videos explaining why they believed Hillary Clinton was routinely abusing kidnapped children in a secret dungeon beneath the pizza parlor. Shortly before leaving to drive to DC, Welch tried to enlist two friends to the conspiracy theory, urging both to watch YouTube videos like "PIZZAGATE: The Bigger Picture."

The video he made from the road mimicked the style of his favorite conspiracy theorists, with Welch speaking directly into the camera as he waxed poetic about tyranny and his personal heroism. But unlike those YouTubers, Welch was about to put conspiracy theory into practice. "Raiding a pedo ring," he texted a friend about his journey to DC, "possibly sacraficing [sic] the lives of a few for the lives of many. Standing up against a corrupt system that kidnaps, tortures and rapes babies and children in our own backyard."

More than three hundred miles later, Welch parked his car outside Comet Ping Pong and retrieved a military-style assault rifle from the back. Then he entered the restaurant. Inside, Comet Ping Pong was packed with its Sunday lunch rush. Parents and children, the very people Welch had vowed to protect in his video, crowded the booths. Their afternoon turned to panic when he started shooting. Families and employees scrambled for the exits as Welch fired multiple shots, including at the lock on a closet door. What looked like a terror attack to patrons and employees was actually a fact-finding mission, Welch later explained to detectives. While he was menacing the restaurant with his rifle, he was also searching for underground tunnels, signs of child sex slavery, anything that would finally confirm the stories he'd learned on YouTube.

Then, as abruptly as he'd stormed the restaurant, Welch stopped shooting. He went outside, where police officers had gathered to demand his exit, and lay on the ground at their command. "Pizzagate," one irate officer announced while Welch mumbled into the pavement about a pedophile ring. "He's talking about Pizzagate."

After the shooting, Pizzagate's highest-profile advocates denounced Welch as "controlled opposition," because they'd found a web page for an amateur actor of the same name. And not even Welch, who had seen the inside of Comet Ping Pong firsthand, was fully dissuaded from the conspiracy theory. "The intel on this wasn't 100 percent," he told the *New York Times*. A judge called it "sheer luck" he didn't hurt anyone.

Unchastened and unchecked, Pizzagate carried on, eventually transferring much of its momentum to QAnon, which borrows many of its foundational claims. In January 2019, twenty-two-year-old Ryan Jaselskis doused a curtain in Comet Ping Pong with lighter fluid and set it on fire while customers—some of them children—were eating dinner. An hour before the arson, according to NBC News, Jaselskis uploaded a YouTube video about QAnon. Though he managed to escape Comet Ping Pong undetected, his act of arson was captured on the now-wary restaurant's security footage, which managers turned over to police. Days later, police arrested him for climbing a fence at the Washington Monument, and identified him as the guy who'd torched a pizzeria across town.

QAnon has a sizable and growing membership overlap with Flat Earth—and both conspiracy theories have a body count. When I asked Flat Earthers at a 2018 conference whether they believed in QAnon, about a year after the theory's emergence, most told me they'd never heard of it or that they were skeptical. By the 2019 conference, however, QAnon had hit the mainstream, with Q supporters running for Congress and scoring retweets from Trump on Twitter. Some diehards treated the theory as a near religion, memorizing Q's posts and citing them by number, as if they were scripture, or printing them out in book form like a religious text. With QAnon's sudden surge in popularity, I didn't have to go looking for its backers at the November 2019 Flat Earth International Conference: two approached me in a hallway to give me free QAnon jewelry.

"About seventy-five to eighty percent of Flat Earthers know QAnon," one of the jewelry-wielding women told me, based on her conversations with Flat Earthers at the conference. She was trying to actively spread Q awareness off-line by distributing cheap QAnon bracelets anywhere people might be receptive to the theory: at Trump rallies, gun shows, and, now, at a Flat Earth conference.

Flat Earth's new embrace of QAnon worried me. Even if my free-jewelry friend had overestimated her figures, I'd watched Q-flavored memes make their way into Flat Earth Facebook groups over the previous year. And in 2019 alone, QAnon had been implicated in a number of violent incidents and at least two deaths.

In January 2019, Buckey Wolfe drove a four-foot sword through his brother's skull. "God told me he was a lizard," Wolfe told 911 dispatchers. "Kill me, kill me, I can't live in this reality anymore."

Wolfe, twenty-six, was a member of the Proud Boys, a far-right paramilitary group that glamorizes violence, often using conspiracy theories to demonize its targets. But his conspiratorial journey, as documented by his favorited YouTube videos, surpassed even the Proud

Boys' weirdest collective paranoias. Wolfe's first "likes" on YouTube were apolitical, mostly music and fitness clips. That changed when he began liking videos by a right-wing vlogger who criticized "social justice" culture. (YouTube was sometimes recommending these videos for people who watch fitness how-tos.) From there, Wolfe appears to have discovered videos about "free energy," the same mythic concept Bramha promised to people who paid $100,000 for a trip to Antarctica. Wolfe's video browsing never returned to normal. He watched videos from Infowars, from white supremacists, and from conspiracy theorists who claimed the government was actively following and harassing them for no discernible reason. Eventually, he landed on videos about QAnon and a sometimes-overlapping theory that claims some people are actually lizards or reptilians in disguise. The fictions of his internet world hacked away at his real life until they destroyed it, taking his brother with him.

While Wolfe was awaiting trial in May 2019, a hero of the QAnon world was found dead. Isaac Kappy, a small-time actor with a role in *Thor*, had rediscovered fame in August 2018 when he gave an interview on Infowars purporting to be a "Hollywood whistleblower" with information on secret pedophilia rings. The remarks followed a monthslong escalating pattern of troubling behavior, including allegedly choking Michael Jackson's daughter Paris and threatening a shootout with police. Less than a year after his InfoWars comments, Kappy jumped to his death from an Arizona bridge, investigators said. His suicide note on Instagram contained an apology to QAnon fans.

Rather than accept Kappy's death as the tragic end to a long, public battle with mental health, QAnon fans declared him to have been murdered in a plot to suppress their conspiracy theory. Believers pointed the blame at Tom Hanks, a Hollywood A-lister whom Kappy had baselessly accused of pedophilia. They dug up one of Hanks's month-old tweets about roadkill, which they said was a coded threat toward Kappy.

"Posted 42 days before his death," one QAnon follower commented under Hanks's tweet. "And he died at age 42."

At least one would-be deadly plot involved a Flat Earther who also believed in QAnon. Kurt Cofano, a Pennsylvania man, spent the spring of 2020 uploading videos about both conspiracy theories to his YouTube channel, where he used a Flat Earth avatar. When racial justice protests swept the nation in May, Cofano began uploading racist, conspiracy-flavored screeds and tweeting threats at protesters. By July, Cofano was uploading videos of himself assembling and exploding homemade bombs, and threatening to drive to DC to blow up the headquarters of some of the government agencies he'd vilified in his video compilations about Flat Earth and QAnon. He was allegedly en route on his destructive road trip when cops pulled him over, likely tipped off by a social media post in which he bragged of having "several life sentences in the trunk of my car." Sure enough, police allegedly found thirty improvised explosives in the back of his Mercedes-Benz.

Cofano didn't kill anyone. But he could have. Pursued to their ends, in true zetetic fashion, conspiracy theories can leave believers doing the deadly, like taking wildly ill-advised trips to Antarctica or trying to blow up government buildings with a luxury car. Conspiracy theories took the life of Buckey Wolfe's brother and upended Wolfe's existence. A year after killing his brother, Wolfe was acquitted of murder by reason of mental incompetence and committed to a hospital for the "criminally insane." Too often, as in Isaac Kappy's case, conspiracy theories end the lives of believers.

Eventually, they came for Mike Hughes.

Hughes's rocket launches were always a dance with disaster. Unlike NASA, which uses fire and fuel to blast into space, Hughes used a clever but temperamental steam propulsion engine.

"That one engine, by itself, could pull a train five miles long loaded with coal up the Wasatch Mountains," Waldo Stakes, Hughes's friend and rocket co-constructionist, told me. The engine worked by heating steam, creating a superpressurized environment, then suddenly releasing the steam to propel the rocket into the sky at terrifying speeds.

"They're about the power of about forty automobiles," Stakes said. He added that the steam could take the sixteen-hundred-pound rocket from zero to "four hundred twenty miles per hour in four or five seconds. There's basically nothing that touches these things. Nothing manned, anyway."

Almost no one dared to pilot the steam rockets besides Hughes. I think he liked it that way. When we'd speak in the year before his final launch, he'd tell me how none of the other famous daredevils would go as far as he had. Evel Knievel didn't have the smarts to build his own steam rockets, he said, and extreme stuntman Travis Pastrana didn't have the guts to ride in one.

And no one could convince Hughes to abandon a stunt once he'd set his mind on it.

"I know I couldn't have talked him out of anything," Faith Garber, his ex-wife, told me. "Nobody could have. He was very driven to do exactly what he was doing."

Mike Hawkins, one of Hughes's close friends from the car-building world, said he called Hughes almost daily, to "just see what he's up to, just scratch his brain on what he's planning and problems that he ran into." Those calls often turned into rocket tech support, Hawkins told me. "I would soundboard some of his problems. There were a lot of problems in the process, because Mike would do things that turn out to be dangerous and he didn't see it—even on the day of that launch."

Hawkins and Stakes were with Hughes on the day of the final launch. But Hughes's heart wasn't in it that day, Hawkins told me. For more than a year, he'd yearned to blast off in his rockoon, the improvised spacecraft he hoped would show him the earth's true shape. On February 22, 2020, however, he was stuck in one of his standard rockets and going only one mile high, due to commitments to a film studio. The launch—which would have been record-breaking, even if Hughes considered it lackluster—was being filmed for a Science Channel show called *Homemade Astronauts*. Hughes had begun to see the show as a barrier to his stratospheric ambitions, Hawkins said.

"Mike was pressured to get the monkey off his back," Hawkins told me. "He wanted to get this launch completed so he could go on to the space project . . . He wanted out."

Hughes tinkered with his rocket formula in the days before the launch, working in a lonely stretch of desert outside Barstow, California. Something about the final hours gave Stakes a bad feeling. "I said, 'You know what, Mike, let's just nix this. Let's not do this,'" Stakes said. A friend had just called him to say he'd had a dream about Hughes crashing his rocket in the desert. Stakes had considered relating the dream to Hughes, but then thought better of it.

"I said, 'I don't have a bad feeling about it, but I don't know if this is a smart thing to do. Let's tell them [the TV crew] to piss off and that if they want to keep the show going, they can. If they don't want it, we'll do it our way. We don't need them.'"

But Hughes stayed the course—sort of. To make it a mile up, his steam-powered rocket needed approximately seventy gallons of water, Hawkins told me. Instead, Hawkins estimated, the rocket was carrying ninety to ninety-five gallons, a figure he described as "pushing the envelope." Hawkins had never even calculated what ninety-five gallons of water would do to the rocket. None of Hughes's team had.

The rocket's landing system was also suspect. Hughes had used recycled parachutes previously (new chutes cost about $4,000, and Hughes was a stickler for his budget), but this time two of his new chutes were an experimental design he'd dreamed up on his own. "I didn't believe in them," Stakes said. "I said, 'I'm not going to go with you; you're just going to kill yourself.'"

"Why, Waldo?" he said Hughes had asked him.

"Because those chutes are garbage," Hughes had responded. "Put rocket chutes on this thing."

Hughes compromised: two conventional rocket chutes and two of his own design. He also outfitted his launching station with last-minute alterations that worried his collaborators. He didn't notice, for instance, that the new ladder into the rocket cockpit would have ripped off the craft's tail fins as they roared from the launchpad. Hawkins did, though, and he rushed to a hardware store to buy a grinder that could trim back the final inches of ladder.

"We would do anything and everything we could to just keep him out of hot water," Hawkins said, but Hughes was set in his ways. "And that's how he was. You don't argue over it because Mike's going to do it."

So with his friends watching and the Science Channel filming, Hughes climbed into his rocket for the last time. He counted down, lifted off, and everything went wrong. The extra water gave him too much steam pressure, tearing a release nozzle and setting it flapping off course. The experimental parachutes deployed during the unsteady launch, catching on the too-close ladder and sending the rocket farther off-kilter.

"He should've had about eight thousand horsepower. It probably went to twelve thousand or fourteen thousand horsepower," Stakes said. "So it had more power, and it wasn't directed. It wasn't focused like it was supposed to be when the rocket came up. It started zigzagging."

The cloud of steam and dust, the white flash of the parachute, the unsteady exhaust trail into the sky: all were over in moments. Thousands of feet up and out of steam, the rocket plummeted toward the ground. Inside, Hughes was likely unconscious, suffering a "redout" from the blood rush to the head that accompanies a dangerous downward acceleration.

"We had radio contact with Mike, but he wasn't answering now," Stakes said. "'Throw the chutes, Mike. Throw the chutes, Mike. Mike, throw the chutes. You've got to,' I was screaming, 'Throw the effing chutes already.' And of course, he never deployed the chutes, because he was out. He didn't see it coming. And if there's a good side to it, he never saw it coming. It would've been like you fall asleep, you wake up, and you're standing before God."

Hughes's death was broadcast live online. The friends who'd traveled to support him had been filming the launch and streaming it on social media. When the rocket hit the ground, the livestreamer whose video I was watching took off running into the desert, out toward the distant dust cloud where his friend had landed. Eventually, someone in a car turned him away. "Why aren't they sending the ambulance?" the streamer called out.

Stakes made it farther, all the way to the crash site. The rocket looked like a piece of crumpled aluminum foil.

The internet's response was swift and cruel. People shared videos of Hughes falling from the sky and joked that he deserved a Darwin Award, a sarcastic accolade for people who die in ridiculous ways. Hundreds of YouTube commenters made a joke about Hughes being a "flat" Flat Earther, as if they were any cleverer than he was, a bunch of anonymous sad sacks writing tired puns in the comments sections of snuff films. I had no patience for that shit. I knew Hughes. I knew him to be a kind eccentric, someone with a strong (albeit unusual) sense of justice. He didn't deserve this.

Then, a couple days after his death, I started questioning how well I knew Hughes at all. Darren Shuster, Hughes's public relations representative, told journalists that Hughes had never been a Flat Earther—that the whole thing was an act for publicity.

"As his PR rep for 17 years, and privy to hundreds of hours one-on-one, I can say with certainty: He was a great American daredevil," Shuster told *Vice News*. "While open to the idea of government conspiracies, he was a daredevil who used flat earth publicity to get worldwide attention. It was a PR stunt. We used the attention to get sponsorships and it kept working over and over again. For the sake of Mike's legacy, it's time to tell the truth."

Thing is, no one who knew Hughes well seemed to agree with Shuster. I mentioned the publicist in passing to Waldo Stakes. Bad move.

"The Shuster guy," Stakes told me, "he wants to promote himself. He said these things about Mike to stir up controversy, like all of a sudden Darren Shuster's got the answers. This guy isn't shit. He won't even talk to you. He'll never meet me face-to-face, because he knows I'll put my boot up his ass."

Shuster and Hughes were on the rocks, and had been for years, Stakes claimed. The supposed rift began when Hughes learned Shuster was a Trump supporter, something Hughes decidedly was not. Hughes "shit a brick," when he learned, Stakes said. "He called him up and said, 'Don't ever call me up again. You're done.' And that was it. He never did anything with us, and that was two years ago."

Shuster claimed otherwise. He told the *New York Times* that Hughes had texted him the morning of the launch. "Is the media going to be there?" Hughes's last message read, according to Shuster.

Shuster gave me a similar line when I emailed him.

"It was part of the PR story to help to get traction with global media. We talked about it many times," he wrote to me. "He would say: 'I'm not saying the world is flat, I'm saying I want to motivate people to discover things for themselves.' And we agreed that nothing gets attention like the then emerging 'flat earth movement' and the whole YouTube rabbit hole thing."

Shuster mentioned that he was working on a screenplay and that he was wary speaking to me because of "how this conflicts with my own writings and projects surrounding Mad Mike Hughes (have turned down Sports Illustrated and many others)." He'd give me a few quotes, he said, but "anything more would require some discussions of a budget."

I don't pay people for interviews. Few journalists do, for ethical reasons, and the last time I could remember being asked for money was in something like 2017, while interviewing someone connected to a very funny but very illegal rental-car scam. Besides, almost everyone in my profession is broke. I told Shuster I'd call anyway. Only an answering machine greeted me. It was the last I heard from him, despite leaving a voicemail and sending repeated emails.

Instead, I called Justin Chapman, a journalist who'd been following Hughes for months while writing a long-form article on the stuntman. Chapman had been one of the only reporters at the scene of Hughes's fatal launch, and Hughes had previously hosted him at his house. I asked Chapman if he thought Hughes had been lying the whole time.

"My sense is he was genuine," Chapman told me. He thought back on his last long talk with Hughes. "Eighty percent of the interview was a rant about conspiracy theories," he said, including those on which Hughes had personally acted. Among those theories was his belief in sovereign citizen legal theory, which certainly didn't buy him any good publicity and, by then, had earned him felony charges for repeated filings.

One of the best predictors for conspiratorial belief is prior belief in other conspiracy theories. Was it possible that Hughes, who had a verifiable commitment to some fringe theories, saw Flat Earth as clear nonsense? Stakes—who is not a Flat Earther and had tried talking Hughes out of the belief—didn't think so.

"Mike [was] a Flat Earther, absolute Flat Earther," he said. Hughes had Flat Earth books that he'd cite when Stakes tried to argue against the theory, he added. "He'd make me nuts with that," Stakes said. He noted that Hughes did his own Flat Earth experiments without publicity, like loading up his limousine with measurement devices and recording altitudes as he drove around the country. And contrary to the claim that Hughes was only into Flat Earth for the money, the theory sent him into the red, Stakes said. In 2019, he told me, "Mike put on a Flat Earth conference himself. He funded it himself, and it ended up costing him three thousand dollars in losses. He lost three thousand dollars on top of the ten thousand dollars he put into it."

Mike Hawkins wasn't a Flat Earther, either, but he told me that he and Hughes were like brothers. I called him on a June afternoon after puzzling through Shuster's messages and listening to recordings of my old interviews with Hughes, playing them on loop trying to catch the sound of a lie. When I reached Hawkins, he was driving Hughes's ashes back to Oklahoma; that's how close the two were. I asked him straight-out: Did Hughes really believe Earth was flat? Hawkins gave me an answer that seemed to reconcile Shuster's and Stakes's warring perspectives.

Mike's path to Flat Earth was "a fine line between two things," Hawkins said. "I'm here to say that it started out as a marketing approach—and it was my idea. Mike was looking for a way to get out there into the public. And I said, 'Well, what you need is a controversy. So you should tell everybody that the earth is flat. That would definitely do it.' That's how it started."

But after publicly associating his name with the theory, the already-conspiratorial rocket man went looking for more information about Flat Earth, Hawkins said. "Mike actually investigated the truth behind it. He wanted to see it for himself. So we went from an idea to an actual investigation." Hughes began networking with more established Flat Earthers and showing up at conventions. "I think that generated awareness and involvement for him. It just went on its course," Hawkins said. "It became something to him."

Faith Garber was also searching for answers after her ex-husband's death and Shuster's public statements. She'd recently spoken to one of her and Hughes's mutual friends, who'd prodded Hughes on his belief shortly before his passing. "You don't actually believe that," the friend told Hughes.

"I don't know," Hughes replied. "I don't know."

Neither did Garber. "I think if I had to guess, I'd say he probably did believe it," she told me.

Zetetic science supports Flat Earth only if no one actually tries it. Samuel Rowbotham knew this. When Globe Earthers tried debating him on zetetic terms, he simply ran away. Many modern Flat Earthers understand this, too. For all their talk of independent thinking and scientific inquiry, most are content to convert based on information they've gleaned secondhand on social media. They leave real zetetic inquiry to the few Flat Earthers who haven't caught on: people like Mike Marshalek, the would-be Antarctic explorer who described Earth as "infinite until proven otherwise," and Hughes, who described Flat Earth as a hypothesis, not an orthodoxy, but was willing to go to end of the earth for answers.

True zetetics like Hughes will never prove Flat Earth theory, because Flat Earth is a lie. Instead, through their experiments, they serve as the collateral damage that lets Flat Earth continue masquerading as a science. Their lives and deaths uphold a Flat Earth fiction that claims the conspiracy is always just on the verge of coming to light, that any one believer can reveal the truth, if only he travels a little higher or a little farther into Antarctica. Flat Earth lured Hughes up into the sky, against all evidence.

Before his launch, I'd doubted Hughes would actually go through with the stunt. I'd doubted so much that I never fully told Hughes, a man I considered a friend, that I thought the launch could kill him. In his absence, while rumors fly about his beliefs, I've begun trusting Hughes's faith more than I did in his lifetime.

In zetetic logic, you are what you do.

If Mike Hughes truly did feign his belief—if he'd fooled his friends, gone into debt for Flat Earth, become one of the movement's most prominent faces, joined a TV show about the theory, all to drum up publicity for a rocket launch—would he be any more alive than he is today?

When I first wrote this chapter, I titled it "Someone Is Going to Die for No Reason." Now that Hughes is dead, I think that title lets Flat Earth off easy. Mike had his reasons. Whatever he privately believed in the moments before his rocket launched, he died in Flat Earth's name.

8 | Flat and Fascist

LOOK, IT'S VERY simple:

"Adolf Hitler. They have reincarnated him. He has been cloned," a top-hat-wearing attendee of the 2019 Flat Earth International Convention said in a now-viral video from the event. "He realized the Flat Earth model was correct and went to seize the Gate of the South in what we call Antarctica—a place called New Berlin, Antarctica. I believe that Hitler sequestered himself and his greatest scientific teams to New Berlin, Antarctica, in the 1940s—in the *early* 1940s—where he built a manufactured city."

As a journalist, I've reported from the ground at white-supremacist marches. I've gotten drunk with anti-fascist activists up and down the East Coast, and one time, after I wrote about an upcoming far-right rally, a guy on the rally's RSVP list got so mad at me that he tried to sneak into my office while I was away at my wedding rehearsal dinner. All this is to say that despite years of monitoring neo-Nazi movements, I've never heard Hitler invoked half as many times as on any given day of any given Flat Earth conference.

Most Flat Earthers, of course, are not neo-Nazis. Mike Hughes wasn't, and neither are any of the conference organizers or Flat Earth Society holdouts or Antarctic explorers I've met. If anything, much of the Nazi chatter comes from well-meaning Flat Earthers who compare everything they dislike to Hitler. According to this crowd, NASA—which, to be fair, absolutely did hire Nazi scientists in its bid to win the space race—is an ongoing fascist plot.

In most social settings, this anti-Nazi position should be pretty uncontroversial. The Flat Earth movement, however, is not a normal social setting.

A second faction of Flat Earthers makes mouth noises about disavowing Hitler, but regards the Holocaust as a hoax. This leaves them in an uncomfortable position of Hitler adjacency. In one of the many Flat Earth Facebook groups I monitor, for instance, I observed a conspiracy theorist asking for Holocaust denial videos—just not overtly Nazi-friendly Holocaust denial videos. "Does anybody have any videos that they can recommend other than [here she named a notorious pro-Hitler video by a major Flat Earth YouTuber]," she asked. "I am NOT praising Hitler so keep the hateful comments to yourselves please."

Then there is the third faction of Flat Earthers, which piled into the comments section of the above Facebook post. This group recommended not just Holocaust denial videos, but undiluted Nazism, memes glorifying Hitler, and antisemitic books by a former Ku Klux Klan leader. While the majority of Flat Earthers are not fascists, if another interest group (say, bird-watchers or people who go to Phish concerts) had the same preponderance of fascist members, you might think twice before joining your local birding club or buying a Phish T-shirt.

Belief in conspiracy theories is a unifying feature of extremist groups of every political and religious stripe. "The frequency of conspiracy theories within all these groups suggests that they play an important social and functional role within extremism itself," wrote the authors of a 2010 study. Conspiracy theories "hold extremist groups together and push them in a more extreme and sometimes violent direction."

Perhaps it was only natural, then, that some Hitler apologists and open antisemites would turn to one of the world's most extreme conspiracy theories to infuse their movements with new urgency. This fusion means that Flat Earth Nazis are, unfortunately, real.

Nothing in the bylaws of Flat Earth theory requires believers to hate Jews. Samuel Rowbotham, who birthed the theory nearly a century before Hitler took power, maintained that both Jewish and Christian texts were inherently Flat, and that the Globe Earth agenda was an attempt to subvert Christianity and Judaism alike. The globe, he wrote, is "a prolific source of irreligion and of atheism, of which its advocates are practically supporters. By defending a system which is directly opposed to that which is taught in connection with the Jewish and Christian religion they lead the more critical and daring intellects to question and deride the cosmogony and general philosophy contained in the sacred books."

But Rowbotham was writing in a different conspiratorial era than Flat Earth Facebook users. The century and a half that separated them saw a new strain of conspiracism rise, with Jews at the center of its suspicion.

Conspiracy theories, historically speaking, have seldom been very good for Jews. As one of the most visible minority groups in Europe for centuries, Jews were frequently made scapegoats for societal ills. Many of these early accusations were religious in nature. One pernicious belief, popularized in the fourth century (and only officially repudiated by the Catholic Church in 1965), held all Jews responsible for the death of Jesus Christ. By the thirteenth century, this rumor had morphed into moral panics about Jews destroying Communion wafers and ritually murdering Christians, a myth known as "blood libel." These myths helped cast Jews as the primary *other* in Christian societies, the shadowy outsider of whom almost anything could be suspected. "It was widely believed in the Renaissance that Jewish males menstruated, for example, which served as one explanation for the famous 'blood libel,'" scholar Stephen Eric Bronner writes in *A Rumor about the Jews*. "The belief that Jews murdered Christian children and consumed their blood in the matzos made for Passover in order to replenish the blood lost in menstruation" endured into the twentieth century in some circles.

When the Black Death ravaged Europe in the 1340s and 1350s, killing up to 60 percent of people in some locales, Jews were again accused of murder. A conspiracy theory emerged, blaming the plague on a powerful rabbi who had allegedly ordered followers to drop poison in major water sources across Europe. In Switzerland, multiple Jews were detained and forced to offer details about the nonexistent poisoning plot. "After a long time, having been subjected again to torture a little, he confessed in the presence of a great many trustworthy persons," reads an account of a so-called confession by a Jewish man named Agimet in 1348. No matter that Agimet's and other Jews' confessions had been obtained by torture, or that the Black Death was a bacterial infection and not the result of poison. Pogroms—ethnic massacres—swept the continent. Historian Jacob von Königshofen, who lived through the pandemic and the subsequent massacre, wrote that approximately two thousand Jews in Strasbourg were rounded up in a single 1349 incident and led to a cemetery to be burned alive. (Some, many of them children, avoided the flames by agreeing to convert to Christianity on the spot.)

For centuries, Jews across Europe faced discriminatory laws, were deprived of citizenship, and were often confined to ghettos. Only between the late eighteenth and early twentieth centuries did Jews earn more or less equal rights through a slow-rolling emancipation move-ment, the result of their appeals to the Enlightenment ideals of universal rights and individual liberties. Some European countries were simulta-neously using Enlightenment ideals to disrupt the ruling order. Rigid monarchies and powerful religious orders gave way to constitutional governments and more secular societies.

Not everyone (monarchists and social conservatives, for example) was on board. The Jews' new freedom and their old role as the bigots' go-to scapegoat made them the face of the Enlightenment for a new anti-Enlightenment backlash. Robert Wistrich, a leading scholar on anti-Jewish hatred, identified the late nineteenth century as the birth of modern antisemitism. Emancipated Jews became associated, for better or worse, with progressive ideals and modernization, Wistrich wrote, "with the Stock Exchange, the press, cultural innovation, greater sexual freedom, radical politics, and the promotion of free-thinking secularism."

Unlike the predominantly religious and ethnic discrimination of the past, the emerging modern antisemitism also viewed Jews as a cultural and political force that was upending local (read: gentile, pre-Enlightenment) tradition. Where Jewish emancipation took place, a wave of this new antisemitism was likely to follow. When Rowbotham first published *Earth Not A Globe* in 1849, it was nearly a decade before the United Kingdom would pass its Jews Relief Act, restoring Jews to equal rights with Christians. Though he raged at emerging secular and scientific trends, Rowbotham never appears to have linked the Jews with this supposed assault on Christianity.

He was among the last generation of conspiracy theorists *not* to do so. A steady and growing drumbeat of conspiracy theories blamed Jews for upheaval occurring at the end of the nineteenth and beginning of the twentieth centuries. In France, the trend manifested in the Dreyfus Affair, a decade-long political scandal that saw an army captain of Jewish heritage falsely accused and convicted of spying for the Germans. The captain, the affair's eponymous Alfred Dreyfus, was later found to be innocent, but the incident radicalized some of his countrymen, mainstreaming a conspiracy theory that characterized Jews as traitors. French antisemitism would become a national export.

A number of French texts from this time period, at least one of them completely satirical, were plagiarized and remixed into *The Protocols of the Elders of Zion*, an antisemitic forgery created by imperial Russia's secret police. The document, a hoax that purports to describe a world-domination plot by Jews and their allies, first circulated in Russia in 1903 amid an ongoing spate of pogroms, and was soon used to blame Jews for the 1905 Russian Revolution. The text, which would provide the justification for violence and genocide against Jews worldwide, became a bible for antisemitism.

"Indeed what the real *Communist Manifesto* was for marxism, the fictitious *Protocols* was for antisemitism," Bronner writes. In keeping with the conspiratorial trope linking Jews to upheaval, a popular and incorrect theory about "Judeo-Bolshevism" accused the religious minority of being behind Marxist rebellions, like the 1917 Russian Revolution.

It's easy to dismiss Flat Earthers as weirdos, an aberrant fringe separate from society at large. The same mistake cannot be made of people who believe antisemitic conspiracy theories. Far from fringe, these theorists include heroes of modern history books. In 1919, for example, the priest who was to become Pope Pius XII observed a short-lived communist uprising in Munich, and falsely identified its leader as Jewish. Winston Churchill, the British prime minister who led the United Kingdom to victory over the Nazis in World War II, was also prone to blaming Jewish people for unrest. In a 1920 article titled "Zionism versus Bolshevism," Churchill accused the Jews of orchestrating every one of the many recent uprisings, particularly the Russian Revolution. (Jews did not orchestrate the Russian Revolution.)

"From the days of Spartacus-Weishaupt to those of Karl Marx, and down to Trotsky (Russia), Bela Kun (Hungary), Rosa Luxembourg (Germany), and Emma Goldman (United States), this world-wide conspiracy for the overthrow of civilisation and for the reconstitution of society on the basis of arrested development, of envious malevolence, and impossible equality, has been steadily growing," Churchill wrote, naming recent agitators in each country. "It played . . . a definitely recognisable part in the tragedy of the French Revolution. It has been the mainspring of every subversive movement during the Nineteenth Century; and now at last this band of extraordinary personalities from the underworld of the great cities of Europe and America have gripped the Russian people by the hair of their heads and have become practically the undisputed masters of that enormous empire."

Churchill's conspiracy theory may have won over readers worried about a communist uprising in Britain, but it didn't hold up to any serious scrutiny. Adam "Spartacus" Weishaupt, the first person Churchill named, was not even Jewish, but the Catholic founder of the Bavarian Illuminati (a group that dissolved quickly before accomplishing much of anything). Goldman, an anarchist, rallied for revolution, but at the time of Churchill's writing had spent many years in prison and had been deported from the United States. Luxemburg, a Marxist philosopher, was already dead, executed by German Freikorps during a brief uprising the previous year. If these were among the most influential "underworld" figures Churchill could conjure, then their "world-wide conspiracy" seemed firmly in check.

Years later, many of the Freikorps who put down Luxemburg's uprising would fall in line with the Nazis and help push an actual plot to upend the German government. The Nazis, in turn, would make use of both *The Protocols of the Elders of Zion* and Churchill in their antisemitic propaganda; a Nazi poster titled "Das Jüdische Komplott" ("The Jewish Conspiracy") described Churchill as one of the "henchmen" under control of "the Jewish Puppeteers." Those conspiratorial claims would provide the justification for the Nazis' murder of some six million Jews in the Holocaust.

Overtly antisemitic conspiracy theories went somewhat out of vogue after World War II ended and the Holocaust's incalculable horrors were revealed. The Elders of Zion were unseated as the primary villains of conspiracy culture, and replaced by imaginary plotters of more ambiguous religious origins, like the fictional New World Order and One World Government. Real entities, like the Bilderberg Group and the United Nations, became the subject of new suspicions. Much of the underlying conspiratorial architecture remained the same, though, as if truthers had been too busy to reimagine world-domination plots and had simply swapped out "the Jews" for another demonized entity. Sometimes, this was almost certainly intentional; for instance, the far-right anti-communist John Birch Society often invoked Jewish families and the myth of Judeo-Bolshevism in its appeals to paranoia.

Conspiracy theories are not all inherently antisemitic, scholar Jovan Byford writes, "but it is also true that discernible within many conspiracy narratives, even those that are not explicitly targeting Jews, are worrying, and often subtle, reminders of the conspiracy theory's earlier, overtly antisemitic incarnations."

Modern conspiracy narratives are so steeped in antisemitic imagery that tropes about villainous Jews can thrive even in populations with virtually no Jewish presence. In 2011, it was reported that only two Jews—a pair of elderly cousins—held Malaysian passports. Nevertheless, a study published the following year found a thriving antisemitic conspiracy culture that strongly correlated with anti-Chinese feelings. "Belief in the Jewish conspiracy theory among Malaysian Malays appears to serve ideological needs and as a mask for anti-Chinese sentiment," giving conspiracy theorists a new sense of control over complex international relations, researchers wrote.

Or take the case of Aum Shinrikyo, the Japanese doomsday cult responsible for the 1995 sarin gas attacks on Tokyo's subway system. Though Jews in Japan were a statistically negligible group (a 1992 estimate put them at fewer than one thousand in a population of 124 million), they became central to Aum's conspiratorial dogma, which warned of an apocalyptic war that would be brought on by the United States and the Jews. Antisemitic writings had seen a surge in Japan in the early 1990s, but Aum Shinrikyo took the paranoia to extremes. Two months before cult members released deadly gas in the subway, the group's monthly publication announced that it "hereby formally declares war on the 'world shadow government' that murders untold numbers of people and, while hiding behind sonorous phrases and high-sounding principles, plans to brainwash and control the rest. Japanese, awaken! The enemy's plot has long since torn our lives into shreds." It was the same conspiracy theory pushed by *The Protocols* and Hitler (Aum Shinrikyo's leader was a fan), retooled for Japan.

So it really doesn't matter that Jews have nothing to do with the shape of the earth. Theories about worldwide domination schemes—be they on a globe or a flat plane—fall so frequently into antisemitic tropes that unless believers explicitly reject these old prejudices, they risk accidentally supporting them. And some Flat Earthers skip right past the accidental antisemitism and lean all the way into its most overt forms.

Such is the case with Eric Dubay, the video maker who kick-started the Flat Earth theory's YouTube renaissance in 2014. Though Dubay is no longer the type to show up to a Flat Earth International Conference (having become "one of our more fringe figures," as Mark Sargent put it to me delicately), his books and videos have achieved massive reach since he emerged on the scene. Parents in Flat Earth Facebook groups still routinely recommend his illustrated Flat Earth children's book for their homeschooled kids.

This is unfortunate, because, unlike other picture book authors, Dubay's side projects involve Flat Earth rap albums with lyrics like "you are blind so fuck what you say, I'll expose the flat Earth and Heil Hitler all day." I'm not quoting him out of context. The line is one of the more polite lyrics I can excerpt from a song called "Blood Rituals," which appears on Dubay's *The Flat Earth Movement* album alongside tracks like "Bruce Hitler" and "Goyim Revolution," which includes clips of longtime Ku Klux Klan leader David Duke. He has multiple Flat Earth albums in this vein, all of them morally and musically exhausting.

YouTube banned some of Dubay's videos for reasons of hate speech in 2018, he claimed. But on an alternative video website, a Dubay "documentary" titled *Adolf Hitler vs. The Jew World Order* has tens of thousands of views. Even within the sphere of Flat Earth belief, the video description is objectively unhinged, arguing incorrectly that Hitler was a misunderstood pacifist. Dubay writes that "unlike the demonic portrait that history has painted of him, Hitler was beloved by his people and he wanted nothing but peace. From 1933-1940 Hitler tried repeatedly to make peace with the Jews and 'allied' forces even calling for complete disarmament on everyone's part. He was nominated for the Nobel peace prize in 1939, the very year he was attacked on his own soil after repeatedly pleading for peaceful solutions. In 1936 99% of German registered voters went out to vote and 98.8% voted for Hitler."

Impressively, almost every point in this video description is either misleading or outright incorrect, from small points like Hitler's Nobel Prize nomination (by a lone anti-fascist who had intended it as a satirical critique of the Nobel process and quickly rescinded the nomination) to history-shaping matters like Hitler's habit of offering countries offensively unworkable peace treaties and invading regardless of whether the treaties were signed.

Dubay's groupies (Dubay has groupies) are unbothered by these historical trifles. Some, in fact, have tried chasing Dubay's niche stardom.

Steven Hildebran, a Colorado man, became locally notorious in 2019 by shouting "Heil Hitler" at LGBTQ events and repeatedly brandishing anti-gay signs outside drag shows, sometimes while dressed in riot gear. He attended at least one far-right rally while carrying a large sign that described the Globe Earth as a Jewish conspiracy, documenting his exploits on Instagram, where he went by "Flat Plane Level Conquered Earth." One of Hildebran's worst digital sins, however, was an attempt to join Eric Dubay in the genre of Flat Earth Nazi rap music. A fan of Dubay's pro-Hitler tirades ("Sieg Heil," he commented on Dubay's *Adolf Hitler vs. The Jew World Order* video), Hildebran managed to be even less skilled than Dubay at rapping.

"Excuse me, but have you researched Flat Earth? We really ought to figure out the universe. Your sense of reality will get hurt. Can't find a picture of the earth's curve," Hildebran mumbled on one of his rap songs, over a beat sampled from what sounded like ice-cream truck music. Elsewhere on the track, he complained: "On Facebook, I always get censored. On Facebook, I'm a habitual offender. I always get caught for pics of Hitler." Another one of his raps is about lynching and burning gay men at a specific LGBTQ-friendly Colorado Springs comics shop.

Not to be outdone, at least one neo-Nazi Flat Earther conscripted an entire heavy metal band to perform a song about the conspiracy theory. Jacob Laskey, an Oregon-based neo-Nazi, spent nearly a decade in prison for drawing swastikas on bricks and throwing them through a synagogue window. After his release from prison in 2015, he began selling Holocaust denial books he'd written behind bars and making Flat Earth videos, including a music video for an anti-globe rock song. Unfortunately for his budding vlog career, the Flat Earth YouTube scene was already supersaturated by the time Laskey started making videos. Before he could achieve any real YouTube fame, he was reimprisoned for stabbing someone.

Dubay might not attend Flat Earth conferences (last I checked, he was living in Thailand), but that hasn't kept a Dubay-style brand of antisemitism from sneaking into the meetups. The 2018 FEIC featured a large merchandise room, like a shopping mall for conspiracy theorists. Spread through a hotel ballroom were tables laden with Flat Earth T-shirts, Flat Earth books, Flat Earth knives engraved by a lady who later accused me of terrible things via email, CDs with Flat Earth music, and a camping stove brand with no clear Flat Earth connection. I had my sights set on a reproduction of a Rowbotham-era Flat Earth map, but over the course of conversations with vendors at three neighboring tables, I decided to forgo the map in favor of buying several bags of junk food from a nearby vending machine and eating them in the mental oasis of the hotel parking lot.

At the first table, I chatted with Mike, a nice man wearing a sonnenrad, one of the most recognizable symbols of the neo-Nazi movement, on a gleaming necklace over his shirt. A sonnenrad, variously called a black sun or a sun wheel, is hard to mistake for anything else. It looks like a crooked wheel, its spokes formed by the same S-shaped runes that formed the Nazi SS sigil. I asked Mike whether he knew it was a Nazi thing.

Sure, he said, he was aware of the sonnenrad's legacy as a "more popularized, misinterpreted trigger symbol," but he was choosing to wear it as "an ancient symbol of the stars. The twenty-four positions of the Big Dipper . . . an ancient, cosmic symbol of peace."

Here's the thing: The swastika, before its appropriation by the Nazis, was a religious symbol associated with faiths like Jainism. It's still a symbol in Jain iconography. But the Nazis made the swastika so synonymous with their administration that, in the Western imagination, it really only signifies Hitler's regime. If you wear a swastika T-shirt on a public stroll in the United States, you're probably a jerk, not a Jain.

Sonnenrad wearers have even less of an excuse. The symbol's pre-Nazi origins are shrouded in historical debate, with the sonnenrad only truly emerging in connection with the Nazi Heinrich Himmler and his genocidal SS forces. After the Nazis' fall, the symbol became popular with neo-Nazis, and featured prominently on the cover of a manifesto by Brenton Tarrant, a white supremacist who murdered fifty-one worshippers at a mosque in Christchurch, New Zealand, in 2019. Tarrant, who livestreamed the massacre on Facebook, titled his manifesto after a conspiracy theory about immigrants "replacing" white populations. The theory is often paired with antisemitic tropes that accuse Jews of organizing mass migration in order to overthrow white majorities. (A different neo-Nazi would cite the same conspiracy theory when he killed eleven worshippers at a synagogue in Pittsburgh in 2018.)

If the swastika is a chart-topping single, the sonnenrad is a deep cut: less mainstream but well known among true fans. Mike's Big Dipper explanation was particularly obscure; I had to Google it to discern what the hell he was talking about, and even then I only got a few hits, largely from the notorious troll forum 4chan, as well as from a blog called *Daily Bitcoin News*, where a blogger explained why various Nazi symbols were, in his opinion, actually not racist.

I moved on to the next vendor table, where I chatted with the saleswoman about the Flat Earth cover-up. I asked her, Who was bothering to conceal the shape of the earth? "The CIA, the FBI," she told me. "The Jews are involved too." She started in on a theory about today's Jews not being "true Jews" but nefarious forces sullying the name of a once-noble people. I excused myself and started flipping through books at the next table, where I picked up a copy of a tome titled *The Greatest Lie on Earth: Proof That Our World Is Not a Moving Globe* and turned to a chapter titled "Mind Control." The second paragraph was a long block quote from *The Protocols of the Elders of Zion*. Much of the book carried on in this manner, wandering off topic from Flat Earth to dive into nearly every antisemitic conspiracy I've ever encountered, including some real throwbacks, like medieval tales of Jews eating Christian children. "Judaism is a religion of hate," author Edward Hendrie writes, characterized by "the hatred of Christians and Gentiles of all races." Hendrie goes big on Judeo-Bolshevism, accusing Russian revolutionary Vladimir Lenin of being a Jewish conspirator, because one of his grandparents might have been a Jew who converted to Christianity. The culmination is a picture of Jews as a political menace and evil incarnate. "Communism reveals Judaism as a satanic conspiracy against God and man," Hendrie writes.

This goes on for more than six hundred pages, and prominent members of the conspiracy community have read each one, multiple times. Texe Marrs, a notoriously conspiratorial (now deceased) radio talk show host and minister, promoted *The Greatest Lie on Earth* and other Hendrie books, in which the author blames Jews for the world's troubles. Nathan Thompson, the founder of the Flat Earth Facebook group, hails the book as a "masterpiece" and drives around with it in his car. Maybe that explains why, when asked in a popular video from a convention, who he thought was concealing the Flat Earth truth, Thompson replied by rubbing his hands together greedily. The gesture appeared to be reference to "the Happy Merchant," a wildly antisemitic cartoon first published on a white-supremacist website with a caption comparing Jews to rats. As if to eliminate any confusion, Thompson clarified that he definitely meant the Jews. "Some *grabblers*, you know," he said, invoking an antisemitic slur. "Most Jewish people are just mom-and-pop deli owners. What I use is the word 'Zionist.' So these are people that are hellbent on world domination."

Thompson's group amassed more than 125,000 members before Facebook removed it in late 2020 (he soon made a replacement group). During the first group's prime, I liked to play a horrible game with myself where I opened up its page and searched for terms like "Hitler" and "Holocaust," just to see what turned up. Though Thompson moderated with an apparent iron fist (swear words resulted in an "IMMEDIATE ban," per group rules), some eyebrow-raising posts managed to slip through every couple days. Often, Thompson was their author. "Everyone here is free to say the Holocaust didn't happen," he posted, evidently unprompted, during the group's first year of existence.

In fairness to Thompson, his is not the only major Facebook group with a pesky Holocaust denial problem. The group Flat Earth No Trolls (forty-eight thousand members in spring 2020) gives Thompson's page a run for its money. One evening in early 2019, I opened Facebook to find both groups independently engaged in heated Holocaust denial. ("Half of you will read this and call me an antisemite, which is a totally meaningless phrase," Thompson was saying. "Nobody has a problem with people speaking Samaritan languages.")

Thompson is, unambiguously, an antisemite, but he's also a nobody outside the Flat Earth scene. His biggest film credits include an appearance in a Flat Earth documentary, and the time he went viral for yelling at the NASA employee in Starbucks. But Owen Benjamin, the headline speaker at the 2019 Flat Earth International Conference, has real Hollywood titles under his belt. An actor and comedian, albeit one currently experiencing a career downturn, Benjamin has a wide reach and a history of grossly antisemitic remarks.

In a 2019 video, he described himself as a "big fan" of Hitler's paintings. Said paintings consist of tepid watercolors that got Hitler twice rejected from art school, and don't merit any praise unless you're trying to kick up some controversy. Except in this case, Benjamin's art critiques were among his least controversial remarks about Hitler.

"Really what he was trying to do was clean Germany, clean it of the parasites, of the fleas. He did not hate Jews. He hated filth and he was trying to clean up," Benjamin said in the video.

In another clip from early 2019, Benjamin trotted out an antisemitic trope to blame Jews for pornography, then incorrectly claimed that in Dante's *Inferno* Jews and gay people were condemned to the innermost circles of hell. "Gays and Jews were considered the worst of the worst," he said. "Why? Because if they get power, they will destroy your entire civilization. Has anyone not seen that happening?" Elsewhere, he has appeared in videos with famous white supremacists and promoted Holocaust denial and fake quotes from the Jewish text the Talmud.

Benjamin likes to complain that his "politically incorrect" comedy has cost him valuable Hollywood deals. The truth is that comedy coddles figures like Benjamin. "Just kidding" is a common last resort for racists trying to avoid consequences. Accordingly, a whole genre of Benjamin-like jokers have sprung up, who say bigoted things and give fans plausible deniability for laughing. An employee style guide from the neo-Nazi news site The Daily Stormer explains the dynamic well. "The tone of the site should be light," reads the manual, which leaked in 2017. "Most people are not comfortable with material that comes across as vitriolic, raging, nonironic hatred. The unindoctrinated should not be able to tell if we are joking or not. . . . This is obviously a ploy and I actually do want to gas kikes. But that's neither here nor there." (Elsewhere in the handbook: "Always Blame the Jews for Everything.")

Without that veneer of comedy, Benjamin would have a harder time getting away with writing and performing songs like "That N**** Stole My Bike." When Benjamin leaned way into overt antisemitism in 2019, at least one of his Jewish former fans had a change of heart. "Some of this stuff really hurts me as a Jew," the ex-fan told the Jewish Telegraphic

Agency. "It made me rethink my whole time with him. Was 'this n-word stole my bike' really actually racist?"

And that's how I ended up listening to Benjamin rail against the Jews to uproarious laughter in a packed FEIC auditorium. "Jewish hats are fucking retarded," Benjamin was saying as I left the room to meet with conference organizer Robbie Davidson. "When you see a guy with a weird hat, don't listen to him about the shape of the earth."

My father is Jewish. I'd mentioned it to a Flat Earth couple that morning, when they asked about my religious beliefs. I'd told them that I respected my father's Judaism and my mother's Christianity but never attached myself to either faith. What I wish I'd said was that my relationship with religion is more complicated than the blunt-force logic and false binaries that conspiracy culture will allow. That I don't subscribe to any religion but that there, among books accusing historical figures of conspiracy for potentially having a Jewish-born grandparent, my religious choices hardly mattered. That I'm not sure whether I'm a Jew but that antisemites are damn certain. That neo-Nazis have read my reporting, recognized my often-Jewish surname, and sent me pictures of the Auschwitz death camp. That a white nationalist YouTuber, visibly drunk, made a video trying to guess how many Jewish grandparents I have. That QAnon believers have added me to a public list of supposed Jews they suspect of crimes (a list that includes several of my gentile journalist peers). That for so many centuries, Jews were defined not by their own choices, but in negation: by the places they couldn't live, the rights they couldn't hold, by the ghettos and cultures that formed in the recesses that Jews were allowed to occupy. That theirs—I'm never sure whether I have the authority to say "ours"—is the history of a people furiously refusing demands to die.

Historian Paul Hanebrink writes that, in the medieval imagination, the figure of the Jew served as an abstract threat around which Christianity—then embroiled in messy sectarian infighting—could rally and solidify. Antisemitic conspiracy theories were a cohesive force.

"Jews and Judaism gave coherence to a variety of cultural visions by suggesting what their inversion might look like," Hanebrink writes. The idea of Jews attaining power conjured to mind a frightening dystopia, one which had to be defeated. "Even as it was imagined, Christian civilization seemed in dire need of defense."

Antisemites need Jews, or else the logic of their world collapses. What I wish I'd told that Flat Earth couple was that I'm an atheist of partial-Jewish heritage, and a Jew when conspiracy theorists need me to be. I wondered whether the couple was among the crowd laughing at Benjamin's jokes.

Out in the lobby, I asked Davidson whether he was worried about antisemitism in the movement and, although I didn't mention Benjamin by name, the comedian's muffled voice was still booming through the auditorium speakers and into the hall.

"Not really," Davidson said, adding that the FEIC speakers had unanimously approved adding Benjamin to the roster. (Davidson had made sure to get their sign-off after the previous year's debacle with Logan Paul.) "Owen will get branded that [antisemitic] all the time, but he's got great Jew friends, right?"

Minutes earlier, Benjamin had described one of his Jewish friends thus: "David Weiss took all his Jew powers of marketing and app making and made it selfless. He's the Selfless Jew," he told the FEIC audience, describing a fellow Flat Earther who'd developed a Flat Earth app. "It was so funny seeing all his Jew powers of marketing and app making, but none of it was out of greed. You know, he's a Jewnicorn." The joke is that unselfish Jews are unicorn-rare.

I called Weiss after the conference. Weiss who, like me, has never actively practiced Judaism, said that he and Owen Benjamin were friends and that he understood Benjamin's remarks to be comedic in nature. People "will make Jewish jokes, and I laugh at them," Weiss said. "They make bald jokes, and I get offended at those, and they make Black jokes and, you know, I look to my left, look to my right, before I laugh to make sure there's no Black people around, but it's just comedy in my opinion."

Weiss said he didn't believe in structural racism. That said, he told me that his friend, a Black Flat Earther "just got so upset at Owen, 'cause Owen was making Black jokes. But they were just jokes."

I asked whether other people in the movement treated Weiss differently for his Jewish heritage. "They try to, but I ignore it and then they just fade away and they don't bother me at all," he said. "You know, people call me the Jewnicorn because I'm a rare Jew. Owen made up that name. Should I be offended? Absolutely not. There's not a lot of Jewish people like me that don't get easily offended at some of these things. And maybe there are—I just don't know them. But anybody that doesn't like me because I'm Jewish—I mean, I barely even know that I'm Jewish. I was born Jewish. I don't practice Judaism."

In the FEIC lobby, as Benjamin's speech about "Jew hats" carried on in the adjacent room, conference organizer Robbie Davidson continued. "But I don't really see antisemitism. I see a lot of people skeptical of Zionists or the Jews in Hollywood, but I don't think it's a blanket statement like 'All Jews are bad.' I just think that, like, a lot of powerful people in Hollywood, they are Jewish families, right? There are bad people in every group. I know people's language can be aggressive, but I think it's more of an immaturity. I think as they mature, they'll kind of see it."

Benjamin was thirty-nine. The ensuing months did not mature him out of antisemitism. Less than a month after the conference, he was banned from Facebook and Instagram for his posts, which included a cartoon mocking teenage Holocaust victim Anne Frank, describing her in sexualized terms and falsely accusing her father of inventing her as a "fanfiction" character. "I never openly mocked the holocaust so much until I found out Anne Frank was fake," Benjamin wrote on Instagram, adding that "I legit don't care if I hurt your feelings Jews." The cartoon had a watermark with the skull-and-crossbones insignia of a Nazi SS division. Benjamin soon returned to Twitter and YouTube (other platforms from which he'd been banned) to tweet conspiracy theories about Jews being the source of all wars, and to more or less abandon all comedic pretense and accuse Jews of being thieves. "What's up with the Jews?" he asked in a video. "Because there is something going on with it." Later in 2020, he would join a wave of antisemites who accused Jews of orchestrating the COVID-19 pandemic.

Contrary to Davidson's suggestion, most people do not undergo a second adolescence that delivers them from bigotry in their late thirties. But Benjamin's slide into open antisemitism aligned with a more global shift in attitudes. The back half of the 2010s, when Benjamin turned a conspiratorial corner, saw rising hostilities against Jews. The Anti-Defamation League, a US organization monitoring antisemitism, saw a 99 percent increase in reported antisemitic incidents from 2015 to 2018. In an ADL survey of US Jews in early 2020, nearly two-thirds of respondents said they felt less safe than they had ten years earlier, with more than 10 percent saying they had made efforts to avoid being identified as Jewish, for fear of antisemitic attacks. The rise in US-based violence mirrored a worldwide trend in organized antisemitic movements. During those years, far-right ruling parties in Poland and Hungary revived old conspiracy theories about Jewish domination plots. Back in the United States, a previously loose coalition of racists unified around the mantle of the "alt-right," a movement that peddled fascist talking points through memes and 4chan jargon. The alt-right movement made itself unavoidable in August 2017, when members held a deadly rally in Charlottesville, Virginia. During a torchlit march, those white supremacists chanted "Jews will not replace us," in reference to a bogus theory about Jews trying to make white people a minority. The following day, a neo-Nazi participant drove his car into a crowd of anti-racist protesters, murdering one and wounding dozens more. In the ensuing years, that killer's ideological allies would release conspiratorial manifestos online when they murdered Muslims at a New Zealand mosque, Latino shoppers in a Texas Walmart, and Jews at synagogues across the United States.

The trend shows no signs of abating. In August 2020, a scheduled Republican National Convention speaker recommended a series of QAnon-associated tweets that also promoted *The Protocols of the Elders of Zion*. "The Protocols of the Elders of Zion is not a fabrication," read one of the tweets she recommended. "And, it certainly is not anti-semetic [sic] to point out this fact." (Her RNC speech was canceled after one of my colleagues at the *Daily Beast* reported on her tweets.) That same year also saw a wellspring of antisemitism related to the COVID-19 pandemic, which conspiracy theorists (some Flat Earthers, like Benjamin, among them) falsely derided as a Jewish world-domination hoax.

Some fascists would rather have nothing to do with Flat Earth—but increasingly, they can't seem to disentangle themselves. When the alt-right adopted a cartoon frog named Pepe as its unofficial mascot, Flat Earthers tagged along by naming as their mascot a nearly identical cartoon character named Fepe. When Andrew Anglin, the founder of The Daily Stormer, poked fun at Flat Earth in an article in April 2017, he sent the site into a bitter feud, with warring factions of neo-Nazis calling each other ridiculous in the comments section. Readers with usernames like InterJew, 3rdRicht, and SouthernFascist abandoned Anglin to leap to Flat Earth's defense. A commenter called WhiteLiberty claimed that scientific experiments are supposed to be reproducible, therefore massive cosmological events are unscientific because they can't be recreated in a laboratory. "You can't reproduce Big Bang. It's not science," WhiteLiberty argued, in a weird interpretation of zeteticism.

Anglin might have been surprised to learn that so many of his readers were Flat Earthers, but I was less shocked. Conspiracy theories are almost always intertwined with each other, and antisemitism—the underpinning of Nazism—is a conspiracy theory itself. It argues that the world is not as it seems and that a murderable minority is to blame.

Over the course of the Trump presidency, the far right mobilized around conspiracy theories about QAnon, voter fraud, and immigration. Just as fear and insecurity turned many people toward conspiratorial belief in the first place, the far right's political program of rage and domination gave those conspiracy theorists a new outlet. In the administration's final months, anti-democracy demonstrators repeatedly gathered at state and national government buildings to falsely accuse Trump's opponents of stealing the election. During one such rally, at the Arizona State Capitol, one demonstrator brought a massive Flat Earth poster. At the largest of these demonstrations, a protest at the nation's capital on January 6, 2021, I spotted at least one vocal Flat Earth fan (Britney Spears's ex-husband Jason Alexander) in attendance. Later, other members of the crowd broke into the Capitol building. Among them was a California man who shared Flat Earth YouTube videos, which a prosecutor would later cite when the man faced federal charges for the Capitol attack. Another rioter was photographed wearing a T-shirt that glorified the Auschwitz concentration camp, where more than a million people were murdered. The T-shirt felt like an attack on memory itself. It reminded me that an uncomfortable number of my fellow citizens regard the Holocaust as a hoax or, worse, a reality that merits only celebration.

I asked David Weiss, the Jewish Flat Earther, about Holocaust skepticism in the Flat Earth movement. He replied that maybe the Holocaust, as well as the perception of Holocaust denialism in Flat Earth, was overblown. Poll any room of one hundred people, not just Flat Earthers, and probably at least one would have their doubts about the genocide, he argued. Hell, even he was questioning some accounts of the Holocaust after watching conspiracy videos on it, although he agreed that Eric Dubay maybe took the theory "too far."

"He put out some good information, and then he poisoned the well with this Hitler stuff," Weiss said.

"Poisoning the well" is an interesting metaphor. A conspiratorial phrase, it refers to attempts to discredit a movement. I hear it often in truther scenes, usually when one theorist accuses another of selling out or betraying the cause.

I can no longer hear it, however, without remembering the victims of literal well-poisoning conspiracy theories: the Jewish people falsely accused of contaminating water supplies during the Black Death. In the plague years, Europeans sought solace by blaming this minority group of outsiders for their troubles. Nearly seven hundred years later, in the plague year of 2020, those same conspiratorial impulses still raged, this time with Flat Earthers like Weiss's friend Owen Benjamin blaming shadowy plotters for the COVID-19 pandemic.

For Jews, the eternal outside group and the family of so many Weisses and Weills, those theories seldom end happily.

9 | Away from the Edge

THE WORLD HAS flattened as I've watched.

I began one morning in late July 2020 the unhealthy way I often do, which meant opening Facebook on my phone and reading updates in Flat Earth groups while my eyes were still unfocused. Everyone was sharing the same video. In it, a group of people in lab coats claimed that the COVID-19 virus, which at that point had killed more than 150,000 Americans, was an overhyped illness that could be cured using a few dubious drugs. The doctors—a hastily assembled coalition of private-practice physicians, backed by conservative lobbyists—trotted out some tired talking points that had circulated among the political right for months. Americans shouldn't have to wear face masks to prevent the spread of the virus, they said, adding that the teachers' unions that wanted to close schools were selfish and that social media companies were unfairly censoring COVID-skeptical conservatives. Et cetera. Even during a once-in-a-century pandemic, this stuff was getting repetitive.

The video had muted notes of conspiracism throughout. "We are not held down by the virus as much as we're being held down by the spiderweb of fear," a doctor said in the clip's opening moments. "That spiderweb is all around us and it's constricting us and it's draining the lifeblood of the American people, American society, and American economy." Blearily, I noted the parallels, probably unintentional, to antisemitic conspiracy theories: the imagery of a spider, the parasite draining volkish blood.

I didn't have to wait long to hear the less muted notes of conspiracy. One of the video's most notable personalities was Stella Immanuel, a pediatrician and minister who had spent years claiming that various illnesses were actually caused by people having sex with demons in their sleep. At other junctures she'd claimed that the government was run by "reptilians," that doctors were using alien DNA to make medicine, including a microchip vaccine that would prevent people from being religious; that "children need to be whipped," and that gay people are terrorists. And here she was among this collective of doctors, falsely claiming to have a COVID miracle cure.

All of this was pretty standard fare for Flat Earth groups, which, with the onset of the COVID-19 pandemic in the spring of 2020, had become host to a dense slurry of medical misinformation. But less common, I realized as I squinted into the bright rectangle of my phone, was the video's spread. Most conspiracy videos I've watched have limited audiences and struggle to crack a million views. Nearly overnight, this video had racked up more than thirteen million views, and when I opened Twitter—ah, that would do it. President Donald Trump and his eldest-and-loudest son had both tweeted the video approvingly, demon-sex doctor and all.

The conspiracy world was leaking into Americans' daily life. It had been for a while.

I began actively monitoring the Flat Earth community in 2017, half as a joke. Whenever the day's news felt too crazy, I could check back in on the Flat Earth movement and feel a sense of comparative normalcy. At least *most* of the country had a firmer tether in reality, I consoled myself in those moments. But the ensuing years stripped me of that smugness. Over the course of a wildly conspiratorial Trump presidency, the United States and the world at large had started to embrace Flat Earth–level delusions.

Some of that unraveling came from public figures' open acceptance of Flat Earth theory. In February 2019, a city council member in Gatineau, Canada, appeared to champion Flat Earth in online writings. That same month, 3 percent of Britons in a two-thousand-person poll stated that Earth was definitely or probably flat, echoing another poll that gave comparable figures of Flat Earth belief for Americans. In June 2019, a minor-league Spanish soccer team changed its name to Flat Earth FC after its owner endorsed the theory. Reality television personality Tila Tequila announced her Flat Earth belief in 2016, as did rapper B.o.B, followed a few years later by Deftones guitarist Stephen Carpenter. Basketball star Kyrie Irving came out as a Flat Earther in 2017 and later retracted his statements, but he accidentally prompted a bevy of professional athletes, like Super Bowl champion Sammy Watkins and Seattle Seahawks backup quarterback Geno Smith, to question the earth's shape.

Reality TV stars and professional athletes like these are, of course, liable to do all kinds of questionable things, like claim to have been Adolf Hitler in a past life (Tila Tequila) or sign with the not-especially-good 2014 Buffalo Bills (Sammy Watkins). But while B.o.B. and Kyrie Irving were giving much-mocked interviews about Flat Earth, a serious conspiratorial movement was entrenching itself in US politics, with real consequences for the world at large.

As it surged in popularity during the Trump presidency, I'd seen the Flat Earth movement grow increasingly entangled with political conspiracy movements like Pizzagate and its successor, QAnon. The Flat Earth Facebook groups I monitored had become awash not just in globe skeptics, but in ones who now accused Hillary Clinton of removing a child's face and wearing it. One book vendor at the 2019 Flat Earth International Conference didn't appear to have any books on Flat Earth at all but urgently wanted to sell me texts about satanic child-trafficking.

Flat Earth wasn't the only community being annexed by this movement, which also believed that Trump was on the cusp of executing his opponents for occult sex crimes against children. By the 2020 election, an increasingly comingled conspiracy movement composed of QAnon and Flat Earth believers was converting a paranoid wing of the Republican Party itself. Ninety-seven QAnon supporters ran for Congress in 2020. Lauren Witzke, a Delaware Republican who won her party's US Senate primary, endorsed both QAnon and Flat Earth, the latter on a radio show hosted by an antisemitic monarchist, who soon became Witzke's campaign manager. Witzke lost to Democratic senator Chris Coons in the general election, but other QAnon candidates had more luck. Two won election to Congress in 2020. One, Rep. Marjorie Taylor Greene of Georgia, had previously made videos endorsing QAnon, and Facebook posts blaming wildfires on lasers in space. She ran unopposed even after she invoked an antisemitic conspiracy theory to call a prominent Jewish philanthropist a "Nazi," and claimed Muslims were carrying out an "invasion of our government." As new wingnuts like Greene took office, the leader of the party was radicalizing in real time. Trump and his campaign appeared to court QAnon fans on social media, with Trump retweeting QAnon personalities fourteen times on a single day in July 2020.

People turn to conspiracy theories in moments of instability. "Conspiracy theories are a natural reaction to social situations that elicit fear and uncertainty," psychologist Jan-Willem van Prooijen writes. "Specifically, the more strongly people experience such aversive emotions, the more likely it is that they assign blame for distressing events to different groups."

Trump, whose chaotic presidency was guided by some of the United States' darkest tendences, might be seen as both a product and an accelerator of those paranoid conditions. He rose to political prominence while pushing a conspiracy theory that falsely claimed Barack Obama, the first Black president, was not born in the United States. Trump and other Western right-wing populists who won elections in the mid-2010s did so in a time of surging income inequality, accompanied by growing fears, on the right, of immigration. Across the pond, following a sustained disinformation campaign that maligned Muslims and immigrants, the United Kingdom voted to leave the European Union in 2016. A 2018 University of Cambridge study found that Trump and Brexit voters were much more likely than their opponents' supporters to believe conspiracy theories about immigration, with nearly half of Trump and Brexit voters believing the government was hiding "the truth" about immigration.

If Americans were already susceptible to conspiratorial belief before the 2016 presidential election, the outbreak of the COVID-19 pandemic in spring 2020 optimized them for it. A once-in-a-lifetime combination of plague and financial meltdown created a firestorm of fear and uncertainty. Lockdown measures, designed to curb the virus's spread by keeping people indoors, drove people online en masse. There, while trying to connect remotely with work or friends, many struck up isolated lives in front of the computer. This constant online-ness exposed perhaps an unprecedented number of people to conspiracy theories. Seventy-one percent of nearly ten thousand Americans surveyed in a June 2020 poll had heard a conspiracy that claimed COVID-19 was planned in advance by powerful elites. A quarter of respondents said they thought the theory was definitely or probably true.

Facebook groups centered around skepticism of COVID-19 soared in membership as the death count climbed. By mid-August 2020, when the virus's US death count had surpassed 163,000, nearly three million COVID-19 truthers were members of 1,150 US-based Facebook groups protesting measures to contain the disease, researchers found. An internal Facebook investigation reported on by NBC News that same month revealed approximately three million members in QAnon Facebook groups, too. (Notably, the Facebook spokesperson who discussed the data with NBC requested anonymity due to fear of harassment from QAnon followers.) A Pew study found that, while only about a quarter of Americans had heard of QAnon in February 2020, nearly half knew about it by September.

Trump, who spent the spring retweeting conspiracy theorists and parroting medical hoaxes on television, did little to inspire sanity. He shared videos of phony doctors like Stella Immanuel (the demon-sex lady). He voiced support for conspiratorial anti-lockdown protesters. When some of those protesters were later implicated in a plot to kidnap the governor of Michigan, Trump doubled down on his criticism of the governor.

It seemed almost inevitable, in these circumstances, that people who would normally scoff at Flat Earthers would begin watching their videos about coronavirus conspiracy theories. Nathan Roberts (one of several Nates to give presentations at the Flat Earth Intentional Conference) racked up millions of views on a video that falsely claimed protective face masks were a human rights violation. Using the same confrontational tactics that made "flat-smacking" videos a hit, Roberts prowled a supermarket, telling people, incorrectly, that they could cite a religious exemption to avoid the store's face mask requirements. Other previously fringe figures, like Stella Immanuel, suddenly became stars among the conspiracy-curious, while documentary-style hoax videos, like *Plandemic*, won over the newly paranoid to become bona fide hits.

All the while, Flat Earth happily merged with other up-and-coming conspiracy theories, sometimes even to other conspiracy theorists' annoyance. "NO FLAT EARTH POSTS OR DISCUSSIONS ARE ALLOWED," read the rules on a Facebook group for a theory about the apocalypse. In Wisconsin, a pharmacist accused of deliberately damaging COVID-19 vaccines (which he believed were harmful) was revealed to be a Flat Earther, who believed the sky is a "shield put up by the Government to prevent individuals from seeing God," according to an FBI agent's testimony.

When Trump contested his election loss at the end of the year (at which point more than a quarter million Americans had died of COVID-19), I watched years of conspiratorial movement-building rally around him. He and his followers alleged an increasingly nefarious and impossible scheme of voter fraud designed to boot him out of office.

Distressingly few elected Republicans challenged Trump's claims to victory. One Republican who did, then congressman Denver Riggleman of Virginia, likened Trump's claims of voter fraud to Flat Earth belief. "You have crossed the Rubicon, you jumped on the crazy train and you're headed into the cliffs that guard the flat earth," Riggleman told *Yahoo! News* in November 2020, when it became apparent that Trump would not concede defeat. In promoting blatantly fake theories about the election, supported by lawyers who tweeted QAnon slogans, Trump was warping truth in ways I used to witness only on small conspiratorial Facebook pages. The fringe wasn't fringe anymore.

Every day that I clocked in to work to report on this alternate reality, I felt like I was back at a Flat Earth conference. When two QAnon-backing lawyers (one of whom had been on the Trump campaign's payroll days earlier) held a rally in support of overturning the election results, they invited onstage a young woman who asked what Trump fans could say "to friends or loved ones who think we're crazy." It was the same question I'd heard during question-and-answer panels at Flat Earth events. As I watched a livestream of that rally, I recognized someone in the comments section as a QAnon follower I'd interviewed previously. Earlier that year, she'd told me she'd converted to conspiracy belief after researching alternative COVID-19 theories.

Other signs of conspiratorial rot appeared in my personal life. A Facebook post about the temporary COVID-related closure of a restaurant in my nine-thousand-person hometown attracted comments full of QAnon memes. A close friend visited her own hometown to find her father promoting dangerous miracle cures based on Stella Immanuel's claims. While I pushed my baby in a stroller during the preelection plague months, a man confronted me on the sidewalk with a baby-in-a-stroller-height dog, yelling "Trump 2020! That mask is for nothing!" very close to my face.

I would like my old neighbors to stop invoking a fictional cannibalism ring when the diner down the road takes basic health precautions during a pandemic. I would like to live through an election devoid of conspiracy theories about vote rigging and racial minorities. But when an increasingly vocal population believes they live on a completely different planet, how can I find common ground for conversation? When some weirdo is sending spittle flying in the direction of my kid while yelling about a hoax he saw on the internet, how am I supposed to politely debunk his premises?

I could try my hand at addressing the QAnon rumors about my local restaurant. Here, I might make my neighbors listen to me by appealing to our common ground. I could point to our shared first-person experiences (like enjoying perfectly nonsatanic meals at the restaurant) that cast doubt on the notion that a bloodthirsty cabal is trying to destroy the Sunday pancake special. I might acknowledge the anxieties and fears that motivate their theories, and point to a resolution on the horizon ("They're reopening for takeout soon"). This dialogue-based approach can work when everyone is on civil speaking terms. I cannot, however, make the yelling guy unsee every Trump-related COVID hoax he viewed during the pandemic lockdown.

These confrontations can feel futile because they are violent outbursts at the end of a long process of radicalization, one that often begins out of sight, especially on the internet. But it's not too late to stop funneling conspiracy theories into internet users' brains and to provide them an off-ramp into reality. One way is for major social media companies to clean up the mess they've made of the internet.

Through their own design, and conspiracy theorists' ingenuity, sites like YouTube and Facebook became hotbeds of conspiratorial belief in the 2010s. After sustained criticism for its recommendation algorithms, YouTube began taking measures to combat disinformation. In 2018, the site unveiled informational boxes under conspiracy videos. These automatically generated fact-checks provided links to sites like

Wikipedia and Encyclopaedia Britannica when YouTube detected that a video was conspiratorial in nature. Videos on Holocaust denialism, for instance, now resulted in a small informational box confirming that the Holocaust did, in fact, happen. Flat Earth videos triggered a box of text asserting that Earth is a sphere. Facebook rolled out its own fact-checking program, enlisting a host of independent researchers to debunk viral posts and flag them with warning signs if they were found to contain misleading information.

Evidence of the efficacy of fact-checks is gloomy, however. On a recent extensive scroll through a large Flat Earth Facebook group, I somehow did not encounter a single hoax flagged as false. Even when fact-checks do appear alongside debunked posts, less than 3 percent of viewers actually bother to read them, according to a study that tracked browser history before the 2016 election. Readers' self-regard might be part of the problem. In a study on attitudes toward censoring Flat Earth content on YouTube, respondents largely opposed taking action against Flat Earth videos, in part because they thought they would never be fooled by one.

All the same, in January 2019, YouTube changed its recommendation algorithm altogether, to start "reducing recommendations of borderline content and content that could misinform users in harmful ways—such as videos promoting a phony miracle cure for a serious illness, claiming the earth is flat, or making blatantly false claims about historic events like 9/11," the company wrote in a blog post.

The result was immediate. Where once Flat Earth videos appeared unbidden in searches, now it's damn difficult to find one at all, even by directly searching "Flat Earth." (Most of the first search results are for scientific videos debunking the theory or for news outlets reporting on the existence of Flat Earth conferences.)

Robbie Davidson, the Flat Earth International Conference founder, told me he can't even find his own videos in a keyword search for them.

"I've got some of my documentaries where you cannot find them," he said. "You can type them in, they exist on my channel, you will not be able to find them. And they're like really weird words. You can put everything in and you'll never find it. They don't exist."

David Weiss, the Flat Earth YouTuber whom Owen Benjamin hailed as a marketing and tech whiz, told me he sometimes finds earnest Flat Earth videos by sorting his search results to show the most recently uploaded videos. "But you won't find the old, the classic, the highest viewed, real Flat Earth information," he said.

Sometimes, YouTube has gone so far as to ban specific conspiracy channels altogether. In August 2018, an informal coalition of social media companies, including YouTube and Facebook, banned Infowars founder Alex Jones from their sites for violating various terms of service, like policies against hate speech. (None of the companies cited Jones's promotion of conspiracy theories in their statements on the bans.) Jones, who had built a paranoid empire with broad reach across social media, said the bans were proof that he was being censored for exposing taboo truths. He claimed he would emerge from the shakeup vindicated and more popular than ever before.

"The more I'm persecuted, the stronger I get," Jones said in a video broadcast days after getting the boot from most social media sites. "It backfired."

The ban did not backfire. Before the bans, Infowars was averaging nearly 1.4 million website hits and video views per day, the *New York Times* reported. Three weeks after the bans, Infowars views had fallen by nearly half, to about 715,000 daily hits. By July 2020, traffic had halved again, down to an average 351,000 views per day. Banning offenders can mean a game of whack-a-mole for social media companies. Jones repeatedly crept back onto the sites that had banned him, despite decrying those same Silicon Valley companies as satanic. Infowars set up Facebook pages for NewsWars, an Infowars clone that ran the banned channel's videos, accumulating tens of thousands of followers and millions of video views in the months after Infowars' ban. Individual Infowars hosts used their personal pages to share the exact brand of racist material that had gotten Infowars banned in the first place, like angry videos about different races' birth rates.

Even individual banned videos can be difficult to keep off-line. In March 2019, when Brenton Tarrant opened fire in a New Zealand mosque on the basis of a racist conspiracy theory, he livestreamed the massacre on Facebook. Facebook cut off the livestream seventeen minutes into the attack and, alongside YouTube and other social media sites, prohibited new uploads of the monstrous footage. Nevertheless, in the hours after the shooting, YouTubers reuploaded the video approximately once every second, YouTube's chief product officer told the *Washington Post*. When YouTube tried using artificial intelligence to recognize and block the videos, uploaders altered the clips, splicing in momentary glimpses of other videos to confuse YouTube's filters. Similarly, when YouTube and Facebook banned COVID-19 hoax videos like *Plandemic*, I encountered altered, difficult-to-detect versions of the clips all over conspiratorial Facebook groups.

In short, bans and moderation work—up to a point. Infowars suffered a massive blow when it lost its social media profiles and, subsequently, nearly three-quarters of its traffic. Anti-fascist activists often work to get neo-Nazis banned from popular websites, because disrupting their online activities and kicking them off these sites makes it harder for fascist types to recruit. When the video-sharing app TikTok blocked hashtags associated with QAnon in July 2020, it removed one of the most straightforward means for Q supporters to discover and network with their peers.

But while Silicon Valley giants like YouTube can curb the spread of conspiracy theories by taking away their artificial algorithmic boost, big tech firms are unlikely to deliver us, as a species, from the meaning-making thought processes that misfire when we craft conspiracy theories. TikTok can ban a hashtag, but it has less control over the feelings of fear and uncertainty that send us searching for alternative explanations. And if we accept that the Facebooks of the world will never be perfect at moderation, it's worth adopting one more paranoia to ask whether we're giving them too much power in the hopes that they will flawlessly execute an impossible task.

Digital privacy activist Evan Greer is an expert on the Patriot Act, the hallmark legislation of post-9/11 surveillance. When Congress moved to renew parts of the Patriot Act that allowed warrantless surveillance of internet activity in 2020, Greer was quoted in a news story about the vote. She shared a link to the article on her personal Facebook page and found that the site had flagged her post as "partly false." One of Facebook's independent fact-checkers appeared to have had a semantic objection to the wording of an entirely separate viral post that linked to the article. Based on the viral post, which Greer did not author, the fact-checker raised a flag about the article itself, lumping it under the same misinformation disclaimer that decorates articles about anti-vaccination and Flat Earth. Shoddy corporate surveillance online had muffled Greer's warning about ominous government surveillance online.

Other activists have found themselves in a similar bureaucratic limbo as Greer while trying to combat misinformation online. In April 2018, before Alex Jones was banned from YouTube, the left-leaning watchdog group Media Matters uploaded a video compiling Jones's most noxious comments. Although Jones was still allowed on the site, YouTube removed the Media Matters video, scolding the group for "harassment and bullying." When YouTube purged racist videos from its platform in 2019, it also deleted videos about racism, including a high school history teacher's educational videos about the Holocaust and an anti-racist activist's videos exposing neo-Nazis. The activist, Daryle Lamont Jenkins, told me he suspected that far-right trolls had flagged the video and that YouTube had automatically deleted it based on their complaints. "My guess is one of our 'fans' might have reported it knowing YouTube won't do a real investigation and just take it down just because they saw the swastika" in the video, Jenkins told me after the purge in 2019. In March 2020, after Facebook turned over some of its content moderation to an artificial intelligence system, it accidentally flagged factual content about COVID-19 as spam while the virus raged.

And these are acts of probably accidental suppression, carried out by corporate entities that only really take action when bullied into it by activists. Codified into law or placed under government oversight, the fight against "disinformation" could also ricochet back onto dissidents, this time with real legal repercussions. In March 2020, Ethiopia passed a law called the Hate Speech and Disinformation Prevention and Suppression Proclamation. On its face, the law was an attempt to combat social-media-based violence, like a series of ethnic conflicts that resulted in at least sixty-seven deaths after online rumors inflamed previous tensions in the country. Critics warned, however, that the legislation's language was overly broad and subject to a range of interpretations, usually at the discretion of government officials. Predictably, within weeks of its passage, the law was reportedly used as the basis to arrest a journalist who published an unflattering report about Ethiopia's handling of the COVID-19 crisis.

Even when content isn't explicitly against the law, social media companies' moderation powers can stray into censorship under enough government pressure. TikTok, a China-based company, secretly ordered employees to censor videos about protests and political movements that opposed the Chinese government, like the 1989 Tiananmen Square protests and the Tibetan independence movement, according to leaked documents obtained by the *Guardian* in 2019. TikTok was also accused of censoring footage of then-ongoing protests in Hong Kong, a charge the company has denied.

Authoritarian regimes aren't the only ones contemplating a crackdown. Democratic US senator Elizabeth Warren made "fighting digital disinformation" a platform in her 2020 presidential campaign. Alongside potentially helpful proposals like publicizing company data and allowing users to opt out of social media companies' opaque recommendation algorithms, her team included a suggestion to create criminal penalties for people who knowingly share disinformation about when and where to vote.

Had Warren's platform moved toward law, it would have likely run into a First Amendment challenge: Social media posts encouraging one's political opponents to vote on the wrong day are obnoxious but are likely protected as free speech. Criminalizing them would mean giving the government the legal muscle to imprison internet trolls—occasionally tempting if you spend enough time online, but ultimately an inhumane practice and probably one that would be used to target the vulnerable, as policing often does. Social networks can rip up conspiracy movements' online architecture, but those often-effective takedowns exist on an uncomfortable spectrum of suppression, somewhere between vital intervention, like banning child-exploitation content, and autocratic moves, like arresting journalists for their reporting.

Speaking of uncomfortable realities, maybe some of Flat Earth's current reach is my fault. Years ago, I started writing about Flat Earth as something close to a joke. I saved the most batshit comments I found in Flat Earth forums. I tweeted about factional rivalries playing out in conspiracy groups. When Trump announced the creation of a Space Force as a new military branch, I convinced my editors at the *Daily Beast* to let me interview the Flat Earth Society about the new organization, on the grounds that Flat Earthers generally think space is a hoax. My colleagues and I put a sarcastic EXCLUSIVE banner on the story and thought it was very funny, and years later—knowing that Flat Earth has torn families apart and that some Flat Earthers are neo-Nazis who make rap songs about killing people like my own Jewish family—I still find the EXCLUSIVE banner, and really the whole article, very funny. It's Flat Earth, for Christ's sake! How absurd! I filed the Space Force story in a couple of hours and rushed out to catch a train to Washington, DC, where I was covering a march of much more explicit neo-Nazis, including one who'd recently threatened on the radio to murder me if I showed up. While I rode down the East Coast, I got a message from the Flat Earth Society, whom I'd just mocked in my online article. I was expecting an angry note, but the group had no ill words for me; they only wanted to point out a typo I'd missed. As my train sped toward Washington, I realized I was approaching a group of people that knew media coverage could hurt them while taking editing notes from a group with no such fears.

I listen to conspiracy theorists' claims about web traffic with almost as much skepticism as I do their opinions on gravity; after all, Alex Jones claimed his social media bans would strengthen him, when the reverse was true. Nathan Thompson, however, might have been on to something when he told me his Flat Earth Facebook group had experienced a membership surge after it appeared in *Behind the Curve*, a documentary about Flat Earth that ran on Netflix.

"Netflix really did a good job, not just spreading awareness, but spreading it internationally, because right after that video dropped, we were getting hundreds of thousands of member requests," he told me. (I watched his group's numbers as they rose, and they don't suggest hundreds of thousands of new requests, but I suspect his group did see a traffic boost.) "So I know that of all the stuff they do to make Flat Earth look stupid or spread disinformation about the leaders in the movement, all it does is add fuel to the fire and make people say, 'Why are they still talking about Flat Earth?'"

Pete Svarrior, the Flat Earth Society spokesperson, told me internet virality brought the group much-needed attention as it was losing ground to other Flat Earthers in 2017. That's when Elon Musk, the billionaire CEO of the space travel company SpaceX, tweeted a joke about the lack of a Flat Mars Society. Svarrior answered sarcastically from the Flat Earth Society account. "Hi Elon, thanks for the question. Unlike the Earth, Mars has been observed to be round," Svarrior wrote. "We hope you have a fantastic day!"

Svarrior's tweet went viral, making headlines and sending the society's Twitter following sky-high. "If you look up the Twitter follower graph, it's publicly available, you will pinpoint the spot where our Twitter account absolutely blew up, and that was the Elon Musk tweet," Svarrior told me. "I'm not going to pretend there is a master plan and that I sat in a corner planning the Elon Musk tweet for days. I saw it, I thought it would be a funny response, so I wrote it. It just happened to work out in this instance. But the overall objective of that account is to get people talking. Especially people who wouldn't be looking for us otherwise."

Robbie Davidson told me his Flat Earth international conferences depend on the crowds of media that attend (that includes me, twice), plus the late-night talk show staffers and the YouTube clowns like Logan Paul who've trolled the events.

"We need it. We need it a hundred and ten percent," he told me, "because with YouTube completely doing the things that they're doing, we need the Logan Pauls, we need the late-night. We need all the media. Because, again, every time they do it, they do us favors, because they say two words: 'Flat Earth.' That's all we need."

Since the beginning, Flat Earthers have made the case that media helps their cause. Newspapers gave Rowbotham free publicity by mocking his upcoming lectures. He encouraged the combative relationship, inviting scientists to attend and make a scene. When the Flat Earth Society relaunched as a web forum a century and a half later, in 2009, its leaders cited recent media attention—news articles and historian Christine Garwood's book *Flat Earth*—as one reason for the reboot. "In the past two years, there has been a major book published about the Flat Earth movement as well as articles on the BBC website and Fox News which included interviews with one of the Society's most prominent members, James McIntyre," leader Daniel Shenton said in a press release about the society's grand reopening.

"There's conferences that couldn't buy this much media," Davidson told me once. "They come pouring in from other countries." And he's right. Since its surge in 2015, Flat Earth theory has inspired television specials, multiple documentaries, and more articles than I can count. This is a book about Flat Earth, and you are very near the end of it.

And yet, at the risk of giving Flat Earthers exactly what they want, we need to pay attention to them. Movements at the peripheries do not always stay on the sidelines. When I read back on my first published interview with the Flat Earth Society, I can acknowledge that its premise was a silly joke that probably gave the society unwarranted publicity. But other passages read like warnings from the future.

"The flat earth and pro-Trump movements share strands of the same conspiratorial, counter-factual DNA," I wrote in a 2018 article, when QAnon was still embryonic. I added that the overlap "has resulted in forums and Facebook groups like the 101-member 'QAnon flat earthers club,' which accuses Hillary Clinton of being a pedophile and German Chancellor Angela Merkel of being Adolf Hitler's daughter. When Earth is flat, other untruths are trivial."

I mean, goddammit.

We need to understand Flat Earth if we are to have any hope of finding our way out of it. Fortunately, some former Flat Earthers have already found life on a post-Flat planet.

A home improvement project left Jose Gonzales struggling to repair his sense of reality. While fixing up his Florida home in 2017, he entertained himself by listening to YouTube videos about outer space. He'd click a video about black holes and let it play in the background while he worked. His story is so common in Flat Earth circles that you can probably guess its outcome. Based on his interest in cosmology, YouTube started recommending Flat Earth videos, he told me. Eventually, he relented to the algorithm and pressed PLAY on one of the recommendations. That first click changed his world.

"Since the first day I clicked on the first video, I couldn't take it off my mind," Gonzales told me of Flat Earth theory. "The only thing I thought about was the shape of the earth, the science. I was like, holy cow. I was looking into the skies like 'This is all a big lie.'"

The theory was all-consuming, Craig Pennock, a British man, told me of his similar YouTube-based conversion that same year.

"I'd always been sort of conspiracy-minded," Pennock said. "I've believed in other things like chemtrails—really deep down the rabbit hole. Flat Earth popped up, and I just sucked it straight in. All it took was a few YouTube videos, and I was hooked."

Both men described Flat Earth as almost addictive, so much so that it began to drive away the real world. Pennock and Gonzales made their own YouTube channels and new Flat Earth friends. They needed those new acquaintanceships as real-life connections disappeared. Gonzales's coworkers made fun of his new beliefs, and hung a Flat Earth picture next to his photograph in the break room of the supermarket where they worked. Pennock said his Flat Earth belief actively pushed away close friends, except for a handful who converted to the theory upon his insistence.

What do you call a close-knit belief group that demands friend-ship-ending fanaticism from members? One that recognizes no per-spectives outside its all-encompassing worldview? One that is obsessed with recruiting but treats ex-members like traitors? If not a cult, then at least something very close to it.

Rachel Bernstein, the cult-exit psychologist, said cults and conspira-torial movements are cousins, in that their followers form insular sects. Followers of both cults and conspiracy theories often grow fiercely pro-tective of their cliques, she told me; you're either helping the movement, or actively hurting it.

True, Flat Earth has no king-like figure at its center, unlike the most infamous cults. Instead, Flat Earth's followers keep each other in line, surveilling each other for signs of deviancy, and corralling themselves closer together, away from the outside world.

Gonzales recalled following other movement members' teachings as if they were gospel. "I didn't do any deep research. I just Googled what Flat Earthers told me to," he said. "They said, 'This is what you're going to read, and this is how you interpret it.'"

Debunking Flat Earth is, again, relatively easy in a good-faith debate. You can watch a ship disappear hull-first behind the horizon as it sails away, or watch the sun set the same way, degree by degree behind the earth's curve as the planet spins toward the dark. You can watch the orbits of stars in the night sky and observe that those slow paths—different in the Northern and Southern Hemispheres—are impossible on a Flat Earth map, which would require stars to streak wildly across the sky at the planet's outer edges. And if you believe in outer space, and don't think NASA is a satanic organization, you can peruse pictures of the globe planet captured from space.

All these methods, however, require genuine willingness to change one's mind. Flat Earthers are maddening to debate, because many simply do not want to be convinced. For some time, Gonzales was the same way.

Determined to replicate other Flat Earthers' experiments, Gonzales acquired a camera with a high-powered zoom, originally owned by a famous Flat Earth YouTuber. ("Not only do I have the camera, I have the camera from *the man*," he recalled thinking.) Yet the magic of its previous owner didn't seem to rub off on Gonzales or his experiments. He tried zooming in on the bottoms of distant buildings where they disappear beyond the curve of the earth—a popular stunt that, if performed incorrectly, can falsely suggest that the hidden buildings reappear with a strong zoom. Instead, Gonzales performed the experiment correctly and discovered that the bottoms of the buildings were still out of sight, no matter how powerful his camera. He did not immediately publish those results.

"I was holding back some observations because I didn't know how to explain it. When I zoomed into a building, I couldn't see the bottom," he said. He opted to share explanations about tricks of the light that might have hidden the buildings from view. "I was sharing a lot of theories with atmospheric conditions."

If conspiracy theorists are like cult members, maybe it's no surprise that they won't abandon their beliefs over a few inconvenient facts. In order to bring believers back from the edge, maybe we need to approach debunking less like a debate and more like holding a friend's hand as they leave a terrible, dependent relationship.

Psychologists working in the cult-exit field offer the same initial piece of advice for people trying to prize a loved one from a controlling group's grasp: Keep in communication with that person. Remind them that another world exists outside of their faith community. This, in itself, can be difficult, especially when the group preaches ideals that are baffling, even immoral, to the person on the outside. But Gonzales and Pennock, who both went all in on Flat Earth and found their way out, describe Globe Earth friendships as the only thing that brought them back to Earth.

Even as he was explaining away the issues with his experiments, Gonzales kept one toe on the round planet. He was part of a public group for debates between Flat and Globe Earthers. By 2018, relations between the warring factions in Gonzales's debate group had soured so badly that the Flat pack expelled the globe fans, who created a separate forum just for the spherically inclined. Gonzales, always friendly, kept in touch with the outcasts. In keeping with cult-adjacent behavior, his Flat peers accused him of being unfaithful to their cause and branded him as a "flip-flopper." So when his doubts started mounting over the failed camera experiment, he took his concerns to the Globe Earth forum.

"I felt like, why am I holding this back? I want to be honest with myself. I want to find Flat Earth," Gonzales said. He told himself he'd share his findings with Globe Earthers first, just to hear their explanations for his photos, which showed buildings half obscured by the planet's arc.

"They were like, 'Yeah, that's the curvature of the earth. Welcome to the globe.'"

Pennock's trip back to the globe also began with Globe Earthers. Conspiracy Catz, a YouTuber who debunks conspiracy theories, uploaded a video dismantling one of Pennock's Flat Earth videos point by point.

"I watched it," Pennock said. "At first I was like, 'No. I don't believe any of it.' But a few of my [Globe Earth] mates around me were saying, 'Dude, you're so wrong. This man has debunked everything you said.' I looked back at it and got this real sick feeling in my stomach that suddenly I'm wrong, and I'd been sitting here on YouTube for six months, probably converting people to Flat Earth belief. Now I know that—oh God."

Gonzales did not immediately abandon Flat Earth, even after he saw proof of the curve through his telephoto lens.

"I wanted to believe so hard," he said. He imagined a future in which Flat Earth was revealed to be reality. He would be vindicated, championed as one of a select few truth tellers who'd been right all along. He was going to be *big*. Those dreams clashed with the evidence of his own eyes. The dissonance between the two became so extreme that he couldn't bring himself to look at a sunset, for fear it would remind him of his doubts. "I didn't want to look up at the sky because the sunrise and sunset are impossible on the flat plane," he said.

Unconsciously, Gonzales was performing an exercise similar to one Bernstein practices with her clients.

"I will have people go through a list: all the times they were told they were going to be poisoned, or their family was going to die, or the world was going to end, or the computers were going to crash," she told me. "They'll usually have a list of twenty or thirty things that never took place. I'll just have them look at the size of that list. Then I'll ask what explanations they were given, and, as they're saying those things, how it sounds to their ear. Often they'll say, 'Oh, it actually sounds like an excuse.'"

Eventually, Gonzales's mental list of globe arguments became too long to ignore. He also remained in the pro-globe forum that had splintered off the Flat Earth debate group. Whenever he grew disillusioned about another Flat Earth talking point, he'd run it by the globe advocates, who debunked it in short order. When the mountain of pro-globe proof became too large to ignore, both Gonzales and Pennock did the most helpful thing they could: they turned their Flat Earth YouTube channels into Globe Earth YouTube channels. Today, Pennock's channel focuses on the psychology of why people believe Flat Earth and similar conspiracy theories. Gonzales's channel hosts professors and airplane pilots who patiently explain why various Flat Earth arguments are bogus.

Pennock and Gonzales both found community in Flat Earth circles online. But crucial for them to move on from the theory was support from real-world communities who welcomed them back when they returned to the globe.

"I was laughed at. I had a lot of issues with my family," Gonzales said of relationships during his time as a conspiracy theorist. "After I left Flat Earth, everything came back to life."

Conspiracy theories preach suspicion and prey on our fears. Inherently divisive, they thrive when we mistrust others and wall ourselves behind our personal paranoias. Fittingly, one of the best ways out of conspiratorial thinking can be to place our faith in others.

Pennock said he might have dismissed Conspiracy Catz's video about him without ever watching it, had Catz not contacted him ahead of time, starting a conversation and earning Pennock's confidence.

"A lot of it is about trust," Pennock said. "I influenced people into Flat Earth belief. It also works the other way around."

Trust can be frightening, especially for people steeped in a paranoid theory. It requires vulnerability and the confidence that something new will be ready to catch and support a person when they finally let go of an idea that has carried them for so long. When Pennock chose to drop out of Flat Earth, a soft landing of empathy was waiting for him. That doesn't mean I'm about to hand out roses to conspiratorial antisemites or the anti-masker who yelled at my infant. But for those willing to abandon their theories, a gentle comedown can help them find solid ground again.

To ease that transition, Bernstein said she sometimes encourages patients to lean into the limbo between faiths.

"I talk to them about 'operating in the gray,'" she said. That means not blindly trusting people or organizations that are likely lying, but also allowing oneself to feel safe, unburdened by the paranoias that power conspiracy theories. "You can be in the middle and be a critical thinker."

I think about the term "operating in the gray" often. I write this nearly a year into a raging pandemic, after months of the sitting president's refusal to embrace his reelection loss. A strange year, when suspicion feels like self-defense and trust comes harder. Some days, amid all this uncertainty, I feel quite like a conspiracy theorist myself.

Knowing as little as I do—as little as anyone does—about the looming future, I understand why my Flat Earther friends want to believe they live in a different world, a finite world that does not expand into the endless vacuum of space but ends with a simple answer in the form of a dome or an ice wall. Flat Earth is a bracket on understanding. It narrows the world to a safe frame.

Now it is dusk, and the lights in my city are coming on as the globe rotates away from the sun. These moments between day and night are the best time to watch the sun sink behind the earth's curve, the way mathematicians and mapmakers of old used to watch ships disappear behind the horizon. It's the gray, the clarity, that comes in the dim in-betweens.

Somewhere, statistically speaking, quite nearby me, a Flat Earther has noted the nighttime and chalked it up to the sun moving across the face of a flat plane. Tomorrow morning, the sun will rise according to our various models, and the day will come again. Either way, at least for now, we'll have to share it.

ACKNOWLEDGMENTS

THIS BOOK IS indebted to countless colleagues, friends, and writers who came before me. Thank you to Justin Miller and Noah Shachtman, who greenlit my first reporting trip to a Flat Earth conference. To my agent, Dan Mandel, who believed in this book from the start. To Abby Muller, who acquired this book and shaped it into the best version of itself. To librarians and historians at the New York Public Library, Cambridge University, and the Zion Benton Public Library, who helped me access records I never would have found on my own. To writers Christine Garwood and Robert Schadewald, whose pioneering works helped me understand Flat Earth's rich history. To innumerable Flat Earthers who were gracious with their time, despite our disagreements. To the Hog Chat, the Heck Chat, and the friends who made 2020 a bearable book-writing year. To my parents, who encouraged me to write from the beginning. Finally to my husband, my first reader, whose support kept me going, and to our son, who raced this book to birth and won.

NOTES

Prologue

2   **embellished Columbus biography**   Darin Hayton, "Washington Irving's Columbus and the Flat Earth," Haverford College, December 2, 2014, https://dhayton.haverford.edu/blog/2014/12/02/washington-irvings-columbus-and-the-flat-earth/.

4   **five criteria**   Jan-Willem van Prooijen, *The Psychology of Conspiracy Theories* (Routledge, 2018), 5–6.

1: In the Beginning

6   **griped about his neighbors**   W. H. G. Armytage, *Heavens Below: Utopian Experiments in England, 1560–1960* (Routledge, 2007), 148.

6   **letter to the commune newspaper**   Hodsonian Community Society, *Working Bee*, December 1, 1840.

7   **on laughing gas**   Society of Rational Religionists, *New Moral World*, vol. 6 (Greenwood Reprint Corporation, 1969), 717.

8   **beyond our control**   Karen M. Douglas, Robbie M. Sutton, and Aleksandra Cichocka, "The Psychology of Conspiracy Theories," *Current Directions in Psychological Science* 26, no. 6 (December 7, 2017): 538–42, https://doi.org/10.1177/0963721417718261.

8   **train line near campus**   Van Prooijen, *Psychology of Conspiracy Theories*, 29–30.

8   **cast them into unemployment**   Joseph E. Uscinski and Joseph M. Parent, *American Conspiracy Theories* (Oxford University Press, 2014), 110–11; van Prooijen, *Psychology of Conspiracy Theories*, 23.

8   **tour of existing Owenite communes**   John Langdon, "'A Monument of Union': Social Change and Personal Experience at the Manea Fen Community, 1839–1841" *Utopian Studies* 23, no. 2 (2012): 504–31, www.jstor.org/stable/10.5325/utopianstudies.23.2.0504.

9   **Super Bowl commercial**   Travis Pittman, "Amazon Super Bowl Ad Asks What
     We Did Before Alexa." WUSA-TV, January 31, 2020, https://www.wusa9.com/
     article/sports/nfl/superbowl/amazon-super-bowl-ad-what-we-did-without-
     alexa/507-d253fd94-8618-40ef-8a64-53902de536ce.

9   **"no God or Creator"**   Robert Schadewald, *The Plane Truth* (2015), www.cantab.
     net/users/michael.behrend/ebooks/PlaneTruth/pages/index.html.

10   **"a beautiful promenade"**   Armytage, *Heavens Below*, 147.

10   **guided by ulterior motives**   Schadewald, *Plane Truth*.

10   **eight inches per mile squared**   Isaac Asimov, "The Relativity of Wrong,"
     Skeptical Inquirer 14, no. 1 (Fall 1989): 35–44, https://web.archive.org/web/
     20210217134045/https://chem.tufts.edu/answersinscience/relativityofwrong.htm.

10   **ice-skaters six miles away**   Stephen Carter, "Be Grateful for Flat-Earthers,"
     Associated Press, January 30, 2016, https://www.pilotonline.com/opinion/
     columns/article_20ec5920-8ae9-5a9c-ab1b-470dad5d2e8a.html.

11   **burgeoning theory**   Ouse Washes, "'Earth Not a Globe': Ouse Washes Flat
     Earth Trials 2015," Cambridge Archaeological Unit, YouTube video, August 11,
     2015, www.youtube.com/watch?v=2z3quJk_mWw.

11   **as a hermit**   Langdon, "'Monument of Union,'" 504–31.

11   **toilet products**   Cambridge Archaeology, "Manea Colony—Archaeology
     of Utopia," YouTube video, September 14, 2017, www.youtube.com/
     watch?v=17A9WmHbdxg.

11   **"useless discussions"**   Armytage, 148.

12   **independent sexual relationships**   Langdon, "Monument of Union," 516–17.

12   **"a little confusion in our Society"**   John C. Langdon "Pocket Editions of the
     New Jerusalem: Owenite Communitarianism in Britain 1825–1855," (DPhil diss.,
     University of York, 2000), 200, https://etheses.whiterose.ac.uk/10872/1/313876
     .pdf.

12   **cast him out**   Armytage, 293.

13   **"Dr. Birley"**   *Dr. Birley's Compounds of Free (or Unoxidised) Phosphorus :
     Fifteen Standard Combinations. A Special Remedy for Each Disease*
     (Gordon, Murray & Co., c. 1900), https://wellcomecollection.org/works/
     b92wbkxn#?c=0&m=0&s=0&cv=0&z=-0.5953%2C-0.0866%2C2.1908%2C1.7317.

13   **anti-vaccine movement continues**   "Autism and Vaccines," Centers for Disease
     Control and Prevention, August 25, 2020, https://www.cdc.gov/vaccinesafety/
     concerns/autism.html.

13   **"they lose a customer"**   Sales text for Mike Adams's *How to Halt Diabetes in 25
     Days*, https://www.amazon.com/How-Halt-Diabetes-25-Days/dp/B001TAI4B2.

14   **phosphoric acid and lime**   Christine Garwood, *Flat Earth: The History of an
     Infamous Idea* (Thomas Dunne Books, 2007), 39.

14   **"chemically generated 'holy water'"**   Parallax, "The Prince of the Power of the
     Air," *Earth Life* 1, no. 1 (March 1873), 4.

14   **role in their son's death**   "Inquests before T. Badger, Esq.," *Sheffield
     Independent*, June 29, 1844.

15   **acid is actually good**   "Samuel Rowbotham," Flat Earth Wiki, Flat Earth
     Society, wiki.tfes.org/Samuel_Rowbotham.

15   the pen name Parallax   Garwood, *Flat Earth*, 45.

15   radical British atheist crew   Garwood, 40.

16   "scheming, but not proving"   Samuel Birley Rowbotham, *Zetetic Astronomy: Earth Not a Globe* (1881), 13.

17   "the great deep"   Rowbotham, *Zetetic Astronomy*, 145.

18   "destruction by fire"   Rowbotham, 145.

18   "incandescent state"   Rowbotham, 148.

18   "befallen mankind"   Anonymous, *Anti-Newtonian* (self-pub., London, 1819), i.

19   for his own purposes   Schadewald, *Plane Truth*.

19   slower-moving center   Mick West, *Escaping the Rabbit Hole: How to Debunk Conspiracy Theories Using Facts, Logic, and Respect* (Skyhorse, 2018), 208–09.

20   religiously anxious   Garwood, 45.

20   "astronomical and geological theories of the day"   Rowbotham, 259.

21   George Washington   Note 1 accompanying "To George Washington, from G. W. Snyder," October 22, 1789, Founders Online, National Archives, https://www.loc.gov/item/mgw441411/.

21   networks of fellow schemers   Jovan Byford, *Conspiracy Theories: A Critical Introduction* (Palgrave Macmillan, 2011) 43–44.

21   "in all its bearings"   Rowbotham, 289.

22   Augustus De Morgan   Augustus De Morgan, *A Budget of Paradoxes* (Open Court, 1915), 88–89, http://www.gutenberg.org/files/26408/26408-h/26408-h.htm.

22   bailed on his own lecture   De Morgan, *Budget of Paradoxes* 88–89.

23   "philosophers and Scientific men"   Garwood, 48.

24   "converts to his system"   Robert Schadewald, "Looking for Lighthouses," *Creation/Evolution* 31 (1992): 1, ncse.com/files/pub/CEJ/pdfs/CEJ_31.pdf.

24   "What do these few . . . prove?"   Schadewald, "Looking for Lighthouses," 1.

25   "This is supposed to be meaningful?"   Tom Bishop, Flat Earth Discussion Boards, Flat Earth Society, https://forum.tfes.org/index.php?topic=11728.msg177985#msg177985.

25   branch in New York   Parallax, "Officers and Council of the New York Zetetic Society, 1873," *Zetetic* 2, no. 8–9 (October–November 1873): 54.

25   "has yet been found"   Common Sense, *Theoretical Astronomy Examined and Exposed* (Job Caudwell, 1864), xiii.

26   "their *mis-calculations*"   Common Sense, *Theoretical Astronomy*, 3.

26   front of Carpenter's book   Common Sense, vi.

26   "for our guidance"   Common Sense, vi.

26   Church of England   Garwood, 73.

26   correspondence with Carpenter   Schadewald, *Plane Truth*.

27   placing Carpenter in his debt   Charles H. Smith, ed., "Reply to Mr. Hampden's Charges against Mr. Wallace (S202: 1871)," Alfred Russel Wallace Page, Western Kentucky University, people.wku.edu/charles.smith/wallace/S202.htm.

27   "more convincing than the ridicule"   Smith, "Reply to Mr. Hampden's Charges."

28   **start the surveying process anew**   Schadewald, *Plane Truth*.

28   **"diametrically opposite decisions"**   Smith, "Reply."

28   **"done with him"**   Smith, "Reply."

28   **"my getting tired"**   "The Rotundity of the Earth," *Essex County Standard*, March 12, 1875.

29   **taking advantage of an idiot**   Garwood, 143.

29   **"never be convinced"**   Dana Hunter, "Wallace's Woeful Wager: How a Founder of Modern Biology Got Suckered by Flat-Earthers," *Scientific American*, January 12, 2015, blogs.scientificamerican.com/rosetta-stones/wallace-8217-s-woeful-wager-how-a-founder-of-modern-biology-got-suckered-by-flat-earthers/.

29   **make his measurements again**   Schadewald, *Plane Truth*.

29   **phoning it in**   "The Bedford Level or Flat Earth Experiments," Welney website, www.welney.org.uk/fens-rivers-washes/flat-earth/experiments.htm?LMCL=VkkSdM.

29   **"until it was over"**   Parallax, *Experimental Proofs (with Illustrative Engravings) That the Surface of Standing Water Is Not Convex but Horizontal. With a Critical Examination of the Recent Attempt to Decide the Question—"Is the Earth a Globe or a Plane?" . . .* (1870), 3–4.

30   **"'save me from my friends'"**   Parallax, *Experimental Proofs*, 7.

2: The Tyrant

32   **in jail for a month**   H. J. Gibbney, "Dowie, John Alexander (1847–1907)," *Australian Dictionary of Biography*, National Centre of Biography, Australian National University, https://adb.anu.edu.au/biography/dowie-john-alexander-3434.

32   **close look at the incident**   Barry Morton, "The Big Con: John Alexander Dowie and the Spread of Zionist Christianity in Southern Africa," Academia.edu, 2013, www.academia.edu/6779053/The_Big_Con_John_Alexander_Dowie_and_the_Spread_of_Zionist_Christianity_in_Southern_Africa_Paper_Presented_at_the.

32   **stories on faith healing**   "Believers in Faith Cures: Birmingham's Religious Circles in a Ferment of Excitement," *New York Times*, May 1, 1885, https://nyti.ms/3ssEvKK.

32   **a local infection**   "Healed by Faith: A Brooklyn Woman Who Believes Her Cancer Has Been Cured," *New York Times*, May 3, 1885, https://nyti.ms/3s0EEPr.

32   **anti-doctor sentiment**   Meredith Mattlin, "Examining the Social Construction of Health, Illness, and Wellness in Anti-Science Communities (master's thesis, Vanderbilt, 2018), https://core.ac.uk/download/pdf/216056116.pdf.

33   **"divine healing"**   Pew Forum on Religion and Public Life, *U.S. Religious Landscape Survey* (Pew Research Center, February 2008), 188, https://assets.pewresearch.org/wp-content/uploads/sites/11/2013/05/report-religious-landscape-study-full.pdf.

33   **prayed for their own health**   Jeff Levin, "Prevalence and Religious Predictors of Healing Prayer Use in the USA: Findings from the Baylor Religion Survey,"

Journal of Religion and Health 55, no. 4 (August 2016): 1136–58, https://doi.org/10.1007/s10943-016-0240-9.

33   **his death in 1896**   "Prof. Carpenter Dead," *Baltimore Sun*, September 2, 1896.

34   **globe belief with heresy**   Schadewald, *Plane Truth*.

34   **marrying outside his faith**   Garwood, 155.

34   **infused with sheet music**   Garwood, 167.

34   **modern-day critics**   Exploring the Plane, "Lady Blount Talks Refraction as Infrared Images Reveal Flat Earth," YouTube video, November 6, 2019, https://www.youtube.com/watch?v=nK0_bVedJDs.

35   **truth to the theory**   Lady Blount, *Adrian Galilio: or, A Song Writer's Story* ("The Faith" Press, 1898), 15–18.

35   **three-sentence article**   "Aero Modeled on Bird," *Washington Post*, October 23, 1909.

35   **more notoriety**   Grant Wacker, "Marching to Zion: Religion in a Modern Utopian Community," *Church History* 54, no. 4 (1985): 509, www.jstor.org/stable/3166516.

35   **without a license**   Randall J. Soland, *Utopian Communities of Illinois: Heaven on the Prairie* (History Press, 2017), 115–17.

35   **laying hands on them**   Morton, "The Big Con."

36   **personally controlled**   Morton, "The Big Con"; Soland, *Utopian Communities of Illinois* 117–18.

36   **great ceiling**   Kyle Munzenrieder, "A Florida State Park Is Dedicated to a Cult That Believed Earth Was Inside Out," *Miami New Times*, January 26, 2016, https://www.miaminewtimes.com/news/a-florida-state-park-is-dedicated-to-a-cult-that-believed-earth-was-inside-out-8203214.

36   **"'Koreshanites' of America"**   Blount, *Adrian Galilio*, 67.

37   **joined Dowie's movement**   Garwood, 189.

37   **"*round* the world"**   Joshua Slocum, *Sailing Alone around the World* (Century Co., 1911), 243.

37   **thousands of dollars back**   Schadewald, *Plane Truth*.

38   **died within the day**   Wacker, "Marching to Zion," 506.

38   **partially paralyzed**   Wacker, 496.

38   **then in Jamaica**   Gibbney, "Dowie."

38   **goings-on in Zion**   Phillip L. Cook, *Zion City, Illinois: Twentieth-Century Utopia* (Syracuse University Press 1996), 193–94.

38   **Satan's grasp**   Cook, *Zion City*, 197–98.

38   **would-be partners**   Garwood, 195–96.

39   **injuring Dowie's son**   Cook, 202–09.

39   **scrubbed his name**   Wacker, 508.

40   **up to $3,500**   Cook, 196.

41   **"I mean business"**   "State Militia to Quiet Zion City," *Inter Ocean*, May 2, 1909.

41   **"two more years"**   "Zion City Jail Is Prepared for Siege," *Inter Ocean*, May 5, 1909.

41 **as they pleased** "Liberals Capture Town Hall in Zion City after Battle," *Inter Ocean*, May 4, 1909.

42 **Chicago newspaper** "Liberals Capture Town Hall," *Inter Ocean*.

42 **"no such thing"** Schadewald, *Plane Truth*.

42 **alternative model of the world** Schadewald, *Plane Truth*.

42 **conventional geography** Vincent Mitchell, "Voliva Dusts off Dirge of Doom to Meet Chaos in Warring Zion," *Chicago Tribune*, June 3, 1934.

42 **did not intervene** "A Page of Opinion and Comment," *Decatur Herald and Review*, June 16, 1919.

43 **"doesn't even mention ameba"** Garwood, 210–11.

43 **wrote of her daughter** Mattlin, "Examining the Social Construction."

43 **North Pole at its center** Garwood, 210–11.

43 **addressed to Voliva** Wilbur Glenn Voliva, ed., *Leaves of Healing*, September 14, 1918.

44 **"*His Holy Name*"** Schadewald, *Plane Truth*.

44 **INFIDEL THEORIES OF MODERN ASTRONOMY** Voliva, *Leaves of Healing*, May 10, 1930.

45 **distance to the sun** Schadewald, *Plane Truth*.

45 **"globular surface"** Voliva, *Leaves of Healing*, May 10, 1930.

47 **even more ears** Tom Kneitel, "WCBD, The 'Flat Earth' Radio Station," *Popular Communications*, June 1986, https://worldradiohistory.com/Archive-Popular-Communications/80s/Popular-Communications-1986-06.pdf.

47 *Dispatch* **quipped** "Over the Edge Is Lost," *Dispatch*, March 31, 1928.

47 **spoiling for a fight** Garwood, 214.

47 **"man has no proof"** Tom Pettey, "Voliva Is Back from Flat Tour around World," *Chicago Tribune*, March 5, 1931.

47 **previously held power** Schadewald, *Plane Truth*.

48 **her children and three others** "Tortured in Rite of Fanatics; Dies," *Chicago Tribune*, September 21, 1907.

48 **faithful to the movement's founder** "Zionites in Africa Revolt against Voliva," *Inter Ocean*, February 21, 1907.

48 **title *The Theocrat*** Cook, 221.

48 **"mercy and kindness"** "Zion Is Wavering with Dowie Home," *Chicago Tribune*, April 29, 1906.

49 **for smoking** Walter Davenport, "They Call Me a Flathead," *Collier's*, May 14, 1927, 30–31.

49 **tobacco juice** Garwood, 200–01.

49 **subject to arrest** Schadewald, *Plane Truth*.

49 **covered at all times** Garwood, 201.

50 **"buttermilk and Brazil nuts"** "Voliva, 65, on Nut Diet; 'to Live to Be 120,'" *Chicago Tribune*, March 11, 1935.

50 **THUGS WILL FIND THIS CITY HOTTER THAN HELL** Schadewald, *Plane Truth*.

50 **START SOMETHING ELSE** Garwood, 199–200.

51   anti-smoking slogans   "Zionites Plan Loud Prayers," *Chicago Tribune*, April 25, 1912.

51   "storm the jail"   "Workmen Rout 200 Zionites with Clubs and Stones," *Chicago Tribune*, April 30, 1912.

51   gun to guard it   "Workmen Rout 200 Zionites," *Chicago Tribune*.

51   made of steel   "Smokers in Zion Burn Signboard," *Chicago Tribune*, May 8, 1912.

51   please not do that   "Eggs and Fists Fly in Zion's Tobacco War," *Inter Ocean*, June 15, 1912.

52   "ballot frauds and intimidation"   "Voliva Is Indicted on Perjury Charge," *Inter Ocean*, October 7, 1911.

52   shady election dealings   "Zion City Leader Must Face Trial," *Inter Ocean*, January 11, 1911.

52   declared him not guilty   "Acquit Voliva of Perjury in Inquiry on Vote Frauds," *Chicago Tribune*, October 25, 1913.

52   Dowie's pallbearers   "Truce at Zion City for Dowie Funeral," *True Republican*, March 13, 1907; "Voliva Fined One Cent, Costs in Libel Case," *Chicago Tribune*, April 1, 1923.

52   "blatherskite" . . . and other insults   "Religion, Libel and Law in Zion City," *Galena Evening Times*, April 30, 1923; "Probe Charge That Libel Jury Was 'Fixed' by Voliva," *Chicago Tribune*, October 21, 1920; "Voliva Goes to Trial by Jury on Charge of Libel," *Chicago Tribune*, October 26, 1922.

52   married one of his congregants   Mitchell, "Voliva Dusts Off."

52    $700,000 loan   "Voliva Is Supreme over 'Zion' Today," *Inter Ocean*, October 1, 1910.

53   industries he controlled   Mitchell, "Voliva Dusts Off."

53   "aged rapidly"   Mitchell, "Voliva Dusts Off."

53   "ruled by one man"   "Voliva Loses First Election in 23 Years," *Chicago Tribune*, April 15, 1934.

53   "Grinny Granny Goodwin"   Schadewald, *Plane Truth*.

54   "human nature from me"   "Foes Complain to Prosecutor of Voliva's Acts," *Chicago Tribune*, April 20, 1934.

54   defeat his rivals   "Victorious Foes of Voliva to Let Zion Pick Its Fun," *Chicago Tribune*, April 4, 1935.

55   play was being held   Schadewald, *Plane Truth*.

55   struck by a plane   Kneitel, "'Flat Earth' Radio Station."

55   chose a globe   Garwood, 217–18.

55   "globe in almost every room"   David Anderson, "Zion Prepares to Dedicate Public School," *Chicago Tribune*, March 10, 1940.

3: The Joke

57   "sloppy push-off"   Terry Coleman, "Globites Are Not Convinced," *Guardian*, January 2, 1969.

57   **full conversion**   Garwood, 221–22.

58   **flat, stationary planet**   Coleman, "Globites Are Not Convinced."

58   **its own dome**   W. E. Hall, "The Plane Truth," *Birmingham Daily Post*, October 24, 1966.

59   **"think for yourselves"**   "Wanted: Flat Earthists!" *Daily Mirror*, August 24, 1956.

59   **Flat Earth Research Society**   Schadewald, *Plane Truth*.

59   *Our Earth Flat, Not Spherical*   Schadewald, *Plane Truth*.

60   **"studied this subject"**   "Letters to the Editor," *Guardian*, August 16, 1962.

60   **"Anti-Vaccination league"**   "Watch Your Step! Earth's Flat—He Says," *Chicago Tribune*, November 19, 1959.

60   **seeing flying saucers**   Patrick Moore, *Can You Speak Venusian?: A Guide to the Independent Thinkers* (Hornchurch, 1977), 115.

60   **"the Conservative Party"**   Samuel Shenton, *The Plane Truth*, Flat Earth Society, 1966, http://www.theflatearthsociety.org/library/pamphlets/Plane%20Truth%20, The%20(Samuel%20Shenton%201966).pdf.

61   **famously racist speech**   Garwood, 231.

61   **"mystery of his beliefs"**   Coleman, "Globites Are Not Convinced."

61   **"beliefs in detail"**   "Lost Persons Fell off Flat Earth, Briton Says," Associated Press, June 6, 1967.

61   **"such a failing"**   Eric Clark, "The Day the World (Nearly) Fell In," *Observer*, August 28, 1966.

61   **"revealed as fact"**   Hall, "Plane Truth."

62   **membership dues**   "Lost Persons Fell off Flat Earth," Associated Press.

62   **"proper service to members"**   Hall, "Plane Truth."

62   **"contacts all over the world"**   "Watch Your Step!" *Chicago Tribune*.

62   **joining the group as a joke**   "Flat," *Daily Mirror*, May 11, 1961.

62   **the trio wrote**   Garwood, 233.

62   **"afraid to admit it"**   "Sittingbourne & Milton," *East Kent Gazette*, January 20, 1961.

63   **bids for his attention**   Garwood, 226.

63   **Bexleyheath Young Conservatives**   Coleman, "Globites."

63   **boundaries that May**   "Flat," *Daily Mirror*.

64   **stars shining through it**   United Press International, "Shepard Will Never Orbit, Flat Earth Society Says," *Battle Creek Enquirer*, May 11, 1961.

64   **"between us and the moon"**   Clark, "World (Nearly) Fell In."

65   **"Studio shots, probably"**   Coleman, "Globites."

65   **"a case against the moon flights"**   John Noble Wilford, "A Moon Landing? What Moon Landing?" *New York Times*, December 18, 1969, https://nyti.ms/3tuD7al.

66   **"God's wonderful breathing system"**   United Press International, "Moon Landing a Hoax, Many Skeptics Claim," *Wisconsin State Journal*, June 15, 1970; Gary Detman, "'Throw God's Wonderful Breathing System out the Door,' Mask Debate Turns Fiery," WPEC-TV, June 24, 2020, https://cbs12.com/news/local/throw-gods-wonderful-breathing-system-out-the-door.

66   *Thirty Billion Dollar Swindle*   Wendy L. Kaysing, "A Brief Biography
     of Bill Kaysing," Bill Kaysing tribute website, http://billkaysing.
     com/biography.php; Richard Godwin, "One Giant . . . Lie? Why So
     Many People Still Think the Moon Landings Were Faked," *Guardian*,
     July 10, 2019, https://www.theguardian.com/science/2019/jul/10/
     one-giant-lie-why-so-many-people-still-think-the-moon-landings-were-faked.

66   **concealing atrocities**   Uscinski and Parent, *American Conspiracy Theories*,
     60–61.

67   **"me or the Society"**   "Mr. Shenton—Still Refusing to Come Round," *Daily
     Mirror*, January 2, 1969.

67   **many IFERS members had quit**   Clark, "World (Nearly) Fell In."

67   **the *Observer* observed**   Clark, "World (Nearly) Fell In."

67   **which was modest**   Coleman, "Globites."

67   **"music-hall joke"**   Clark, "World (Nearly) Fell In."

68   **"America is especially interested"**   Hall, "Plane Truth."

68   **"accept it from the start"**   Garwood, 315–16.

68   **prove the planet's shape**   Ronald Yates, "Flat Earth Society Is in Its Own
     World," *Chicago Tribune*, August 26, 1977.

68   **everything Johnson had suspected**   Schadewald, *Plane Truth*.

68   **like bats**   Schadewald, *Plane Truth*.

68   **"never hung by her feet"**   Associated Press, "Flat Earth Group Holds Steadfast,"
     Montgomery Advertiser, June 26, 1977.

69   **burn down a Masonic lodge**   Mark Serrels, "The Bizarre Tale of the Flat-Earth
     Convention That Fell Apart," CNET, May 11, 2018, https://www.cnet.com/news/
     the-bizarre-tale-of-the-australia-flat-earth-convention-that-fell-apart.

69   **married in 1962**   Garwood, 323.

70   **a mere curiosity**   Garwood, 274.

70   **heart complications**   Garwood, 279.

70   **"charm, coherence and sincerity"**   Mike Jelf, "Desert Researcher 'Proves' It:
     Really! The Earth IS Flat," *Independent Press-Telegraph*, November 18, 1973.

70   **"attempted to find out"**   Richard W. O'Donnell, "No Way around It, They Dig
     Flat Earth," *Boston Globe*, July 28, 1975.

70   **"infinite in size"**   Jelf, "Desert Researcher."

70   **end of Shenton's reign**   Jelf, "Desert Researcher."

71   **"believing that the world is flat"**   O'Donnell, "They Dig Flat Earth."

71   **"a Hard Core of Stalwarts"**   Charles K. Johnson, "News Bulletins," *Flat Earth
     News*, July 1978.

72   **"the Plan, anyway"**   Johnson, "News Bulletins."

72   **the strings of world power**   Michael Barkun, *A Culture of Conspiracy:
     Apocalyptic Visions in Contemporary America* (University of California Press,
     2013), 50–51.

73   **"flat-earth map as their symbol"**   Robert Schadewald, "Earth Orbits? Moon
     Landings? A Fraud! Says This Prophet," *Science Digest*, July 1980.

73   **2001: A Space Odyssey**   Schadewald, "Earth Orbits?"

73   **"not reality in it"**   Beth McLeod, "The Great Moon Hoax," Cox News Service, *Escondido Times-Advocate*, July 23, 1994.

74   **"there were skeptics"**   McLeod, "Great Moon Hoax."

74   **comparatively sane**   *Hot Seat*, episode 165, guests Alan Katz, Joel King, and Charles Johnson, aired September 6, 1986, on KDOC-TV.

75   **"get to you sometimes"**   Schadewald, *Plane Truth*.

75   **"spherical tendencies"**   Garwood, 328.

75   **"full speed FORWARD"**   Johnson, "Personal," *Flat Earth News*, March 1994.

76   **"really at a loss"**   Bhavna Mistry, "Fire Destroys Records of Flat Earth Society Leader," *Los Angeles Daily News*, September 29, 1995.

76   **"forcing myself to go on"**   Diane White, "Is a Round Earth Just a Flat-Out Lie?" *Boston Globe*, October 14, 1996.

76   **wrote to reenlist**   White, "Flat-Out Lie?"

76   **whatever lay beyond**   Schadewald, "Earth Orbits?"

4: The Reboot

80   **children or young adults**   Tim Miller, "The Electronic Fringe," *Washington Post*, July 14, 1985, www.washingtonpost.com/archive/lifestyle/magazine/1985/07/14/the-electronic-fringe/17955294-9c94-4b5d-99e4-9af799b45eae.

80   **calls for assassinations**   Kathleen Belew, *Bring the War Home: The White Power Movement and Paramilitary America* (Harvard University Press, 2019), 120–21.

80   **militias and libertarians**   Elizabeth Weise, "Internet Provided Way to Pay Bills, Spread Message before Suicide," Associated Press, March 28, 2007, https://archive.seattletimes.com/archive/?date=19970328&slug=2531080.

81   **alien abduction insurance**   Edith Lederer, "Alien Abduction Insurance Cancelled," Associated Press, April 2, 1997.

81   **quirk of computer geeks**   Weise, "Internet Provided Way to Pay Bills."

82   **"hamster insurrectionist group"**   Fake Flat Earth Society home page, Wayback Machine, Internet Archive, February 26, 2000, https://web.archive.org/web/20000226041945/http://alaska.net/~clund/e_djublonskopf/flathome.htm.

82   **"interesting and/or revolting websites"**   Kate Silver, "Site Specific," *Miami Herald*, November 30, 2001.

82   **"government-run re-education centers"**   "Welcome to Y2K Newswire," November 18, 1999, Wayback Machine, Internet Archive, https://web.archive.org/web/19991118033625/http://www.y2knewswire.com/.

82   **"into the year 2000"**   Jonathan Chevreau, "Who's Afraid of the Big, Bad Y2K Bug?" *National Post*, March 6, 1999.

83   **threatened to sue him**   Mitch Ratcliffe, "Mike Adams' Last Gasp," *ZDNet*, December 9, 2009, www.zdnet.com/article/mike-adams-last-gasp/.

83   **"Who will be next?"**   Paul Janensch, "'Astroturf' Threatens E-mail Form of Letters to Editor," *Great Falls Tribune*, February 1, 2003.

84   **"too sensitive for public release"**   "New to Y2K Newswire," Y2K Newswire, http://web.archive.org/web/19991128093829/www.y2knewswire.com/new.htm.

84   **cost $569**   Kelly Weill, "The New Infowars Is a Vitamin Site Predicting the Apocalypse," *Daily Beast*, June 8, 2019, www.thedailybeast.com/ how-natural-news-became-a-conspiracy-hub-rivaling-infowars.

84   **internet sales blitz**   Ratcliffe, "Last Gasp."

84   **link to that website from other pages**   Safiya Umoja Noble, *Algorithms of Oppression: How Search Engines Reinforce Racism* (New York University Press, 2018), 46–47.

84   **registered a number of websites**   Ratcliffe, "Last Gasp."

85   **"killing knife"**   Charlie Warzel, "Alex Jones Will Never Stop Being Alex Jones," *BuzzFeed News*, May 3, 2017, www.buzzfeednews.com/article/charliewarzel/ alex-jones-will-never-stop-being-alex-jones.

85   **crackdown on civil liberties**   "Infowars," *Alex Jones' Infowars*, October 9, 1999, http://web.archive.org/web/19991009085521/infowars.com:80.

85   **"Military helicopters 'invading'"**   "Helischool," *Infowars*, October 6, 1999, http://web.archive.org/web/19991006222627/www.infowars.com/helischool.html.

85   **"controlled bombing"**   Jeremy Stahl, "Where Did 9/11 Conspiracies Come From?" *Slate*, September 6, 2011, http://www.slate.com/articles/news_and_ politics/trutherism/2011/09/where_did_911_conspiracies_come_from.html.

86   **predominantly Muslim**   Ed Pilkington, "Registry Used to Track Arabs and Muslims Dismantled by Obama Administration," *Guardian*, December 22, 2016, www.theguardian.com/us-news/2016/dec/22/ nseers-arab-muslim-tracking-system-dismantled-obama.

86   **Abu Ghraib prison**   Alex Jones, "Martial Law 9/11: Rise of the Police State," 2005.

86   **allowed them to happen**   Anna Merlan, *Republic of Lies: American Conspiracy Theorists and Their Surprising Rise to Power* (Metropolitan Books, 2019), 84; Jeremy Stahl, "The Rise of 'Truth,'" *Slate*, September 6, 2011, http://www.slate. com/articles/news_and_politics/trutherism/2011/09/the_rise_of_truth.html.

88   **"it got me thinking"**   Daniel Shenton, "We Have a New Friend of the Flat Earth!" Flat Earth Society, November 1, 2009, www.theflatearthsociety.org/ forum/index.php?topic=33875.0.

88   **the same conclusions**   David Adam, "The Earth Is Flat? What Planet Is He On?" *Guardian*, February 23, 2010, https://www.theguardian.com/global/2010/ feb/23/flat-earth-society.

89   **"leaders who came before him"**   Shenton, "We Have a New Friend."

89   **"Five liars"**   "When Did You Become a Believer," Flat Earth Society, September 2, 2006, www.theflatearthsociety.org/forum/index.php?topic=4614.0.

89   **new interest among journalists**   Flat Earth Society, "The Flat Earth Society Officially Reopens to New Members," news release, October 30, 2009, www .theflatearthsociety.org/library/pressreleases/flat_earth_society_press_release.pdf.

90   **"amazing tool for communication"**   Flat Earth Society, "Officially Reopens."

90 **niche punk-rock scene** "Bullying at Gananda School Has Officials Worried," WHEC-TV, October 16, 2006, https://web.archive.org/web/20061027222640/ https://www.whec.com/index.asp?template=item&story_id=20466.

90 **"unseen forever"** Adam, "Earth Is Flat?"

91 **555 people** "Membership Register," Flat Earth Society, 2016, https://www .theflatearthsociety.org/home/index.php/about-the-society/membership-register.

91 **male-to-female ratio** "The Flat Earth Society–Statistics Center," as of April 6, 2021, Flat Earth Society, https://www.theflatearthsociety.org/forum/index .php?action=stats.

92 **"why can't I just hover"** Eric Dubay, *The Atlantean Conspiracy* (self-pub., 2009), 302.

92 **"so I wrote about it"** Eric Dubay, "Who Brought Back the Flat Earth?" March 7, 2016, International Flat Earth Society, https://ifers.123.st/ t190-who-brought-back-the-flat-earth.

93 **antisemitic JewWorldOrder** Kate Starbird et al., "Ecosystem or Echo-System? Exploring Content Sharing across Alternative Media Domains" (paper presented at Twelfth International AAAI Conference on Web and Social Media, Association for the Advancement of Artificial Intelligence, June 27, 2018), http://faculty.washington.edu/kstarbi/Starbird-et-al-ICWSM-2018-Echosystem-final.pdf.

94 **"first Internet blockbuster"** Nancy Jo Sales, "Click Here for Conspiracy," *Vanity Fair*, October 10, 2006, https://www.vanityfair.com/news/2006/08/ loosechange200608.

94 **"goddamned weird"** Rick Paulas, "The '9/11 Was an Inside Job' Guy Has Some Regrets," *Outline*, August 25, 2017, https://theoutline.com/post/2179/ reflecting-on-loose-change-in-the-age-of-fake-news-9-11-inside-job.

94 **modest conspiratorial stances** Eric Dubay, "Eric Dubay Answers Everyone's Flat Earth Questions," YouTube, February 22, 2019, https://www.youtube.com/ watch?v=0NM5q22j5VI.

96 **message was bolded** "About FEIC," Flat Earth International Conference (USA) 2018, https://fe2018.com/about/about-us/.

97 **"will not let you down"** "Alex Jones and Donald Trump: How the Candidate Echoed the Conspiracy Theorist on the Campaign Trail," *Frontline*, July 28, 2020, PBS, https://www.pbs.org/wgbh/frontline/article/alex-jones-and-donald-trump-how-the-candidate-echoed-the-conspiracy-theorist-on-the-campaign-trail/.

97 **1.5 million followers** Sacha Feinman, "Meet the Internet Entrepreneur Profiting off the Anti-Vaxxer Movement," *ThinkProgress*, March 10, 2015, http:// thinkprogress.org/meet-the-internet-entrepreneur-profiting-off-the-anti-vaxxer-movement-2e3ba8f791b9/.

97 **leading US Conspiracy pages** Weill, "Vitamin Site."

98 **most viewed anti-vaccination posts** Alexis C. Madrigal, "The Small, Small World of Facebook's Anti-Vaxxers," *Atlantic*, February 27, 2019, https://www .theatlantic.com/health/archive/2019/02/anti-vaxx-facebook-social-media/583681.

98   **banning Natural News**   Kelly Weill, "Facebook Removes Conspiracy
Site Natural News," *Daily Beast*, June 10, 2019, www.thedailybeast.com/
facebook-removes-conspiracy-site-natural-news.

98   **"D-Day against the tech giants"**   Beth Mole, "Facebook Bans Health
and Conspiracy Site Natural News [Updated]," *Ars Technica*, June 10, 2019,
arstechnica.com/science/2019/06/natural-news-hawker-of-vitamins-and-far-
right-conspiracies-banned-from-facebook.

5: The Rabbit Hole

102   **orders from the government**   Q drop #760, February 15, 2018.

102   **withholds important stories**   Lee Rainie, Scott Keeter, and Andrew Perrin,
"Trust and Distrust in America," Pew Research Center, July 22, 2019,
www.pewresearch.org/politics/2019/07/22/trust-and-distrust-in-america.

104   **"steer you toward Crazytown"**   Kevin Roose, "The Making of a
YouTube Radical," *New York Times*, June 8, 2019, www.nytimes.com/
interactive/2019/06/08/technology/youtube-radical.html.

105   **"structural problem"**   Guillaume Chaslot (@gchaslot), "A few example of flat
earth videos that were promoted by YouTube #today," Twitter, November 18,
2018, 8:21 a.m., https://twitter.com/gchaslot/status/1064554284757340161.

105   **promoted Flat Earth as reality**   Guillaume Chaslot, "How YouTube's A.I.
Boosts Alternative Facts," *Medium*, March 1, 2017, https://guillaumechaslot
.medium.com/how-youtubes-a-i-boosts-alternative-facts-3cc276f47cf7.

105   **they saw on YouTube**   Ian Sample, "Study Blames YouTube for Rise in
Number of Flat Earthers," *Guardian*, February 17, 2019, www.theguardian.com/
science/2019/feb/17/study-blames-youtube-for-rise-in-number-of-flat-earthers.

106   **embrace of Flat Earth**   "Paulista é Preso por Vender Terrenos em Cidade para
ETs," Terra Networks, March 27, 2000, www.terra.com.br/brasil/2000/03/27/
011.htm.

106   **pro-alien "knowledge seekers"**   Danielle Valentim, "Terraplanista e
Defensor do ET Bilu Diz Que Criticas Vêm de 'Colega Enciumado,'" *Campo
Grande News*, August 22, 2019, www.campograndenews.com.br/lado-b/
comportamento-23-08-2011-08/terraplanista-e-defensor-do-et-bilu-diz-
que-criticas-vem-de-colega-enciumado; Guilherme Caetano, "Zigurats, a
Comunidade Brasileira Que Se Prepara para o Dia do Apocalipse," *Época*,
September 16, 2019, epoca.globo.com/brasil/zigurats-comunidade-brasileira-
que-se-prepara-para-dia-do-apocalipse-23846792.

107   **heavy social media users**   Rafael Garcia, "7% of Brazilians Believe That Earth
Is Flat," *Folha de S.Paulo*, July 15, 2019, www1.folha.uol.com.br/internacional/en/
scienceandhealth/2019/07/7-of-brazilians-believe-that-earth-is-flat.shtml.

107   **"more of a joke"**   Mark Sargent, *Flat Earth Clues: End of the World* (self-pub.,
2019), 25.

107   **"and one more after that"**   Sargent, *Flat Earth Clues*, 26–27.

108   **invited Sargent onto his podcast**   "CCR 089: Flat Earth with Mark Sargent,"
Canary Cry Radio, April 11, 2015, https://www.canarycryradio.com/2015/04/11/
ccr-089-flat-earth-with-mark-sargent.

114   **"very dangerous"**   Darlene Superville, "Trump Accuses Google of 'Rigged'
Search Results," Associated Press, August 28, 2018, https://www.pbs.org/
newshour/politics/trump-takes-on-google-in-complaints-about-social-media.

114   **"news on the president"**   Paula Bolyard, "96 Percent of My Google Search
Results for 'Trump' News Were from Liberal Media Outlets," *PJ Media*, August
25, 2018, https://pjmedia.com/news-and-politics/paula-bolyard/2018/08/25/
google-search-results-show-pervasive-anti-trump-anti-conservative-bias-n60450.

114   **pandemic was a hoax**   Lachlan Cartwright and Justin Baragona, "Fox News
Cuts Ties with Diamond & Silk," *Daily Beast*, April 27, 2020, www.thedailybeast
.com/fox-news-cuts-ties-with-diamond-and-silk.

114   **violated site rules**   Andrew Kirell, "Diamond & Silk Claim Facebook Never
Contacted Them. Facebook Emails Prove Otherwise," *Daily Beast*, April 12, 2018,
www.thedailybeast.com/diamond-and-silk-claim-facebook-never-contacted-
them-facebook-emails-prove-otherwise.

114   **government action against Google**   Kelly Weill, "Trump Threatens to Regulate
'Rigged' Google after Right-Wing Blog Post" *Daily Beast*, August 28, 2018, www
.thedailybeast.com/
trump-threatens-to-regulate-rigged-google-after-right-wing-blog-post.

115   **"expect massive casualties"**   FBI, "FBI Arrests Cave Junction Man on Charges
He Threatened YouTube Employees and CEO," news release, September 21, 2018,
https://www.fbi.gov/contact-us/field-offices/portland/news/press-releases/fbi-
arrests-cave-junction-man-on-charges-he-threatened-youtube-employees-
and-ceo.

115   **arrested for his threats**   Kelly Weill, "QAnon Fan Arrested for Threatening
Massacre at YouTube Headquarters," *Daily Beast*, September 27, 2018,
https://www.thedailybeast.com/qanon-fan-arrested-for-threatening-
massacre-at-youtube-headquarters.

116   **ad revenue was distributed**   Stephanie Gosk et al., "YouTube Shooter Nasim
Aghdam's Father Baffled by Her Violence," NBC News, April 4, 2018, www.
nbcnews.com/news/us-news/youtube-shooter-nasim-aghdam-was-vegan-who-
had-complained-about-n862586.

116   **feeling much better**   Nick Morgan, "Cave Junction Man Admits to
Threats against YouTube CEO," Wayback Machine, Internet Archive, *Mail
Tribune*, February 20, 2020, https://web.archive.org/web/20200224015404/
https://www.mailtribune.com/news/crime-courts-emergencies/
cave-junction-man-admits-to-threats-against-youtube-ceo.

116   **three conspiracy theories**   "Continuing Our Work to Improve
Recommendations on YouTube," *YouTube Official Blog*, January 25, 2019,
https://blog.youtube/news-and-events/continuing-our-work-to-improve.

117 **"grow the problem"** Jeff Horwitz and Deepa Seetharaman, "Facebook
     Executives Shut Down Efforts to Make the Site Less Divisive," *Wall Street Journal*,
     May 26, 2020, www.wsj.com/articles/facebook-knows-it-encourages-division-
     top-executives-nixed-solutions-11590507499.

118 **banned all Flat Earth posts** Nibiru Countdown, private Facebook group,
     www.facebook.com/groups/129108597264997.

119 **hard-core neo-Nazism** Ryan Broderick, "I Made a Facebook Profile,
     Started Liking Right-Wing Pages, and Radicalized My News Feed in
     Four Days, *BuzzFeed News*, March 8, 2017, www.buzzfeednews.com/article/
     ryanhatesthis/i-made-a-facebook-profile-started-liking-right-wing-
     pages-an.

119 **#VaccinateUS** David A. Broniatowski et al., "Weaponized Health
     Communication: Twitter Bots and Russian Trolls Amplify the Vaccine Debate,"
     American Journal of Public Health 108, no. 10 (October 1, 2018): 1378–84,
     https://doi.org/10.2105/AJPH.2018.304567.

120 **"discredit and silence" him** John F. Burns, "British Medical Council Bars
     Doctor Who Linked Vaccine with Autism," *New York Times*, May 25, 2010,
     www.nytimes.com/2010/05/25/health/policy/25autism.html.

121 **no official stance on vaccinations** N. F. Johnson et al., "The Online
     Competition between Pro- and Anti-Vaccination Views," *Nature* 582 (May 13,
     2020): 230-33, https://doi.org/10.1038/s41586-020-2281-1.

121 **"old IBM model"** Meredith Wadman, "Vaccine Opponents Are Gaining in
     Facebook 'Battle for Hearts and Minds,' New Map Shows," *Science*, May 13, 2020,
     www.sciencemag.org/news/2020/05/vaccine-opponents-are-gaining-facebook-
     battle-hearts-and-minds-new-map-shows.

121 **truther movements online** Susan Dominus, "The Crash and Burn of an
     Autism Guru," *New York Times*, April 20, 2011, www.nytimes.com/2011/04/24/
     magazine/mag-24Autism-t.html.

122 **top-performing vaccine posts** Madrigal, "Small, Small World."

122 **One such Red Ice article** Kelly Weill, Anti-Vaxxers Are Cozying Up to
     the Far Right Online," *Daily Beast*, March 2, 2019, www.thedailybeast.com/
     anti-vaxxers-are-cozying-up-to-the-far-right-online.

122 **online hate groups** Nicolás Velásquez et al., "Hate Multiverse Spreads
     Malicious COVID-19 Content Online beyond Individual Platform Control,"
     Cornell University, April 21, 2020, https://arxiv.org/abs/2004.00673.

122 **the guise of vaccination** Jack Goodman and Flora Carmichael, "Coronavirus:
     Bill Gates 'Microchip' Conspiracy Theory and Other Vaccine Claims Fact-
     Checked," BBC, May 30, 2020, https://www.bbc.com/news/52847648.

122 **a laboratory error** Will Sommer "Discredited Doctor and Sham 'Science'
     Are the Stars of Viral Coronavirus Doc 'Plandemic,'" *Daily Beast* May 8, 2020,
     www.thedailybeast.com/plandemic-the-viral-coronavirus-documentary-stars-
     a-discredited-doctor-and-sham-science.

122   **with the conspiratorial internet**   Davey Alba, "Virus Conspiracists Elevate a New Champion," *New York Times*, May 9, 2020, https://www.nytimes .com/2020/05/09/technology/plandemic-judy-mikovitz-coronavirus-disinformation.html.

122   **slickly produced video**   Brandy Zadrozny and Ben Collins, "As '#Plandemic' Goes Viral, Those Targeted by Discredited Scientist's Crusade Warn of 'Dangerous' Claims," NBC News, May 7, 2020, www.nbcnews.com/tech/tech-news/plandemic-goes-viral-those-targeted-discredited-scientist-s-crusade-warn-n1202361.

123   **"wouldn't have found out about QAnon"**   Kelly Weill, "How 'Plandemic' Lures Normies down the Rabbit Hole," *Daily Beast*, May 12, 2020, www.thedailybeast .com/how-conspiracy-theory-flick-plandemic-lures-normies-down-the-far-right-rabbit-hole.

124   **deleted her social media accounts**   Sophie Tanno, "Vegan Chef and 'Flat-Earther' Is Branded a 'Covidiot' after Accusing Supermarket Staff of Discrimination for Not Letting Her into Store without a Mask," *Daily Mail*, May 18, 2020, https://www.dailymail.co.uk/news/article-8330603/Woman-loses-cool-supermarket-wont-let-without-mask.html.

6: Alone in a Flat World

127   **church that she later quit**   David Gilbert, "Finding Hope on a Flat Earth," *Colorado Community Media*, December 11, 2018, https:// coloradocommunitymedia.com/stories/finding-hope-on-a-flat-earth,274158.

127   **"Jesus and the online Flat Earth community"**   NoLiesDomedSkies, "What Happens When You Become a Flat Earther," YouTube video, August 14, 2018, www.youtube.com/watch?v=F1EA_SV4CVs.

128   **a threatening "outgroup"**   Jan-Willem van Prooijen and Karen M. Douglas, "Belief in Conspiracy Theories: Basic Principles of an Emerging Research Domain," *European Journal of Social Psychology* 48, no. 7 (December 2018): 897–908, https://doi.org.:10.1002/ejsp.2530.

128   **an anti-Muslim threat**   Ali Mashuri and Esti Zaduqisti, "The Effect of Intergroup Threat and Social Identity Salience on the Belief in Conspiracy Theories over Terrorism in Indonesia: Collective Angst as a Mediator," *International Journal of Psychological Research* 8, no. 1 (January 2015): 24–35, https://doi.org/10.21500/20112084.642.

128   **Black and gay populations**   Jasmine Garsd, "Long before Facebook, The KGB Spread Fake News about Aids," NPR, August 22, 2018, https://www.npr.org/ 2018/08/22/640883503/long-before-facebook-the-kgb-spread-fake-news-about-aids.

129   **"loss, weakness, or disunity"**   Uscinski and Parent, *American Conspiracy Theories*, 131.

129   **"fear of being socially excluded"**   Van Prooijen and Douglas, "Belief in Conspiracy Theories."

130   "shut the Flat Earthers up"   Q drop #2622, December 12, 2018.

130   "no relationship with me or my kids"   Jesselyn Cook, "'I Miss My Mom':
Children of QAnon Believers Are Desperately Trying to Deradicalize Their
Own Parents," *HuffPost*, February 11, 2021, https://www.huffpost.com/entry/
children-of-qanon-believers_n_601078e9c5b6c5586aa49077.

130   "not the man I married"   "Brainwashing Our Kids," coolmom321, February 14,
2021, https://www.reddit.com/r/QAnonCasualties/comments/ljpjnp/
brainwashing_our_kids/.

131   "His burden"   K. T. Nelson, "What I Learned inside the Lonely, Sad World of
QAnon Facebook Groups," *Vice*, January 21, 2019, www.vice.com/en_us/article/
gyapg7/what-i-learned-inside-the-lonely-sad-world-of-qanon-facebook-groups.

132   "I know that's a lie"   All Gas No Brakes, "Flat Earth Conference," YouTube
video, January 3, 2020, youtu.be/H110vCGvTmM.

134   "I am shaking"   "Flat Earth Believer Confronts a NASA Employee in
Starbucks," *Daily Mail*, July 10, 2017," https://www.dailymail.co.uk/video/news/
video-1498765/Flat-Earth-believer-confronts-NASA-employee-Starbucks.html.

135   debunked by actual neuroscientists   Megan Molteni and Adam Rogers,
"The Actual Science of James Damore's Google Memo," *Wired*, August 15, 2017,
www.wired.com/story/the-pernicious-science-of-james-damores-google-
memo.

136   yelled at students playing at recess   Ariel Gilreath and Conor Hughes, "Flat
Earth Advocate Arrested after Yelling at Greenville County Elementary School
Students," *Greenville News*, March 2, 2020, https://www.greenvilleonline.
com/story/news/2020/03/02/flat-earth-advocate-nathan-thompson-arrested-
greenville-sc space-fake/4928578002.

138   surrender all his possessions   *Michael Jay Hughes a man vs. Mark K. Sargent a
man*, May 3, 2019, Superior Court of California, County of San Bernardino.

140   "wasn't chemistry there"   Noel Joshua Hadley, "Everything That Was Beautiful
Became Ugly: Escaping Flat Earth with Patricia Steere," *The Unexpected
Cosmology*, July 3, 2019, https://theunexpectedcosmology.com/everything-that-
was-beautiful-became-ugly-escaping-flat-earth-with-patricia-steere.

140   looking for her true love   Patricia Steere, "Narcissistic Personality Disorder
Smear Campaign. My Story. Show 1," YouTube video, December 31, 2019.

142   accusing Michelle Obama   Alexander Kacala, "Infowars' Alex Jones
Has a Long History of Inflammatory, Anti-LGBTQ Speech," NBC
News, August 7, 2018, https://www.nbcnews.com/feature/nbc-out/
infowars-alex-jones-has-long-history-inflammatory-anti-lgbtq-speech-n898431.

142   abused and/or eaten by Democrats   Ali Breland, "Why Are Right-Wing
Conspiracies So Obsessed with Pedophilia?" *Mother Jones*, July/August 2019,
www.motherjones.com/politics/2019/07/why-are-right-wing-conspiracies-
so-obsessed-with-pedophilia.

142   the conspiratorial clique   #DenounceQ, https://twitter.com/hashtag/
denounceq.

7: Mike

150 **wrote a short article** Kelly Weill, "Logan Paul Sued over Flat Earth Mockumentary by Guy Trying to Launch Himself into Space on Homemade Rocket," *Daily Beast*, April 12, 2019, https://www.thedailybeast.com/logan-paul-sued-for-flat-earth-mockumentary-by-mad-mike-hughes.

150 **"termites to wood"** Michael Hughes, What Does a Limo Driver Know about NASCAR (self-pub., 2007), 11–12.

152 **"science and science fiction"** Dave Williams, "Odd Launch This Weekend," Associated Press, November 25, 2017, https://apnews.com/article/aa6d27e6031c4409a10240d83fb9f932.

152 **"certain death"** Børge Ousland, "Børge Ousland: How I Crossed Antarctica Alone," *Guardian*, December 13, 2013, https://www.theguardian.com/travel/2013/dec/13/borge-ousland-how-i-crossed-antarctica.

156 **"personal luxuries"** Paul On The Plane, "Flat Earth Antarctic Expedition 2017," YouTube video, June 10, 2017, https://www.youtube.com/watch?v=7QBpi47ma84.

157 **suppress its believers** Paul On The Plane, "2017 Antarctica Expedition – REAL or HOAX?" YouTube video, August 17, 2017. https://www.youtube.com/watch?v=pp_b1H8SHAo&t=0s.

157 **starting at $11,900** Over the Poles home page, Wayback Machine, Internet Archive, May 12, 2018, https://web.archive.org/web/20180512054019/https://www.overthepoles2018.com/.

157 **in whiteout conditions** Hugh Morris, "The Trouble with Flying over Antarctica—and the Airline That's Planning to Start," *Telegraph*, April 17, 2019, https://www.telegraph.co.uk/travel/travel-truths/do-planes-fly-over-antarctica/.

158 **"I hope you understand that one day"** "Edgar Maddison Welch, 'Pizzagate' Gunman," video, "Pizzagate's Violent Legacy, *Washington Post*, February 16, 2021, https://www.washingtonpost.com/dc-md-va/2021/02/16/pizzagate-qanon-capitol-attack.

158 **"PIZZAGATE: The Bigger Picture"** *United States of America v. Edgar Maddison Welch*, affidavit filed December 12, 2016, in US District Court for the District of Columbia, https://www.courthousenews.com/wp-content/uploads/2017/03/pizzagate-affidavit.pdf.

158 **"in our own backyard"** Merlan, *Republic of Lies*, 60.

158 **actor of the same name** Nathan Francis, "Edgar Maddison Welch PizzaGate Theory: Was the Comet Ping Pong Shooter a Crisis Actor? New Conspiracy Theory Takes Hold [Debunked]," *Inquisitr*, December 6, 2016, https://www.inquisitr.com/3772621/edgar-maddison-welch-pizzagate-theory-was-the-comet-ping-pong-shooter-a-crisis-actor-new-conspiracy-theory-takes-hold-debunked/.

159 **"wasn't 100 percent"** Adam Goldman, "The Comet Ping Pong Gunman Answers Our Reporter's Questions, *New York Times*, December 7, 2016, https://www.nytimes.com/2016/12/07/us/edgar-welch-comet-pizza-fake-news.html.

159 **"sheer luck"** Matthew Haag and Maya Salam, "Gunman in 'Pizzagate' Shooting

Is Sentenced to 4 Years in Prison," *New York Times*, June 22, 2017, https://www.nytimes.com/2017/06/22/us/pizzagate-attack-sentence.html.

159   **torched a pizzeria across town**   Brandy Zadrozny and Ben Collins, "'Pizzagate' Video Was Posted to YouTube Account of Alleged Arsonist's Parents before Fire, NBC News, February 14, 2019, https://www.nbcnews.com/tech/social-media/pizzagate-conspiracy-video-posted-youtube-account-alleged-arsonist-s-parents-n971891.

160   **"can't live in this reality anymore"**   Sara Jean Green, "'God Told Me He Was a Lizard': Seattle Man Accused of Killing His Brother with a Sword," *Seattle Times*, January 9, 2019, https://www.seattletimes.com/seattle-news/crime/god-told-me-he-was-a-lizard-seattle-man-accused-of-killing-his-brother-with-a-sword/.

161   **Wolfe's first "likes" on YouTube**   Travis View (@travis_view), "I was looking at the 'likes' on the Youtube page of Buckey Wolfe," Twitter, January 10, 2019, https://twitter.com/travis_view/status/1083437810634248193.

161   **apology to QAnon fans**   Jennifer Smith, "Haunting Video of 'Thor' Actor Isaac Kappy . . . ," *Daily Mail*, May 15, 2019, https://www.dailymail.co.uk/news/article-7033879/Haunting-final-video-Thor-actor-Isaac-Kappy-committed-suicide.html.

162   **his Mercedes-Benz**   "Authorities: Whitehall Man Threatened Government, Had Homemade Explosives," *Pittsburgh Post-Gazette*, July 14, 2020, https://www.post gazette.com/news/crime-courts/2020/07/14/mt-lebanon-bomb-explosives-kurt-cofano-whitehall-fbi-atf-allegheny-county-threats/stories/202007140103.

166   **"time to tell the truth"**   Mack Lamoureux, "'Mad Mike' Hughes Was a Daredevil First, Flat Earther Second," *Vice*, February 25, 2020, https://www.vice.com/en/article/939nnz/mad-mike-hughes-was-a-daredevil-first-flat-earther-second.

167   **"Is the media going to be there?"**   Aimee Ortiz, "Mike Hughes, 64, D.I.Y. Daredevil, Is Killed in Rocket Crash," *New York Times*, February 23, 2020, https://www.nytimes.com/2020/02/23/us/mad-mike-hughes-dead.html.

8: Flat and Fascist

171   **"a manufactured city"**   All Gas No Brakes, "Flat Earth Conference."

172   **ongoing fascist plot**   "The Dark Side of the Moon," *Throughline*, NPR, October 24, 2019, https://www.npr.org/transcripts/772742561.

172   **"sometimes violent direction"**   Jamie Bartlett and Carl Miller, *The Power of Unreason: Conspiracy Theories, Extremism and Counter-Terrorism* (Demos, 2010), 4–5. http://www.demos.co.uk/files/Conspiracy_theories_paper.pdf?1282913891.

173   **"prolific source of irreligion"**   Rowbotham, 259.

173   **to replenish the blood lost**   Stephen Eric Bronner, *A Rumor about the Jews: Reflections on Antisemitism and the Protocols of the Learned Elders of Zion* (St. Martin's Press, 2000), 45.

174 **man named Agimet** Jacob Rader Marcus and Marc Saperstein, *The Jew in the Medieval World: A Source Book, 315–1791* (Hebrew Union College Press, 1999), 51–53.

174 **convert to Christianity** "Jacob von Königshofen, the Black Death and the Jews (1348–1349)," Primary Texts on History of Relations, Council of Centers on Jewish-Christian Relations, https://www.ccjr.us/dialogika-resources/primary-texts-from-the-history-of-the-relationship/black-death.

175 **"free-thinking secularism"** Robert S. Wistrich, *Antisemitism in the New Europe* (lecture, Frank Green Lecture Series, Oxford Centre for Hebrew and Jewish Studies, 1994), https://www.ochjs.ac.uk/wp-content/uploads/2011/09/2nd-Frank-Green-lecture-Antisemitism-in-the-New-Europe.pdf.

176 **"the fictitious *Protocols*"** Bronner, *A Rumor about the Jews*, 1.

176 **Pope Pius XII** Paul Hanebrink, *A Specter Haunting Europe: The Myth of Judeo-Bolshevism* (Belknap Press, 2018), 15.

176 **"masters of that enormous empire"** Winston Churchill, "Zionism versus Bolshevism: A Struggle for the Soul of the Jewish People," *Illustrated Sunday Herald*, February 8, 1920, https://archive.org/details/ZionismVsBolshevismByWinstonChurchill.

177 **"the Jewish Puppeteers"** "Nazi Propaganda Poster Entitled, 'Das Judische Komplott' ('The Jewish Conspiracy'), Issued by the 'Parole Der Woche," a Wall Newspaper (Wandzeitung) Published by the National Socialist Party Propaganda Office in Munich," US Holocaust Memorial Museum, https://collections.ushmm.org/search/catalog/pa1156252.

178 **"overtly antisemitic incarnations"** Byford, *Conspiracy Theories*, 96.

178 **Malaysian passports** Andrew Harris, "Life in Jewish Malaysia," *Australian Jewish News*, July 17, 2009, https://ajn.timesofisrael.com/life-in-jewish-malaysia.

178 **"mask for anti-Chinese sentiment"** Viren Swami, "Social Psychological Origins of Conspiracy Theories: The Case of the Jewish Conspiracy Theory in Malaysia," *Frontiers in Psychology* 3, no. 280 (August 6, 2012), https://doi.org/10.3389/fpsyg.2012.00280.

178 **Jews in Japan** Jennifer Golub, *Japanese Attitudes Toward Jews* (American Jewish Committee, 1992), http://www.ajcarchives.org/ajc_data/files/889.pdf.

178 **"torn our lives into shreds"** Ely Karmon, "The Anti-Semitism of Japan's Aum Shinrikyo: A Dangerous Revival," International Institute for Counter-Terrorism, October 15, 1999, www.ict.org.il/Article.aspx?ID=1322#gsc.tab=0.

179 **banned some of Dubay's videos** Eric Dubay (@ericdubay), "Eric Dubay Banned from YouTube AGAIN!" Twitter, December 28, 2018, 9:52 p.m., https://twitter.com/ericdubay/status/1078891565299392512.

180 **rescinded the nomination** "Facts on the Nobel Peace Prize," Nobel Prize, www.nobelprize.org/prizes/facts/facts-on-the-nobel-peace-prize.

180 **dressed in riot gear** "Neo-Nazi Flat Earther Steve Hildebran (CO), Colorado Springs Anti-Fascists," September 1, 2019, https://cospringsantifa.noblogs.org/post/2019/09/01/neo-nazi-flat-earther-steve-hildebran.

181   **reimprisoned for stabbing someone**   Kelly Weill, "Flat Earther Also Supported Neo-Nazis, Police Say. He's Not the Only One," *Daily Beast*, May 28, 2019, https://www.thedailybeast.com/flat-earther-skyler-butts-also-supported-neo-nazis-police-say-hes-not-the-only-one.

183   **eating Christian children**   Edward Hendrie, *The Greatest Lie on Earth: Proof That Our World Is Not a Moving Globe* (Great Mountain, 2016), 441.

183   **"of all races"**   Hendrie, *Greatest Lie*, 436.

183   **"conspiracy against God and man"**   Hendrie, 409.

183   **comparing Jews to rats**   All Gas No Brakes, "Flat Earth Conference"; "The Happy Merchant," Anti-Defamation League, https://www.adl.org/education/references/hate-symbols/the-happy-merchant.

185   **"Has anyone not seen that happening?"**   Jared Holt, "Owen Benjamin's Rhetoric Is Growing More Extreme," Right Wing Watch, March 18, 2019, www.rightwingwatch.org/post/owen-benjamins-rhetoric-is-growing-more-extreme.

185   **the Talmud**   Bethany Mandel, "How Did Conservative Comedian Owen Benjamin Became a Darling of the 'Alt-Right'?" [sic], Jewish Telegraphic Agency, April 8, 2019, www.jta.org/2019/04/08/opinion/how-did-conservative-comedian-owen-benjamin-became-a-darling-of-the-alt-right.

185   **"Always Blame the Jews for Everything"**   Ashley Feinberg, "This Is the Daily Stormer's Playbook," *HuffPost*, December 13, 2017, www.huffpost.com/entry/daily-stormer-nazi-style-guide_n_5a2ece19e4boce3b344492f2.

185   **"really hurts me"**   Mandel, "Comedian Owen Benjamin."

187   **"in dire need of defense"**   Hanebrink, *A Specter Haunting Europe*, 28.

188   **"I legit don't care"**   Zachary Petrizzo, "Alt-Right Comedian Owen Benjamin Banned from Instagram over Anti-Semitic Memes," *Daily Dot*, January 27, 2021, www.dailydot.com/debug/owen-benjamin-banned-instagram.

189   **"something going on with it"**   Claire Goforth, "Banned 'Alt-Right' Comedian Returns to Spread Coronavirus Misinformation," *Daily Dot*, March 24, 2002, www.dailydot.com/debug/owen-benjamin-youtube-twitter.

189   **increase in reported antisemitic incidents**   Idan Zonshine, "Far-Right Extremists Spreading Antisemitic Conspiracies about COVID-19, *Jerusalem Post*, June 14, 2020, https://www.jpost.com/diaspora/antisemitism/far-right-extremists-spreading-antisemitic-conspiracies-about-covid-19-631209.

189   **fear of antisemitic attacks**   Anti-Defamation League, "ADL Survey Finds American Jews Feel More Threatened Than at Any Time in Past Decade," news release, April 21, 2020, www.adl.org/news/press-releases/adl-survey-finds-american-jews-feel-more-threatened-than-at-any-time-in-past.

189   **Jewish domination plots**   Edit Inotai and Claudia Ciobanu, "Antisemitism Creeps Back as Hungary and Poland Fail to Draw Red Lines," *Balkan Insight*, September 11, 2020. https://balkaninsight.com/2020/09/11/antisemitism-creeps-back-as-hungary-and-poland-fail-to-draw-red-lines/.

190   **RNC speech was canceled**   Will Sommer, "RNC Speaker Cancelled after
Boosting QAnon Conspiracy Theory about Jewish Plot to Enslave the World,"
Daily Beast, August 25, 2020, www.thedailybeast.com/rnc-speaker-boosts-
qanon-conspiracy-theory-about-jewish-plot-to-enslave-the-world-1.

190   **world-domination hoax**   Eric Cortellessa, "Conspiracy Theory
That Jews Created Virus Spreads on Social Media, ADL Says,"
Times of Israel, March 14, 2020, https://www.timesofisrael.com/
conspiracy-theory-that-jews-created-virus-spreads-on-social-media-adl-says.

190   **weird interpretation of zeteticism**   David Futrelle, "There Are, for Real, Nazi
Flat Earthers, and They Need to Fall off the Edge of the World," *We Hunted the
Mammoth*, April 10, 2017, https://wehuntedthemammoth.com/2017/04/10/there-
are-for-real-nazi-flat-earthers-and-they-need-to-fall-off-the-edge-of-the-world/
comment-page-1/.

191   **massive Flat Earth poster**   Lennie Clark (@lenniearizona), "Flat Earth
believers in the Az capital to support Trump lol," Twitter, November 28, 2020,
11:17 a.m., https://twitter.com/lenniearizona/status/1332765607381540864.

191   **charges for the Capitol attack**   Bob D'Angelo, "Capitol Rioter Dubbed
'Doobie Smoker' Will Remain in Jail," Cox Media Group, KIRO-TV,
February 12, 2021, https://www.kiro7.com/news/trending/capitol-rioter-
dubbed-doobie-smoker-will-remain-jail/4CARCOWX3ZDU5KRZB4ZU3IH
Y4I.

9: Away from the Edge

193   **"spiderweb of fear"**   "America's Frontline Doctors SCOTUS Press
Conference Transcript," *Rev*, July 27, 2020, www.rev.com/blog/transcripts/
americas-frontline-doctors-scotus-press-conference-transcript.

194   **"children need to be whipped"**   Will Sommer, "Trump's New COVID Doctor
Believes in Alien DNA, Demon Sperm, and Hydroxychloroquine," *Daily Beast*,
July 28, 2020, www.thedailybeast.com/stella-immanuel-trumps-new-covid-
doctor-believes-in-alien-dna-demon-sperm-and-hydroxychloroquine.

195   **council member in Gatineau, Canada**   "Quebec Municipal Councillor
Questioned Earth Is Round," CBC News, February 5, 2019, www.cbc.ca/news/
canada/ottawa/nathalie-lemicux-gatineau-earth-round-1.5007009.

195   **Flat Earth belief for Americans**   Ellen Manning, "This Is How Many British
People Think the Earth Is Flat," *Yahoo! News*, May 9, 2019, https://news.yahoo
.com/three-in-100-britons-think-the-earth-is-flat-143259242.html; Signe
Dean, "No, One-Third of Millennials Don't Actually Think Earth Is Flat,"
ScienceAlert, April 3, 2018, www.sciencealert.com/one-third-millennials-
believe-flat-earth-conspiracy-statistics-yougov-debunk.

195   **Spanish soccer team**   Rafa Mainez, "Spanish Club Changes Name to Flat Earth
FC," *Marca*, June 29, 2019, https://www.marca.com/en/football/spanish-football/
2019/06/29/5d17aa04268e3ecb4f8b458d.html.

195   **Tila Tequila . . . Stephen Carpenter**   Brian Feldman, "Inside 'Flat Earth,' Tila
Tequila's New Belief System and the Wokest Conspiracy Theory of 2016," *New
York*, January 7, 2016, https://nymag.com/intelligencer/2016/01/consider-the-
flat-earth-theory.html; Lauren Said-Moorhouse, "Rapper B.o.B Thinks the Earth
Is Flat, Has Photographs to Prove It," CNN, January 26, 2016, https://www.
cnn.com/2016/01/26/entertainment/rapper-bob-earth-flat-theory/index.html;
wookubus, "Deftones' Stephen Carpenter Explains His Flat Earth, Anti-Vax,
Simulation Theory, Etc. Beliefs," Theprp.com, November 12, 2020, https://www
.theprp.com/2020/11/12/news/deftones-stephen-carpenter-explains-his-flat-earth-
anti-vax-simulation-theory-etc-beliefs.

195   **Kyrie Irving . . . Geno Smith**   "Kyrie Irving on Flat-Earth Comments: 'I'm
Sorry,'" NBA.com, October 1, 2018, https://www.nba.com/news/kyrie-irving-
regrets-flat-earth-comments; Nick Veronica, "Sammy Watkins Is a Flat-Earther,"
Buffalo News, September 20, 2017, https://buffalonews.com/sports/bills/sammy-
watkins-is-a-flat-earther/article_e5e3409a-320b-544a-937d-5bfobd3f4e61.html;
Ryan Wilson, "Geno Smith: I May Be with Kyrie Irving on 'This Whole Flat
Earth vs. Globe Thing,'" CBS Sports, February 25, 2018, www.cbssports.com/nfl/
news/geno-smith-i-may-be-with-kyrie-irving-on-this-whole-flat-earth-vs-globe-
thing/.

195   **Adolf Hitler in a past life**   Rachel Mcgrath, "Tila Tequila Pays Tribute to
Adolf Hitler on His Birthday in Twitter Rant," *Daily Mail*, April 21, 2016,
www.dailymail.co.uk/tvshowbiz/article-3552058/Tila-Tequila-pays-tribute-
Fuhrer-birthday-epic-Twitter-rant-Jews-black-people-gays.html.

196   **Ninety-seven QAnon supporters**   Alex Kaplan, "Here Are the QAnon
Supporters Running for Congress in 2002," Media Matters, November
9, 2020, https://www.mediamatters.org/qanon-conspiracy-theory/
here-are-qanon-supporters-running-congress-2020.

196   **Witzke's campaign manager**   "Will Sommer, "New QAnon-Allied GOP Senate
Candidate Also Pushed Anti-Semitism, Flat Earthism, and 9/11 Conspiracies,"
Daily Beast, September 16, 2020, https://www.thedailybeast.com/new-qanon-
allied-gop-candidate-lauren-witzke-also-pushed-anti-semitism-flat-earthism-
and-911-conspiracies.

196   **lasers in space**   Zack Beauchamp, "Marjorie Taylor Greene's Space Laser and
the Age-Old Problem of Blaming the Jews," *Vox*, January 30, 2021, https://www
.vox.com/22256258/marjorie-taylor-greene-jewish-space-laser-anti-semitism-
conspiracy-theories.

196   **"invasion of our government"**   Ally Mutnick and Melanie Zanona,
"House Republican Leaders Condemn GOP Candidate Who Made Racist
Videos," *Politico*, June 17, 2020, https://www.politico.com/news/2020/06/17/
house-republicans-condemn-gop-candidate-racist-videos-325579.

196   **Trump retweeting QAnon personalities**   Tina Nguyen, "Trump Isn't Secretly
Winking at QAnon. He's Retweeting Its Followers," *Politico*, July 12, 2020, https://
www.politico.com/news/2020/07/12/trump-tweeting-qanon-followers-357238.

196   **"assign blame for distressing events"**   Van Prooijen, *Psychology of Conspiracy Theories*, 22.

197   **leave the European Union**   Viren Swami et al., "To Brexit or Not to Brexit: The Roles of Islamophobia, Conspiracist Beliefs, and Integrated Threat in Voting Intentions for the United Kingdom European Union Membership Referendum," *British Journal of Psychology* 109, no. 1 (2018): 156–79, https://doi.org/10.1111/bjop.12252.

197   **"the truth" about immigration**   "Brexit and Trump Voters More Likely to Believe in Conspiracy Theories, Survey Study Shows," University of Cambridge, November 23, 2018, www.cam.ac.uk/research/news/brexit-and-trump-voters-more-likely-to-believe-in-conspiracy-theories-survey-study-shows.

197   **definitely or probably true**   Katherine Schaeffer, "A Look at the Americans Who Believe There Is Some Truth to the Conspiracy Theory That COVID-19 Was Planned," Pew Research Center, July 24, 2020, www.pewresearch.org/fact-tank/2020/07/24/a-look-at-the-americans-who-believe-there-is-some-truth-to-the-conspiracy-theory-that-covid-19-was-planned.

197   **nearly three million COVID-19 truthers**   "Dashboard: New Far-Right Groups on Facebook Protesting COVID-19 Stay-at-Home Directives," Institute for Research and Education on Human Rights, August 6, 2020, www.irehr.org/covid19updates/dashboard-new-far-right-groups-on-facebook-protesting-stay-at-home-directives.

197   **harassment from QAnon followers**   Ari Sen and Brandy Zadrozny, "QAnon Groups Have Millions of Members on Facebook, Documents Show," NBC News, August 1, 2020, www.nbcnews.com/tech/tech-news/qanon-groups-have-millions-members-facebook-documents-show-n1236317.

197   **heard of QAnon**   "5 Facts about the QAnon Conspiracy Theories," November 16, 2020, Pew Research Center, https://www.pewresearch.org/fact-tank/2020/11/16/5-facts-about-the-qanon-conspiracy-theories.

198   **criticism of the governor**   Craig Mauger, "President Trump Tweets on Kidnapping Plot, Criticizes Gov. Whitmer," *Detroit News*, October 8, 2020, https://www.detroitnews.com/story/news/politics/2020/10/08/president-trump-tweets-kidnapping-plot-criticizes-gov-whitmer/5932010002/.

198   **religious exemption**   "Nathan Roberts," Flat Earth International Conference 2018, https://fe2018.com/speakers/nathan-roberts; Devon Link, "Fact Check: Civil Rights Act of 1964 Does Not Create Religion-Based Exemption from Mask Mandates," *USA Today*, August 6, 2020, https://www.usatoday.com/story/news/factcheck/2020/08/06/fact-check-1964-law-does-not-create-religious-exemption-masks/5530976002.

198   **FBI agent's testimony**   Justin Rohrlich, "Wisconsin Vaccine Saboteur Steven Brandenburg Is a Flat-Earther, FBI Document Reveals," *Daily Beast*, January 31, 2021, https://www.thedailybeast.com/wisconsin-vaccine-saboteur-steven-brandenburg-is-a-flat-earther-fbi-document-reveals.

199   **Trump would not concede defeat**   Jon Ward, "Trump and His Followers
      Are on the 'Crazy Train' with Unhinged Election Conspiracies, Republican
      Congressman Says," *Yahoo! News*, November 12, 2020, https://www.yahoo.com/
      news/trump-and-his-followers-are-on-the-crazy-train-with-unhinged-election-
      conspiracies-republican-congressman-says-213451478.html.

199   **small conspiratorial Facebook pages**   Jessica Guynn, "Trump Allies Banned
      from Twitter Still Spreading QAnon, Election Fraud Conspiracy Theories There,"
      USA Today, February 25, 2021. https://www.usatoday.com/story/tech/2021/02/25/
      trump-twitter-ban-qanon-election-fraud-conspiracy-lies/6818001002.

199   **Trump campaign's payroll**   Maggie Haberman and Zolan Kanno-Youngs,
      "Trump Weighed Naming Election Conspiracy Theorist as Special Counsel,"
      New York Times, December 19, 2020, https://www.nytimes.com/2020/12/19/us/
      politics/trump-sidney-powell-voter-fraud.html.

200   **automatically generated fact-checks**   Neal Mohan and Robert Kyncl,
      "Building a Better News Experience on YouTube, Together," *YouTube
      Official Blog*, July 9, 2018, https://blog.youtube/news-and-events/
      building-better-news-experience-on.

201   **found to contain misleading information**   "Facebook's Third-Party Fact-
      Checking Program," Facebook Journalism Project, https://www.facebook.com/
      journalismproject/programs/third-party-fact-checking.

201   **study that tracked browser history**   Scott K. Johnson, "Data
      Shows Who Was Reading 'Fake News' before 2016 US Election,"
      Ars Technica, March 4, 2020, arstechnica.com/science/2020/03/
      data-show-who-was-reading-fake-news-before-2016-us-election.

201   **never be fooled by one**   Asheley R. Landrum and Alex Olshansky, "Third-
      Person Perceptions and Calls for Censorship of Flat Earth Videos on YouTube,"
      Media and Communication 8, no. 2 (2020): 387–400, http://dx.doi.org/10.17645/
      mac.v8i2.2853.

201   **"reducing recommendations of borderline content"**   "Continuing Our Work,"
      YouTube Official Blog, January 25, 2019, https://blog.youtube/news-and-events/
      continuing-our-work-to-improve.

202   **nearly 1.4 million website hits**   Jack Nicas, "Alex Jones Said Bans Would
      Strengthen Him. He Was Wrong," *New York Times*, September 4, 2018, www
      .nytimes.com/2018/09/04/technology/alex-jones-infowars-bans-traffic.html.

202   **Infowars hosts used their personal pages**   Kelly Weill, "Infowars Makes a
      Stealth Return to YouTube," *Daily Beast*, January 12, 2019, www.thedailybeast.
      com/infowars-makes-a-stealth-return-to-youtube.

203   **confuse YouTube's filters**   Elizabeth Dwoskin and Craig Timberg, "Inside
      YouTube's Struggles to Shut Down Video of the New Zealand Shooting—
      and the Humans Who Outsmarted Its Systems," *Washington Post*, March 18,
      2019, www.washingtonpost.com/technology/2019/03/18/inside-youtubes-
      struggles-shut-down-video-new-zealand-shooting-humans-who-outsmarted-
      its-systems.

203 **network with their peers**   Marianna Spring, "QAnon: TikTok Blocks QAnon Conspiracy Theory Hashtags," BBC News, July 24, 2020, www.bbc.com/news/technology-53528400.

204 **raised a flag about the article**   Evan Greer, "Facebook Told My Followers I Was Spreading Misinformation about Government Surveillance. I Wasn't," *Medium*, May 23, 2020, https://fightfortheftr.medium.com/facebook-told-my-followers-i-was-spreading-misinformation-about-government-surveillance-i-wasnt-63622dd7ae56.

204 **"harassment and bullying"**   Sam Levin, "YouTube Under Fire for Censoring Video Exposing Conspiracy Theorist Alex Jones," *Guardian*, April 23, 2018, www.theguardian.com/technology/2018/apr/23/youtube-alex-jones-sandy-hook-media-matters-video.

204 **purge in 2019**   Kelly Weill, "YouTube Crackdown on Extremism Also Deleted Innocent Videos," *Daily Beast*, June 6, 2019, www.thedailybeast.com/youtube-crackdown-on-extremism-also-deleted-videos-combating-extremism.

205 **accidentally flagged factual content**   Jay Peters, "Facebook Was Marking Legitimate News Articles about the Coronavirus as Spam Due to a Software Bug," *Verge*, March 17, 2020, www.theverge.com/2020/3/17/21184445/facebook-marking-coronavirus-posts-spam-misinformation-covid-19.

205 **Ethiopia passed a law**   "Ethiopia: Bill Threatens Free Expression," Human Rights Watch, December 19, 2019, www.hrw.org/news/2019/12/19/ethiopia-bill-threatens-free-expression; Simon Marks, "67 Killed in Ethiopia Unrest, but Nobel-Winning Prime Minister Is Quiet," *New York Times*, October 25, 2019, www.nytimes.com/2019/10/25/world/africa/ethiopia-protests-prime-minister.html.

205 **basis to arrest a journalist**   Edrine Wanyama, "Ethiopia's New Hate Speech and Disinformation Law Weighs Heavily on Social Media Users and Internet Intermediaries," Collaboration on International ICT Policy for East and Southern Africa, July 22, 2020, https://cipesa.org/2020/07/ethiopias-new-hate-speech-and-disinformation-law-weighs-heavily-on-social-media-users-and-internet-intermediaries; "Ethiopian Journalist Yayesew Shimelis Detained Following COVID-19 Report," Committee to Protect Journalists, April 1, 2020, https://cpj.org/2020/04/ethiopian-journalist-yayesew-shimelis-detained-fol/.

205 **leaked documents obtained by the** *Guardian*   Alex Hern, "Revealed: How TikTok Censors Videos That Do Not Please Beijing," *Guardian*, September 25, 2019, www.theguardian.com/technology/2019/sep/25/revealed-how-tiktok-censors-videos-that-do-not-please-beijing.

206 **when and where to vote**   "Fighting Digital Disinformation," Warren Democrats, https://elizabethwarren.com/plans/fighting-digital-disinformation.

206 **EXCLUSIVE banner**   Kelly Weill, "Flat Earthers Call Trump's Space Force Idea 'Impossible,'" *Daily Beast*, August 10, 2018, https://www.thedailybeast.com/flat-earthers-call-trumps-space-force-idea-impossible.

207   **Flat Mars Society**   Elon Musk (@elonmusk), "Why is there no Flat Mars Society!?" Twitter, November 28, 2017, 10:13 a.m., https://twitter.com/elonmusk/status/935572279693516800.

207   **"Hi Elon"**   Flat Earth Society (@FlatEarthOrg), "Hi Elon, thanks for the question," Twitter, November 28, 2018, 3:01 p.m., https://twitter.com/FlatEarthOrg/status/935644892721762305.   .

208   **grand reopening**   Flat Earth Society, "Officially Reopens."

209   **"other untruths are trivial"**   Weill, "Space Force Idea."

214   **psychology of why people believe**   SeekTruth SpeakTruth, YouTube, https://www.youtube.com/channel/UC8QUo98zQ7HlFFykAcoZ3EA.

214   **arguments are bogus**   Jose JG, YouTube, https://www.youtube.com/channel/UCMvoiw6N8xRFvggBignzK8g.

KELLY WEILL is a journalist at the *Daily Beast*, where she covers extremism, disinformation, and the internet. As a leading media voice on the role of online conspiracy theories in current affairs, she has discussed Flat Earth and other digital fringes on ABC's *Nightline*, CNN, Al Jazeera, and other national and international news outlets. She lives in New York. Follow her on Twitter: @kellyweill.